Homage to a Broken Man

Peter Mommsen

Homage to a Broken Man

The Life of J. Heinrich Arnold

With a Foreword by Eugene H. Peterson

PLOUGH PUBLISHING HOUSE

Published by Plough Publishing House
Walden, New York
Robertsbridge, England
Elsmore, Australia
www.plough.com

ISBN: 978-0-87486-613-1
19 18 17 16   8 7 6 5 4

A preliminary version of this book appeared in 2004 in a limited edition. The present 2015 edition is extensively revised and expanded, and now includes an essay on sources, an index, and photographs.

The epigraph from Thornton Wilder is taken from his play *The Angel That Troubled the Waters* (New York: Coward-McCann, 1928). The quotation is abridged.

Photographs courtesy of family collection. Copyright © 2015 by Plough Publishing House. All rights reserved.

A catalog record for this book is available from the British Library.
Library of Congress Cataloging-in-Publication Data

Mommsen, Peter, 1976-
  Homage to a broken man : the life of J. Heinrich Arnold / Peter Mommsen,
with a foreword by Eugene H. Peterson.
     pages cm
  Includes index.
  ISBN 978-0-87486-613-1 (hardcover)
  1. Arnold, Heini, 1913-1982. 2. Bruderhof Communities--History.
3. Bruderhof Communities Church International--Clergy--Biography. I. Title.
  BX8129.B68A846 2015
  289.7'092--dc23
  [B]

                              2015021274

Printed in the United States of America

To Christoph and Verena

Without your wounds where would you be?
The very angels themselves cannot persuade the wretched
and blundering children of earth as can one human being
broken in the wheels of living. In love's service,
only the wounded soldiers can serve.

Thornton Wilder

Contents

Foreword

Eugene H. Peterson

As a pastor, i have spent most of my adult life looking for connections between the lives of those with whom I am living and the stories of the men and women I read about in the Bible. Just as the entire biblical revelation comes to us in the form of story, so today nothing less than great storytelling is adequate to render the intricacy of creation and redemption in our own lives.

Peter Mommsen's new biography of his grandfather, *Homage to a Broken Man*, tells a story worthy to take its place in the company of the "greatest story ever told," as an extension of that biblical story into the circumstances of our contemporary lives. Today too, as in the days of old, God calls out the most unlikely heroes, uses imperfect people for his glory, and remains faithful to his people no matter how far they stray.

As I read this book lines from Psalm 118 came to mind: "The stone that the builders rejected has become the cornerstone." Anticipating his imminent crucifixion, Jesus used these words to describe himself. It struck me as an apt text to describe the "broken man" of this story as well, a follower of Jesus who was also a "stone that the builders rejected." Though J. Heinrich Arnold never doubted his calling to serve Christ in a common life together with these brothers and sisters – he shepherded a fledgling movement of Christian communities through a cataclysmic chapter of history and its own turbulent growing pains—he would never have chosen to lead. Humble by nature, mystical by bent, and a farmer by training, he was soon sidelined by more ambitious and manipulative men. We can be glad the story doesn't end there.

Another scripture this story will evoke, I must admit, is Jesus' counsel to his followers as he prepares them for what will most certainly come as they give witness to his new life of love and salvation: "One's foes will be members of one's own household" (Matt. 10:36). This book will give you a whole new appreciation for Bonhoeffer's well-worn phrase, "the cost of discipleship." It's hard to believe what Arnold put up with from those closest to him, but what emerges is an exceptional personal story of faithfulness and forgiveness, one that in turn rekindled the fires of first love in an entire church community.

One of the most soul-damaging effects of modern life is the obfuscation of story: the fragmentation of story into disconnected anecdotes, the reduction of story to gossip, the dismemberment of story into lists of formulae or rules. In most of the words that come before us each day—delivered via television, internet, newspaper, billboard, and gossip—there is rarely any story beyond the immediate event. There is very little that connects to the past, reaches into the future, or soars to the heights. Instead of connecting us with a deeper reality, such words disconnect us, leaving us in a boneyard of incident and comment.

On the other hand, every time someone tells a story and tells it well and truly, the gospel is served. Out of the chaos of incident and accident, story-making words bring light, coherence, meaning, and value. If there is a story, then maybe, just maybe, there is (must be!) a Storyteller.

Baron Friedrich von Hügel, the Austrian writer and theologian, was fond of saying, "There are no dittos among souls." At school I learned to marvel that no two snowflakes are alike, no two oak leaves identical. How much more unique is each human being! A true hearing of the gospel always takes in the specifically personal. "I have called you by name" (Isa. 43:1) has become an essential element both in my personal life and pastoral vocation.

Meanwhile the culture in which we are immersed is constantly at work eroding the uniqueness of named persons by giving them labels: ectomorph, unsaved, anorexic, bipolar, single parent, diabetic, left-brained. The labels are marginally useful for understanding some aspect of the human condition, but the moment they are used to identify a person, they obscure the very thing I am most interested in: the unprecedented, unrepeatable soul addressed by God.

Every time someone is addressed by name and realizes that in the encounter they are being treated as one-of-a-kind – not as a customer, not as a patient, not as a voter, not as a sinner – the gospel is served. Saving love is always personally specific, never merely generic. Christ's mercy is always customized to an individual, never swallowed up in an abstraction.

A good writer gives us eyes to see past the labels, ears to hear beneath stereotyping clichés. Peter Mommsen is such a writer. By the time you finish the book you will have made a new friend in J. Heinrich Arnold. In fact, this book introduces us to a whole cast of characters whose stories can heighten our own awareness and sensitivity to the life of Christ being lived in us. If nothing else, I hope that after reading *Homage to a Broken Man* you will never again doubt that "in all things God works for the good of those who love him" (Rom. 8:28).

Evil is not, as some think, the greatest mystery. The mysteries of goodness and redemption far exceed it, but they can be entered only when evil is faced. These mysteries become apparent when we find companions like those brought to life in the pages of this book, in communities like the Bruderhof, and in unassuming and patient leaders like J. Heinrich Arnold.

Author's Note

THIS BOOK IS THE TRUE STORY of one man's quest to follow his calling—a story of what Dietrich Bonhoeffer calls costly discipleship. It's not the tale of a saintly superhero: as the following pages make plain, my grandfather was no stranger to weakness or failure. Still, my aim has been to recount an exemplary life, one that I hope will mean as much to the reader as it means to me.

In telling this story, my approach has been to focus on decisive moments in my grandfather's spiritual journey. This means, by way of tradeoff, that I've sacrificed any attempt to be comprehensive, omitting dozens of people and episodes that might have earned a mention in a more conventional biography. It means, too, that I've given most attention to my grandfather's formative years, so that much of the text is essentially a series of portraits of the subject as a young man. (This book makes no claim to be a history of the Bruderhof, the Christian community in which he served as a pastor.)

My grandfather was never famous. During his life, his influence—profound as it was for those who knew him—spread no farther than a few thousand people. To write about such an ordinary, even obscure, person goes against the starting assumption of traditional biography, a genre that was invented (to use Petrarch's phrase) to record the doings of "illustrious men": history's great statesmen, heroes, geniuses, villains, and saints. My grandfather doesn't fit the bill.

Why write his biography then, or read it? Because, I believe, his story is universal—it's a story that matters. His courage, humility, and downright doggedness in following his calling, no matter the cost, speaks to an inborn yearning shared by millions. If this is true, the usual benchmarks that biographers apply to their subjects—success, prominence, impact—suddenly seem beside the point, their value relativized. As a certain rabbi said two thousand years ago, "The last shall be first, and the first shall be last."

Quotations and dialogue are based on participants' recollection or are reconstructed from written sources. In a handful of cases noted in the index, I've changed the names of people whose role in the story is minor.

Opa

THE MORNING MY GRANDFATHER DIED, I told everyone in my kindergarten class, "Today Opa went to heaven!" My teacher, a long-time friend of our family, started to cry, but her tears made no sense to me. Who wouldn't be proud to have a grandfather in heaven?

Of course, I would miss him. Opa and Oma lived in an apartment in our house, and ever since Oma (my grandmother) had died two years before, he had been sick and rarely left it. My mother, the seventh of their nine children, is a doctor, and Opa had a buzzer by his bed for calling her at night. She spent at least an hour or two in his room every day, sitting at his bedside while I played on the floor. I loved bouncing on his bed and — when he let me — on him. There was a sort of trapeze suspended above his pillow that he used for pulling himself up. It was perfect for swinging on, and then letting go of, to land on his stomach.

On some afternoons my mother wouldn't let me use the trapeze. "Let Opa rest," she'd say, and then I'd have to content myself with just sitting next to him. It was probably on one of those days that I noticed the little black cross that hung on his wall. It fascinated me, though I didn't know what I know now: that he had made it as a boy for Tata, an aunt who had been like a second mother to him.

Opa listened to Bach by the hour. Whenever I hear *Saint Matthew Passion* I'm transported back to the times I helped bring him his lunch.

He is sprinkling so much salt on the sliced tomatoes that they look frosted, despite my mother's protests. He grasps the teapot handle with fingers twisted by disease. Having poured the tea, he heaps a mound of saccharin tablets (he had diabetes) onto his spoon, and stirs.

When he told me he loved me, his words came out in a rich tenor, unhasty and heavily accented. I loved his room and its smell — asparagus, European cologne, burgundy. But what I loved most about it was something a child would never think to speak of, let alone explain. He simply drinks it in, eagerly and without question. Even as an adult, I cannot really articulate it, except to say this: whatever it was that drew me to his bedside was, for years, the most powerful thing in my life — a sure point to return to when everything else went wrong.

Twelve years after Opa died, I sat in the hall of the Harvard Freshman Union listening as President Neil Rudenstine prepared us for the rest of our lives. "You're the best there is, the crème de la crème," he told the 1,600 new freshmen, and I believed him with all my heart. For the next three years I kept on believing. A tumor of the soul was gradually taking over everything I thought and did. This was not Rudenstine's fault: he was only doing his job. But my arrival at college coincided with the start of a new, aggressive phase of the disease.

I was funded by generous financial aid and became a moderately successful student. I worked at the literary magazine, drank a lot when I could, and proved my lack of talent at rugby and crew. On my twenty-first birthday I woke up on a futon, hung-over from champagne and sweaty in a crumpled tuxedo, feeling hollow and desperate. For years a sense of guilt had pursued me with a terrible constancy, and I had managed to evade it. No longer.

Just then, when everything seemed at its cheapest and falsest, I realized I had a choice to make. Either I could turn my back on any integrity I had left, or I could stop, turn around, and retrace my path until I got back to something I was sure of.

And so I backtracked to my great-grandmother, Opa's mother. She is only an image in my mind. I see her descending the staircase on her electric lift. She's coming down from her apartment to our breakfast, where she will sit by Opa's side, picking delicately at a boiled egg in a cup.

I see Oma, too. She is warm and energetic and resolute in the way she moves. She reads stories to us on the sofa, and never forgets to bring a gift on birthdays or at Christmas. She is also strict. Once, at breakfast, I disobeyed her. That is something Opa never tolerated, not from his children, and not from his grandchildren either. Opa said to my father, "Marcus, that boy needs a spank." (I was barely two, according to my mother's diary.) But even at that moment I wasn't afraid of him. With Opa you were always secure.

Not long after, Oma is diagnosed with cancer. She lies on a sofa in her living room where she can watch the neighborhood children as they walk to and from school. She dies shortly before my fourth birthday.

But most of all, I remember Opa. After Oma's death, my cousin Norann and I make him a Valentine out of shiny red paper. It is from Oma, we tell him when we bring it to his room. Opa beams at us as he takes it. He makes us sit on his bed, and tells us stories – about the monkey he kept as a pet when he lived in South America; about the time he had to drive a rich lady through a jungle in his horse wagon, and the horse died. He is a great storyteller, smiling infectiously, surrounded by gales of laughter.

Looking back, I realize that many of my cousins knew Opa far better than I. My mother says I would often refuse to show affection to him. He had a candy dish on the dresser by his bed. Sometimes I came down the hall to his room just for the candy, refusing even to say goodnight to him. My parents were embarrassed, but he just chuckled, "It's OK, it's a free country."

When I was six I caught my first fish, a twelve-inch bass. I can still feel the thrill as the red bobber went under. Someone cleaned it for me, and (maybe because I hated fish) I suggested giving it to Opa. He ate all of it. It was just a month before he died.

During his last days my mother forbade jumping on the bed, and sometimes my cousins and I couldn't even go in the room. Then we would content ourselves with visiting him through the window. Standing in the garden, we'd peer through the pane and sing his favorite songs. Sometimes he lay quietly, trailing oxygen tubes, his eyes closed. At other times he'd gaze back at us, and smile or try to wave.

After Opa's death, I came to accept that he was gone, but I never forgot him. Everything I had experienced as a child lived on. As I turned into a teen, though, life became more complicated, and he grew more and more distant. I even began to chafe at his memory. Sure, I'd always love him, but just who was he? I knew what he had done for most of his life—he was a pastoral counselor, though he would have hated the term. I also knew he had been highly regarded for his sensitivity and humility. But that didn't explain the riddle of conflicting reactions to him. Why did the mere mention of his name seem to polarize people even after he was gone?

Most adults I knew, including my father's parents, loved Opa deeply and spoke of him almost reverently. They claimed he was the most significant person they'd ever met, that he had changed the whole course of their lives. Others felt differently. One estranged cluster of relatives was said to despise him and everything he stood for, even though they hadn't seen him in several decades. And then there was the story about an attempt on his life by a man he had counseled years before. The would-be sniper boasted that he had had Opa in his sights before changing his mind and deciding not to pull the trigger.

At Harvard, despite what I had claimed in my application essay, love of learning was not the point. The point was new power in a new world—a world where I could do as I liked.

There were good moments. Arguing about Coleridge and Virginia Woolf with a group of friends amid the smell of cardamom and hookah smoke in the Algiers Coffee House. Sitting across from Cornel West, just he and I in his office, having an informal tutorial, talking about social justice and Reinhold Niebuhr and W. E. B. DuBois, about his growing up Baptist and my background in a religious community. The Charles River at dawn, with the sun coloring the water as I sculled under the arched bridges. But even at its best, I knew that this life wasn't it. I knew where I had come from. Opa and Oma would never want me to lead the life I was heading toward.

Nor did my parents and the rest of my family. They saw that I was in trouble and urged me to take a break from Harvard. I was far from keen on the idea, and for months I argued, negotiated, threatened, blackmailed them emotionally. My father and mother didn't give in; eventually I did. After my junior year, I boarded a plane heading for backwoods Nicaragua. It was time for me to get in touch with real people, my father told me.

A classics and literature major, I feigned interest in the promise of a multicultural adventure, but underneath I was far from eager. Who'd trade Cambridge for getting his hands dirty among day laborers? All the same, I was soon working on an organic farm on Ometepe, a two-volcano island in the middle of Lake Nicaragua, about an hour's ferry ride from the mainland.

I gradually make friends with my coworkers, most of them hired for $3.50 a day from the nearby village. I learn their Spanish, which is seemingly free of consonants. I go armadillo hunting on the volcano with Jairo and his cousin Luís. Luís's family is considered poor, living high up the mountain where basketball-size chunks of lava make the fields hard to cultivate. Like a lot of the farmers here, he has a backpack pesticide sprayer with which he drenches his crops, and himself, with chemicals long banned in the United States. Though he can't be more than twenty, his hair is falling out.

Luís is well off compared to Raquel, an Indian-featured woman whose shack stands a few hundred yards from my apartment, a room in a bungalow newly built for American missionaries. Raquel has seven children, ages two to thirteen. All suffer from parasites; one has malaria; the three youngest have bloated bellies as seen in photographs of Sudan. Raquel grows vegetables on her patch of land, but has no regular income. There is no man in the house.

Then, on a trip to the doctor on the mainland, Raquel finds out that she has cancer of the uterus. The exam was free, but not the treatment. When my boss hears about her diagnosis, he starts giving her money each month for pills. Nevertheless, the tumor grows, and a couple months later Raquel dies in agony. My boss and I are mystified, but not the orphaned children. They explain that she has been using her extra pay to put food on the table.

It's a common enough story, for all I know. But it happened a stone's throw from my house.

One thing my friends from the village are always asking me when we meet is *¿Por qué triste?*—"Why are you sad?" It takes me off guard; sometimes they ask me this even when I am smiling. But they can see right through me and sense my desperation.

I know I'm on the wrong track. Some nights I am feverish with guilt over the hell I have put my parents through and over my secret sins. I feel corrupted and unsound.

"You bastard, you soak up love from everyone around you," I tell myself. "Where do all your big plans for yourself leave Luís and Raquel? You know you were not made for all that selfish crap. What will you have to look back on when you die?"

Deep inside, like a trapped dormant spore, is the memory of what it felt like to be in Opa's presence. Because it is holy and dangerous, I have kept it hidden, almost forgotten.

Now I need it. I thumb through Opa's books, never daring to read too much at a time. I read one of the writers that I've heard he loved, the thirteenth-century mystic Meister Eckhart, who writes about repentance, conversion, and union with God. "No one must imagine that it is impossible for God to be born in him," I read, "for it is God who does it. Some may say they do not have it. To this I say that I am sorry. But if you do not desire it, I am still more sorry. If you cannot have it, then at least have a longing for it! And if you cannot have the longing, then long to have the longing!"

"That's where I am," I think. "But now what?" Then, one hot afternoon around Christmas, I'm working on the field where my boss is experimenting with growing watermelons in small high-yield plots. My job is to hand-weed around the vines. The air is thick with the smell of the lake, heavy and sweet and sticky, like a rotting papaya. I watch the herons flying over me, their wings gleaming white in the shimmering sun. I myself feel dirty and desolate. I am kneeling by the side of the row, crying and praying. I'm not sure exactly what I'm saying to God. I only know that I am sorry, that I want to find my way home, that I am willing to do anything and give up everything.

I am not transformed overnight, but it is a turning point. I leave Ometepe soon afterward, not to finish college but to continue my search. I know I need to repent and be forgiven. From then on I am pulled closer, sometimes losing focus, sometimes trying to make a slip for it or wavering in my loyalties—but still never doubting where I want to go. Even in the midst of the pain of self-recognition, the prospect of a new life exhilarates me. No turning back.

It's summer, and I'm back home in upstate New York with my cousins, Chris, Priscilla, and Emmy, and my sister Marianne. We're all in our twenties; we've all been trying our wings and making mistakes. Now we find that we're all heading in the same direction. It takes me by surprise. We are just discovering where we came from, asking our parents questions and digging through Opa's and Oma's papers. Some of our discoveries sober us; others make us laugh. Some make us angry.

Standing by Opa's grave one evening, we start talking about him. Long past midnight we are still there, remembering stories. How he faced down the Nazis. How he was separated from his family and sent to work in a leper colony. How we wish we could talk to him.

All of us have heard about Opa from people who knew him as a counselor or friend, and at times the golden memories have left each of us cold. We don't want a saint for a grandfather: we want a man we can approach. True, he made an enormous impact on those who knew him and those who have read his books. But that's only several thousand people. He wasn't famous. Yet just because he wasn't famous, in the same way most of us will never be, we want to ask him a few questions. Embarrassingly basic questions, such as, "What am I here for?" "How can I relate to others?" "What matters in life?" "What about God?"

That night I realized that Opa had always stayed inside me. His once-bright image had receded, as if across a widening chasm, and grown distant and blurred. But now I knew I must retrieve it for good.

As I pieced together his story, amassing what became an unexpectedly vast collection of source material, I began to get answers. Three times I tried writing his life, and three times I had to stop. At one point I felt so confronted by his presence that I could not bear reading what he had written any longer. It was a year before I could begin the project again. This story is still alive. It can get to you.

That is how this book came to be. Like many things that are wonderful or heartrending, the story starts in Berlin.

2

Revolution

Berlin, 1919

After breakfast, when there was a break in the shooting, the boy in the sailor suit went down the *Landauerstrasse* toward school. On the way, he had to cross a trench the soldiers had dug across the street. They had piled up the dirt and pavement to make a barricade and thrown some planks across it as a bridge. The five-year-old walked out to the middle of the plank and looked down at the helmeted men below him. As usual, they were smoking cigarettes and waiting. This was the daily truce that the government and the revolutionaries had scheduled in order to keep the school system running. "Be careful and hurry," his mother had told Heiner. "Soon the guns will start up again."

Every day the soldiers shouted up "Good morning" to the boy. Heiner liked them because they were cheerful and friendly, unlike the neighborhood children, who were mean. It was all because of his father, people said. The other men on the block wore the patriotic ribbon on their suit lapels: the red, white, and black of the imperial German flag. But Dr. Eberhard Arnold wore the red ribbon of the international workers' movement. No wonder the children yelled at Heiner and called him a name neither he nor they understood: *"Spartakist! Spartakist!"*

Heiner had no idea that the Spartacus League, a revolutionary Marxist group, had helped force the end of the war by calling general strikes, then turned to fighting in the streets to establish a socialist republic. He asked his father what the taunt meant. "It was the first serious conversation I had with him," he would later recall. In fact, Eberhard, a Protestant theologian, was no Communist, and he abhorred the violence. But he did believe in justice for the working class. "They have suffered the most during this terrible war."

There were other words Heiner had learned. *Abdicate* meant that the Kaiser had abandoned his country and fled to Holland. *Armistice* referred to Germany's humiliating defeat. *Assassinate*—that meant the military was hunting down the revolutionaries his parents talked about at home, people with names like Rosa Luxemburg and Karl Liebknecht (who were arrested in the Wilmersdorf suburb where Heiner lived, then murdered).

Some things did not need explaining, like the columns of veterans who marched through the center of the city chanting "Hungry, hungry, we are hungry!" For the last two years of the war, even the well-to-do had eaten turnips and little else. Boiled turnips, turnip pancakes, turnip jam made with saccharin for lack of sugar. Now the war was over, but food was scarcer than ever. Children in the slums were dying of hunger. Heiner knew this, because the grownups often whispered about it. City officials wrapped the lightweight bodies in newspapers and carried them out of Berlin to be buried.

Living in the house with Heiner were Emy-Margret and Hardy, who were older, Hans-Hermann, who was a year younger, and baby Monika. The grownups were his father, his mother Emmy, and his mother's sister Else von Hollander, or Tata, as everyone called her. Papa was an editor at Furche, a publishing house, and Tata worked there too as his assistant. They left the house together early in the morning, and when Heiner woke up they were usually gone.

In the evening, when Berlin echoed with gunfire, Emmy and the children would sit in the living room waiting till Eberhard and Tata arrived home. Emmy would fidget, get up, sit back down, and say for the umpteenth time, "They are still not back!"

Once the daily rite went on like this for five hours, until at eleven, they finally heard a key in the lock on the front door. Papa looked pale and said, "The street car got stuck in a firing zone. We had to lie on the floor of the car until the bullets stopped."

Thursdays meant early to bed. That was the night Eberhard and Emmy held "open evenings," and guests swarmed through the dining room and the parlor. Heiner hated being alone with Hardy and Emy-Margret upstairs. Outside, the machine guns seemed to be tack-tack-tacking up and down the block—they always sounded much closer than they really were at night. On the other hand, it was fun to eavesdrop on the grownups downstairs. Open evenings were for serious discussion, not partying. They talked about the weakness of the government, the bankruptcy of German culture, and a group called the Bolsheviks who had recently taken over Russia. They talked about themselves too, circling week after week back to the same strange question, "But what shall we do?"

No one would have believed that Heiner could understand any of it. But though he could barely read yet, he knew how to listen carefully, and he absorbed, little by little, much of what he heard. He knew that the crowd downstairs included leaders from both of the factions that were fighting outside. On the conservative side were Papa's colleagues from the publishing house. Heiner and his siblings had to kiss their hands in the correct way, and knew better than to comment on their warts and moles. These people wore dark clothes and starched collars and parted their hair in the middle. They addressed one another formally and rarely smiled. When they greeted his mother, they called her Frau Doktor. Heiner and his siblings called them "the pious people." At their head was Papa's boss, Georg Michaelis, whom people addressed as "His Excellency." During the war he had been the imperial chancellor.

The pious people were often surprised to meet Eberhard and Emmy's "other" friends. Artists. Social workers. Radicals. Students. Health reformers and teetotalers. Jews.

With such a variety of guests, discussions often erupted into vehement disagreements. And yet the guests kept coming back. Even if no one could agree on the best route into a better world, no one could deny that the old one had collapsed. Everyone saw the need for a new society. And Eberhard put their longing into words.

Heiner felt a certain excitement whenever his father began to speak: "We people of today need an upheaval – the complete reversal and re-evaluation of all norms and social conditions. . . . The answer will be found in the teachings of Jesus."

Many of the guests were openly incredulous: "But is that realistic? Can we actually build a society based on the Golden Rule? Isn't that fanaticism? How is it possible to truly love your enemy?"

It was around this time that Eberhard decided to return to public speaking in addition to his publishing work. He had been evangelizing at Salvation Army meetings ever since his teens. Back then, his parents had been appalled; his father had even said the scandal would force him to resign his professorship (it didn't). Now that Eberhard was a father himself, he often took his sons to the Army's meetings in the poorest areas of Berlin. What impressed Heiner most was the Mercy Seat – the penitents' bench at the front of the hall. Men and women came up from the audience to kneel there – steadied, if they were drunk, by the arm of an officer. As they confessed their sins in whispers, the brass band played and the crowd roared out revival hymns. "What do you think that woman confessed?" the children would speculate. "She sure took long enough."

But now Eberhard's vision ranged far beyond revival meetings. Heiner would sometimes find the soft green carpet of his mother's drawing room covered with posters. Huge black billboard letters announced his father's themes: "World Revolution and World Redemption." "The Bankruptcy of the Religious System."

"Nietzsche's Challenge to Christianity." "The Enslavement of the Masses." "The Worth of the Individual." "The New Youth and its Spirituality." The children were occasionally allowed to go along to a lecture. How proud they were of their father then, as his resonant voice filled the hall! Sometimes the audience exceeded a thousand, but Eberhard gave no hint of shyness. Striding from the podium to the back of the hall and then to the front again, he seemed to demand a response from each listener as he boomed, "Where do *you* stand? Which side are you on? How are you going to change your life?"

Dr. Arnold was known for taking his own sermons to heart. Indeed, he was in the middle of bringing his family's lifestyle into line with new, uncomfortably radical convictions. The greed and social inequalities of the decades leading up to the Great War had caused the death of millions, he believed. And so, to show their solidarity with the underclass, he and Emmy tried to shed their bourgeois privileges. The two servant girls were invited to move into the master bedroom, and Eberhard and Emmy occupied their quarters. The maids were also invited to eat at the family table instead of in the kitchen. For their part, the servants grumbled at having to learn dining-room etiquette, but they soon saw that the new regime would have its advantages. Tata and Emmy began to do the dishwashing, and Eberhard announced that he would take over the job of shining the household's shoes each evening. One night he forgot. Next morning the servants knocked on his study door full of reproaches: "Herr Doktor — our shoes . . . Herr Doktor has forgotten to polish them."

As the summer of 1919 began, the worst of the fighting in the streets was over. The new government forces had suppressed the revolutionaries. But at home the changes had only begun. One hot afternoon, Emmy and the children stood looking down the street from their balcony waiting for Eberhard to return from a weekend student conference. That was him, unmistakably, approaching from far down the street. But where were his usual dark street suit, stiff-collared shirt, tie, and briefcase? He was wearing a simple shirt, short trousers, and hiking boots. His jacket was under his arm, and his collar unbuttoned. Moreover—it couldn't be—his legs were bare of stockings. Emmy didn't know whether to laugh or cry, and started doing both. "But my Ebbo, what on earth are you doing?" she called down. Eberhard hallooed up at her, laughing heartily.

Inside, the children stared and stared at their outlandish father, while he told Emmy eagerly about what he had found at the student conference. It was known as the Youth Movement, and both of them had been hearing about it for months, but this was his first actual encounter with it. The movement's leaders, he said, were mostly young men who had returned from the front. They called the war a crime. They despised hypocrisy. What good, they asked, could there be in a "civilization" that had invented bayonets and poison gas? How godly was a clergyman who blessed deadly bombs?

People in the Youth Movement foresaw a society without class divisions, where everyone would live in harmony and love. They hated the bleakness of city life, the stuffiness of middle-class social life—especially church—and the snobbery of the German universities. They dreamed of (and in many cases established) rural communes and folk schools; they revitalized local traditions and railed against conformity. "You should see them," Eberhard told his wide-eyed children, "when they go hiking in the woods. They take blankets and a cooking pot strapped to their knapsacks, waving the banner of their particular troop, cooking in the open air, and sleeping under the stars or in barns." In the evenings, Eberhard went on, they built a fire and danced around it. And, to show their disgust for bourgeois fashion, the men dressed just as he had come home today, while the women favored peasant blouses and colorful flowing skirts.

There were so many different branches of the German Youth Movement after World War I that it was impossible to define them easily. There were Catholics, Protestants, Jews, and pagans; Zionists and communists; anarchists, medievalists, naturists, feminists, and nationalist reactionaries. What distinguished the best of them, Eberhard told his children, was that they questioned everything: "Is it genuine, or is it fake?" If something was genuine, they embraced it. That alone enamored him enough to want to join their ranks.

As Eberhard talked, he grew as animated as when he used to evangelize at the Salvation Army. But he didn't have to say much more to convince Emmy. From that day on, no one in the family wore conventional styles again, Tata included. She dyed her office blouse in red writing ink (to show her support for the workers' movement) and was soon taking friends to join the spontaneous folk-dancing sessions in the parks at the center of Berlin.

Eberhard's new wardrobe and new line of arguments – for social justice and peace, against class division and war – raised eyebrows at work. It was just in these days that His Excellency Michaelis was rounding up evangelical support for the German National People's Party, a rightwing political machine, and he made it clear that Eberhard's "fanaticism" boded ill for his career.

But Eberhard was not concerned about advancement. He was seeking, as he put it, "a completely new life." He found inspiration first and foremost in the ancient Jewish prophets and their vision of a peaceable kingdom. He was also intrigued by a contemporary seer: Gustav Landauer, an anarchist, pacifist, mystic, and the author of a widely read book on socialism, who believed the time was ripe to turn the prophets' vision into a concrete reality. Landauer proposed establishing self-supporting rural settlements in which the seeds of a new society could be nurtured. (Tragically, he was murdered in Munich in the chaotic days of early 1919, when a short-lived revolution there was brutally suppressed.)

Even in the best stores, food was scarce, tasteless, and expensive. Commercial bakers cut sawdust into their flour, so that eating bread gave the children stomach aches. By 1920, the Arnold children were so malnourished that all but one of them qualified for the extra food given out at school through a relief service set up by English Quakers. That one was Heiner, who was tall for his age. Never mind that he was just as famished as Hardy and Emy-Margret, who had taken to worrying that life in heaven might be too focused on harp playing and not enough on eating. Every morning the six-year-old had to stand aside, watching as the others got in line for a breakfast roll and cup of hot chocolate.

Luckily the Arnolds, as other families of their means, were still able to rent an allotment garden outside the city. Before the war it had been for roses; now it was home to two goats (for milk) and produced potatoes and radishes too. Eberhard even planted tomatoes, which were then considered exotic and known as *Liebesäpfel* or "love apples." Emmy served them to guests as a rarity, to the delight of the children, who eagerly awaited the involuntary grimace that marked the moment a guest realized these apples were a little different.

It was fun to help Papa lay out the garden beds and stamp down the paths between them. The children followed him as he took big jumps with both feet together, shouting out a rhyme: "The kangaroo, the kangaroo! He opens his eyes and shuts them too." Afterward, while their father thinned or weeded, the children played in the garden shed. Large enough to fit a small stove, a table, and chairs, it made a perfect playhouse.

One weekend the family arrived to see laundry waving from a line that someone had erected above their garden. Eberhard strode to the shed and knocked. The door opened and Fritz Schwalbe, an anarchist acquaintance who sometimes came to his lectures, appeared.

"What a surprise to find you here!" said Eberhard, slightly taken aback, but extending a hand.

"But Dr. Arnold, everyone knows you are opposed to private property. And so . . . we've moved in!"

Eberhard smiled and did not object. But since Fritz had brought along a young woman who was not his wife, the children were forbidden to visit the garden plot as long as the squatters continued to live there.

Meanwhile the Arnold's own home looked less and less like a respectable townhouse. Open evenings ceased as a once-a-week event and became a way of life. Now the black-clad pious people rarely came. Replacing them was a new kind of guest: homeless war veterans and former prostitutes trying to get their lives back together. And, of course, *Wandervögel,* or "birds of passage," as Youth Movement hikers were known. Hand-kissing and formal titles were gone; everyone simply used first names. When the weather was good, the guests took over the front lawn. Sometimes they danced; sometimes they invited Heiner, Hardy, and Emy-Margret to play circle games with them. Best of all, they often stayed the night, sleeping on dining room chairs or on the sofas in the drawing room.

Street fighting flared up again in March 1920 during the Kapp Putsch, a coup by rightist factions in the army. The workers' parties responded with a general strike, and soldiers and paramilitaries traded fire. One day during the worst of the violence, Lieutenant Helmut von Mücke, a highly decorated marine officer, telephoned to say he was coming to visit. He appeared at the door shortly afterward and, over coffee, asked Eberhard to take on the new Department of Youth that the rebel government planned to establish. Eberhard declined: "My calling is a different one." Then, as the crisis played out, he did what he could to minimize the casualties by inviting home and calming those he knew on both sides of the conflict, while Emmy stretched her skills as a hostess to make sure that visitors from opposing factions did not meet. By the end of the affair, he had managed to persuade a local Communist faction to reduce its "black list" of military officers they planned to assassinate.

In the weeks that followed the failed Kapp Putsch, evening discussions at the Arnolds grew ever more heated. "We have talked long enough. We must finally act!" "Certainly. But how?" Gradually, a consensus grew: it was not enough to throw out the old conventions and fashions and ideas. The very foundation of middle-class existence—private property—must be abandoned. What could

Jesus' command to "love your neighbor as yourself" mean, if it didn't mean making sure that one's neighbor had the same access to education, healthcare, housing, and food?

Then came the day when a working-class man who had heard Eberhard speak at a public lecture hall appeared at the door with an envelope in his hand. He was shown to the drawing room and offered a seat, but as Eberhard walked in, he found the man about to leave. "Dr. Arnold, I came here with a donation for your work. But now that I am here"—he scanned the opulent furnishings around him—"I see it is not needed." He left. Eberhard spoke of the incident with shame for weeks.

And what was one to make of the first Christian community at Jerusalem, as described in the Book of Acts? It read, "The multitude of those who believed were of one heart and soul; and no one said that any of the things which he possessed was his own, but they had everything in common. . . . There was not a needy person among them, for as many as were possessors of lands or houses sold them, and brought the proceeds of what was sold. . . . Distribution was made to each as any had need." Wasn't such a community the answer to all their questions?

Next, debate centered on where such a settlement might thrive best. "In the city," insisted the suburban middle-class idealists: "That way we can do social work among the urban poor." "In the country," insisted the urban working-class radicals, "so that the workers' children can grow up in a healthy environment, away from the slums."

In the end, it was the family pediatrician who had the final word on the subject. Heiner's younger brother Hans-Hermann, who was four, had once run energetically around the house. Now, because of inadequate nutrition, he had lost the ability to walk, and dragged himself around using his arms. As for the other four Arnold children, especially the youngest, Monika, their health was also poor. "Your children are in danger," the doctor warned Emmy. "Take them out of the city. They need clean air and a wholesome farm diet."

And so it was that by early June of 1920, astonished friends found the Arnolds packing up their house in order to leave what Eberhard had recently taken to calling "the dying metropolis." Their destination was said to be a tiny village near Schlüchtern, in a rural area whose landscape was dotted with *Siedlungen* (communal settlements), folk schools, and other similar ventures. Schlüchtern was known as a mecca for the "new German youth." Moreover, it was the home of Georg Flemmig, a kindred spirit who had invited Eberhard to join him in forming an independent publishing house.

"What about the children? Where will you stay?" relatives asked. They knew the Arnolds had found an empty villa for sale, but now the owner was hedging. And as for the temporary lodging Eberhard had arranged, it was almost laughable: three small, unfurnished rooms at the back of a country inn across the road. But the Arnolds were undaunted. They were bound and determined to throw away everything. Rumor had it that they were even surrendering their life insurance policy for cash.

His Excellency Michaelis's wife visited Emmy to dissuade her from joining Eberhard in the event that he really took this "unusual step." Her mission failed. As Frau Michaelis later told a mutual friend, "She is even more fanatical than he is! There is nothing we can do."

3

Sannerz

June 1920

The children crowded out of the train and into the June evening. There on the platform, waving, stood their father and mother, who had traveled ahead a few days before. Eberhard had hired a horse-drawn farm wagon to take the luggage to their new home. As the children climbed onto their seats, Emmy placed a cornflower garland on each of their heads. She had also tied bunches of flowers to the wagon frame.

It was a perfect night for a city boy's first drive through the country. Fireflies glimmered in the hedgerows, and a bird called from the black woods. Heiner stared in awe. The sight was supernatural, magical.

An earthier reality hit him as the wagon passed through the first village, where a steaming dung heap (prime fertilizer) marked the entry to each homestead. So this was the country – a fairy tale with a reek to it.

The wagon entered another cluster of houses, and it was time to get off. But where were their living quarters? "Follow me," Emmy called to the children, and led them to the back of the inn, and up a rickety flight of stairs. Here, in three rooms previously used for apple storage and saddle-making, was their new home. Hardy and Emy-Margret stared, enthralled, at the exposed rafters and the rough-hewn floor boards. It was so different from Berlin. And that smell: over-ripe apples and a faint stench of hogs from the stall downstairs.

The last luggage unloaded, Eberhard tipped the wagon-driver, and it was time for supper. Herr Lotzenius, the innkeeper, brought fresh bread, butter, and milk. "Eat as much as you like!" Emmy said happily. Heiner dug in, but found it tasted strange. He would gladly have traded the butter for the war-ration margarine he was used to.

The first morning, he set out to explore. On two sides of the village rose steep, thickly wooded hills. Animals he had only heard about in fables could be seen on the grass right outside the inn: pigs, sheep, oxen, and—were they cows? Soon he would learn to tell them all apart. The big animals didn't scare him, but the geese filled him with terror. Whenever they caught him alone they would rush at him, stretching out their necks like snakes with hissing beaks and venomous little eyes.

Heiner wandered out to inspect a cart parked in the road. It carried a monstrous wooden cask, and on one end was a spigot. He turned it just a little. A spurt, and then a jet of foul, cocoa-brown slurry gushed over him and the cart. He twisted the valve frantically, but the wrong way, and the torrent only increased. "Herr Lotzenius, a spring has opened up!" he yelled. Finally he managed to stop the flow. When he looked up there was a ring of bystanders, watching and laughing at him. He tried to wipe the liquid excrement from his clothes, and ran.

Tucked away in southern Hesse, Sannerz was scenic but isolated. There was one small store, but not much else. It had no train station and no post office to put it on the map. Most of its three hundred inhabitants were Catholic and poor. Some tried to make ends meet by farming their small holdings; others hired themselves out as day laborers. Still others worked for the largest employer in the village: Sannerz Tile Manufacturing. Every morning, people of all ages could be seen trooping toward the smokestack that towered above the kiln works.

It was a different world entirely from the broad avenues and town-houses of the capital — even a child could sense that. But it was only as an adult that Heiner would realize how thoroughly his parents had burned their bridges in coming here. Of course, that was just what they had intended. As Eberhard saw it, they had moved away from the bright lights of Berlin to follow a commandment that most people regarded as an idealistic, if noble, impossibility: "Love your neighbor as yourself." To him and Emmy — and Tata — it *was* a possibility. But it required a completely new mode of life. "Aren't the poor and the exploited our neighbors?" he would argue.

"We want to be part of the stream of the Spirit that began at Pentecost. The first believers in Jerusalem distributed all their goods. 'They were of one heart and one soul, and shared all things in common.' As soon as the Spirit was poured over them, nobody could hold onto property any longer.

"We want a genuine school of life, where the simplest work becomes a physical and artistic experience, where there is freedom from intellectualism and its pitfalls, where a new man can emerge, a creative man whose culture expresses what is real.

"We do not need theories or idealistic goals or prophets or leaders. We need brotherhood and sisterhood. We need to *live* Jesus' Sermon on the Mount. We need to show that a life of justice and forgiveness and unity is possible today."

Only a handful of people in Sannerz were acquainted with such ideas, or with Eberhard's plan to build up a *Siedlung* in their midst. But that did not dampen their excitement over the coming of the "Doctors," as they called the family collectively. The Doctors meant money for the village. Laundresses, seamstresses, and wagon-drivers all calculated what new business they could expect. Lotzenius wondered how many new guests would patronize his inn. From the start, the Arnolds were popular.

On their side, Eberhard, Emmy, and Tata were thrilled to live in a farming village, and made an effort to blend in where they could. Soon Heiner, Emy-Margret, and Hardy were attending the village's one-room school. In another departure from Berlin, their new schoolmaster used a birch rod to keep order, and the frequent beatings seemed brutal to Heiner. To his classmates, they were a matter of course. One boy showed him how to fill a pig bladder with red ink and stuff it down the seat of your pants, so that when the cane struck, fake blood would run down your legs.

Not that any of the Arnold children was in danger of being caned — their social standing made that unthinkable. But the same privilege that saved them from punishment netted them the resentment of their classmates, and after a few days of being held up as shining examples, Heiner and Hardy stopped going to school. When the school bell rang, they went down to the village stream to make boats and dams and watermills. Eberhard found out soon enough, and sternly demanded an explanation. When the boys told him their reasons, he arranged for a friend to tutor them at home.

To Heiner, it was heaven: lessons were irregular, and for most of the day he could do as he liked. Before long he was going in and out of neighbors' homes as freely as his own, and chattering in the local dialect as easily as his peers. Their friendly mothers were quick to serve him cake or sausage — and also quick to set him to chores. But even that was fun. In the city, you went to a confectioner for preserves. Here in Sannerz, people made their own. Jam-making, a social event that lasted a whole day (the traditional recipe called for fifteen to twenty hours on the fire) meant gathering around a huge copper vat to watch the plums or pears boil down, spiced with green walnut hulls. While the old women and mothers told stories or sang hymns, the strongest boys took turns with the stirring paddle.

While Heiner explored Sannerz, Emmy kept house, and Eberhard worked with Tata in the new publishing house. The work swallowed hours of their time: reading through prospective manuscripts and acquiring or rejecting them; working with authors, printers, and postmasters; finding a bookkeeper and a proofreader; and composing countless fundraising letters to bring in sorely needed capital. On sunny days the two would sit outside under the trees as Eberhard dictated and his sister-in-law filled one blank sheet after the next.

Then there was the future of the planned settlement to attend to. If it was ever going to take off, they must find the money to buy the two-story yellow brick villa across the road. Months passed, but finally the owner offered a reasonable contract. In autumn, thanks to a timely gift from a wealthy friend, a shipping magnate in Hamburg, the Arnolds were finally able to lease the house.

Some time later, the moving wagons arrived, loaded high with the furniture Emmy had inherited. While the village children watched, Empire-style chairs emerged, and then a mahogany sofa with red plush cushions. A huge formal dining table followed, and finally, a cabinet and chairs emblazoned with the family's coat-of-arms.

In a way, Emmy and Tata were as out of place in Sannerz as their heirloom furniture. One of the patrician clans that used to rule the German-speaking port cities on the Baltic coast, the von Hollanders had furnished their ancestral city of Riga with mayors, merchants, and *philosophes* for nearly three centuries. True, the family had come on hard times – their financial investments in Latvia had become worthless, and the Bolsheviks had confiscated a country estate worth a million rubles. But the von Hollanders never lost their aristocratic sense of honor. Emmy's father, for instance, a professor of law at Halle University and former head of the Association of German Nobility, used to provide the servants with sausage and beer for supper, even though the family dined only on bread and tea.

Eberhard admired his father-in-law for his "undaunted idealism." The two of them had disagreed on almost everything else. From the first day they met, their relationship had been marked by tension. It had started one day in the spring of 1907, when a fashionably dressed stranger had appeared at the von Hollander house, introduced himself, and asked for Emmy's hand. Eberhard, it turned out, was a doctoral candidate, a forceful young man known as a leader in the Christian revival then flourishing among Halle's educated citizens. He had met Emmy, he said, at a recent Bible study.

At first Emmy's parents grudgingly blessed the young couple's plans to get married. It helped that Eberhard came from a respectable family—his father Carl Franklin Arnold was a professor of church history at Breslau University, and on his mother's side he was descended from a long line of theologians. (In later years, Eberhard would remain well connected with academic theology through his Bultmann cousins in Oldenburg, including Rudolf Bultmann, the influential New Testament scholar.)

But it didn't take long before the von Hollander parents grew alarmed by the radical turn their daughter and her fiancé were taking in seeking to live out their Christian convictions—and Else was if anything even more extreme. It was one thing to go to revival meetings. Both sisters had always been religiously inclined: Emmy had been trained as a nurse by an order of Lutheran deaconesses, and Else, though an artist by nature, showed just as much excitement in her newfound faith as in her painting. Yet Eberhard's constant talk of putting faith into practice unnerved the von Hollander parents, as did his disregard for ecclesiastical authorities, whom he accused of diluting the gospel. And his arrogance! In one letter he had written, "I declare war on the existing church systems." They forbade their daughters to attend any more public gatherings and summoned a psychiatrist for Else, who ordered two weeks of strict bed rest to cure her of "unhealthy excitement."

Neither of the young women gave in—their conversion was nothing if not real, they insisted. The crisis came not long afterward, when first Else, then Eberhard, and finally Emmy had themselves re-baptized, thereby excluding themselves from the Lutheran fold, and—much worse—bringing the shame of scandal on the entire family circle.

There were bitter rows at home, and gossip and speculation. "One can understand such extremism from Eberhard," people said. "He's been a firebrand since his youth. But the von Hollander sisters? They used to be such sweet young ladies." Emmy's parents attempted to cancel the engagement and then turned her out of the house (friends in Berlin took her in). Yet all three young people were undeterred. Eberhard and Emmy married just before Christmas 1909, and soon Else was working as his assistant. By the time Heiner was born four years later, on December 23, 1913, she had become an inextricable part of the family.

Snow was blowing over the lonely Tyrolean manor house where the Arnolds were living on the day the baby boy was born, and it was still blowing as a bad case of double pneumonia threatened to take him again two weeks later. Yet Else was there, and over the next several anxious weeks she hardly ever left his room, nursing him slowly and carefully back from the brink. She never slept, it seemed, but constantly checked his temperature and rearranged the wet sheets that she had hung around his crib to humidify the air. When at long last it was clear that the baby had pulled through, Emmy pressed him to her heart and said with tears of gratitude, "From now on he belongs as much to Else as to me." Which is just how it turned out. When asked as a boy who his parents were, Heiner used to answer, "Papa and Mama. And Tata."

In 1921, another von Hollander daughter joined her "irresponsible" relatives in Sannerz. Moni was a midwife in Halle with her own flourishing practice. At first she intended to stay in Sannerz only shortly—just a visit to reconnect with her sisters. But Moni noticed that lunch and dinner were not being served on time. Sometimes the meals were even two hours late. Emmy and Tata looked overworked, and among the many guests who overran the house, only a handful were competent enough to lighten their load. She decided to move in and set the house in order.

After Moni's arrival, meals were more punctual. But as she soon found out, there was no money to improve the basic fare. Often as not the only dish for lunch and dinner was potato soup and the odd pot of greens. (For several months the alternative was tinned potato hash, donated by a wealthy Christian family who had hoarded it during the war. The children ate it guiltily, remembering how many had starved back in Berlin.) Breakfast was oatmeal, day in and day out. Firewood was hard to come by, as were other basic necessities, and when money came in from Eberhard's publishing work, it often went right out again to pay off a loan from the previous month.

Fortunately Heiner's mother and her sisters knew how to celebrate. When the first hard-won fruits of the garden finally came in, they decorated the harvest wagon and danced on the front lawn. When Eberhard bought a new goat, they festooned the animal with wildflower garlands and led it through the village in a triumphal procession, with the children following behind.

The sisters also knew how to laugh. No matter how well-worn a joke, they loved to retell it. "Moni, do you remember the time we went to that revival conference?" Emmy would begin. "After the hostess showed us to our room, I found the bed was filthy. I went to her for fresh sheets, and she stood there in amazement. 'But Emmy, all five people who slept in the bed before you were missionaries!'"

They laughed, too, when others might have cried or grown upset. "It's only one step from the sublime to the ridiculous," they would remind each other, when daily life took a turn toward the absurd. There were plenty of such moments, as on the day the community lost its only cow. The responsibility for milking and feeding her fell to a young member of the household called Otto. But Otto was a poet, and if a verse entered his mind while he was milking, so be it: the milking must wait. Half an hour might pass, and then an hour, and still Otto sat locked in his bedroom, writing, as the jilted cow bellowed in pain. Eva, who was in love with Otto, made sure that no one distracted him at such times. Tiptoeing through the house with her finger on her lips, she shushed the children: "Please be quiet! Otto is writing poetry!"

The cow took her revenge. As time went on, she gave less and less milk, and when she grew so thin that Eberhard could hang his hat on her jutting bones, he saw that there was no other alternative but to sell her. With her went the children's supply of milk and butter.

In general, food was always short, unless you counted the wild spinach the children were sent out to pick. From the first month the family had moved into the villa, they had been besieged by a steady army of guests—more than two thousand came during the first year alone—and since then, the stream of visitors had never stopped. Some were merely curious, and quickly moved on; others stayed longer, sometimes for days. All tended to arrive unannounced. But here again, Moni and Emmy were as likely to laugh as to sigh. If more showed up for dinner than expected, they would simply try to stretch what they had: "Ten were invited; twenty have come—put water in the soup, and bid them welcome!"

Many of the guests were college-age hikers who came wearing bright, peasant-style costumes with guitars slung over their backs. They regarded Dr. Arnold's settlement as a bastion of Youth Movement values and guarded it carefully against infiltration. If a fellow guest came wearing long trousers (bourgeois!) instead of shorts, he might wake the next morning to find them cropped at the knees. In theory, guests helped with the house and garden work. In practice, many worked only when they "felt the inner urge." Emmy did not trust them with her vegetables, and lugged the watering can and weeded the beds herself.

Politically minded guests flocked to Sannerz too, intrigued by Eberhard's stubborn refusal to condone violence and his simultaneous passion for social justice and worldwide brotherhood. Arguing that private property was theft, and that even the most advanced civilization was rotten if it was built on the backs of the poor, Eberhard and Emmy preached a communism of love. Here, no one claimed anything as his own: every bit of income, and every piece of property belonged to *die Sache*—the cause. "How can we, who want to share the suffering of the masses, keep anything at all for ourselves?" Emmy wrote. "We want to give away all we have to those who want to serve the same spirit of love with us. For us, the desire to own nothing is like an article of faith."

Not all who visited Sannerz came with a sound mind or a spotless reputation. Every few months an unkempt man who called himself "Nature's Apostle" would appear. His wanderings took him from town to town campaigning for healthy living, barefoot and clothed in little more than a porous undergarment he advertised as "Dr. Lama's underwear." A family showed up dressed as wildflowers and wouldn't say anything except, "We come from the woods; we live in the woods; we shall return to the woods." One young visitor had such qualms about harming other forms of life that he wouldn't eat anything (he later died of starvation).

Eberhard could enjoy a good laugh, but he drummed it into his children never to make fun of anyone for their peculiarities. He said that learning to show love to absolutely everyone was the single most important goal of education—far more important than academics or practical skills. "To make another human being feel like a fool is a terrible sin," he once told Heiner. "It is soul murder."

Adam von Adamsky, a twenty-year-old blacksmith with enormous biceps, had just been released from prison when he arrived at Sannerz. One day he asked Heiner, "What can I do for Tata? She looks so thin. What does she like?"

"Chocolate," Heiner said. It was a luxury they almost never saw.

"And your father. . . What would he enjoy?"

"Let me think. Maybe a bottle of wine."

Adam disappeared, and came back the next evening with a sack full of gifts for everyone in the household. A few hours after his return, the police were knocking at the door. Adam whispered to Heiner, "I'm going to hide in the hayloft until they're gone. Tell me when I can come down."

The officers, having seen Adam at the villa, explained that he was wanted. Just yesterday, they said, he had robbed the cashbox of a nearby smithy. But Eberhard did not know where Adam was, and the officers left. As soon as they were gone, Heiner went to the barn and shouted up the all clear.

When Eberhard saw Adam, he demanded, "What have you done?"

"*Ach,* Eberhard, I only did it because I love you. I wanted to make you and Tata happy."

"But I hope you have not been stealing again!"

"If you had, would you admit it?" Adam retorted. Then, without another word, he strode off down the road.

Unwed mothers often stayed at the house for months. Some had been referred by the municipal welfare office in Berlin. They knew that between Moni's midwifery skills and Eberhard's generosity, both mother and baby would be well taken care of. Others were casualties of Fritz Schwalbe, the young anarchist who had squatted in the Arnolds' old allotment garden. According to pattern, whenever Fritz's girlfriend of the moment became pregnant, he would send her on to Sannerz. Each one told Heiner a suspiciously similar tale: poor Fritz had been outrageously mistreated by women all his life, until at last he had found his true love—her.

One young woman who came, a shy, depressive creature, had been convinced by the man who seduced her that if she bore his baby, it would redeem humankind.

Heiner was troubled by such sad characters. On the other hand, his favorite visitor was Hans-in-Luck, a Pied Piper who liked to appear when the moon was shining. Hearing the notes of his ocarina before he arrived, the Arnold children would run out to meet him in their nightgowns, with the village children close behind them. Hans-in-Luck (his legal name was Hans Fiehler) looked like he had stepped out of a fairy tale. He wore black pantaloons and a scarlet waistcoat, and his name was embroidered on the back in big gold letters. He sported a red nightcap, and introduced himself by saying, "I am Hans-in-Luck, and I am looking for peace among nations."

During the Great War, Hans-in-Luck had killed a man in hand-to-hand combat, and he told Heiner how his guilt, and then remorse, had changed his entire outlook on life. He was now traveling through Germany, he said, to spread the hope of universal peace – "the springtime of the world." Hans-in-Luck was a poet and musician, always improvising and composing, or penning a new ditty. Everywhere he went, he carried a violin, a set of ocarinas, and his accordion.

Once a visiting parson entered the house to find Hans-in-Luck and Fritz painting the walls of the corridor with rainbows and sinking battleships. "Where are you from?" he asked Fritz abruptly.

"From jail. I'm an anarchist," came the reply.

"And you?" he asked, turning to Hans-in-Luck.

"The lunatic asylum."

It was not the sort of introduction one expected at a Christian home.

Hans-in-Luck's pranks were sometimes risky. Once between visits to Sannerz, he approached an army general widely blamed for losing the war. It was at a time when runaway inflation had wiped out almost everyone's savings, and many were unemployed and starving. Hans-in-Luck made the man a proposal: If you want to restore your good standing with the public, take your field kitchens into the city and feed the poor. I'll stand by and make a film of it all. Remarkably, the general agreed to the plan. Hans-in-Luck stood with his camera in the street surrounded by army men, commanding the general, "Stand up smartly!" "Dish it up yourself!" When all the food had been distributed, the general pulled Hans aside to retrieve the footage. Hans-in-Luck snapped open the camera. It was empty. "My goodness, I must have forgotten the film at home!" he protested. The general and his staff were livid, but Hans-in-Luck had the crowd on his side.

To accommodate guests, especially during weekend retreats or conferences, Eberhard converted the barn behind the villa into a youth hostel. Almost every evening Heiner talked with the young men and women staying there as they mingled outside, cooking on an open fire or trying out new melodies on their guitars and violins. From them he got an education in a wide variety of worldviews. He listened and argued with vegetarians, nationalists, and communists; artists and seminarians; yogis, anarchists, and proletarians.

The last two types were Heiner's heroes, and one of them, Christel Girbinger, became his best friend. Heiner had met him at a conference at Pentecost 1921, when, bored by the endless discussions, he had wandered away to look for someone to play with. Christel had been sitting at the edge of the woods, and with his bushy beard and eye glasses, Heiner assumed that he must be an old man—at very least, thirty. He was actually much younger, as Heiner found out after challenging him to a game of tag. That night Christel brought Heiner home on his shoulders—and stayed on as a member of the household.

Christel was a printer, a carpenter, and a Bavarian, but first and foremost a *proletarian*. "Look here," he advised Heiner, "Don't learn too much in school. If you learn too much, you will become like your father. He means very well and wants to be one of us, but he will never be able to understand the working class. He's got too much education."

One day Heiner told his teacher, Trudi, "Christel says that if I can learn to be a good carpenter, I don't need to learn anything else."

"But if you can't do arithmetic you can't measure the wood."

"Fine, then I will learn arithmetic. But not how to write."

"Then how will you write letters when you're away from home?"

"Oh, Trudi," he said, brightening, "I'll have a Tata, and she will type them for me."

Trudi hoped that Heiner's determination to be a proletarian would prove a passing whim. But he did not waver. He refused to learn, and his grades got worse and worse. Meanwhile his classmates assumed he was slow. Only Christel seemed to understand, and he encouraged Heiner to dig in his heels: "School and everything connected with learning destroys all friendship between us workers and you children of intellectuals. You must rebel!"

Christel always spoke of the millions who suffered exploitation but deserved justice. "A way must be found for the masses!" he would say, his eyes flashing. "It is the greed of the rich and educated that condemns them to misery." Christel's personal motto was "Always seek freedom." Heiner listened, and never forgot.

4

Breakup

It was the summer of 1922, and Eberhard's settlement was entering its third year. Casual visitors still came and went by the dozen, but the core household had multiplied and grown. Apart from the children and long-term guests, there were twenty-three full members. Neuwerk, the publishing house, was putting out a popular journal on religion, social issues, and current events; and in the line of books, Eberhard was developing an impressive list of titles, among them a collection of fairy tales, a Jewish scholar's history of anti-Semitism, and a volume on medieval women mystics. Speaking engagements at universities were making Eberhard's name known up and down Germany.

But despite the vitality of the Sannerz settlement, its members were living hand to mouth. Post-war inflation rose, then soared, and by the time Neuwerk subscribers paid their invoices, the payment had often lost much of its value. Eberhard took Jesus' words literally: "Do not worry. Look at the birds. They do not sow or harvest, and yet their heavenly Father feeds them. How much more will he feed you, his children?" Not that he wasn't a stickler for good business practice—he had a committee of auditors certify the community's books, and in members' meetings he reviewed reports on profits and expenses item by item. All the same, he insisted that faith, not money, was what mattered.

Eberhard disliked fretters and long-term planners. "Worry is just another form of materialism," he would say. Sannerz was for people of the spirit, not managers and accountants. When finances were especially tight, Heiner heard him say, "The money is there; we just haven't got it yet."

In July, the Arnolds took a train to Bilthoven in the Netherlands, where they planned to spend some days with a Quaker whose regular donations helped keep Sannerz's publishing venture afloat. Kees Boeke was an educator and anarchist pacifist with such unyielding principles that at that time he refused to pay taxes or even use the mail. (Later he founded a school patronized by the Dutch royal family; his 1957 book *Cosmic View* showing the universe from galactic to microcosmic scales would go on to inspire the IMAX film *Cosmic Voyage*.) His wife Betty, a Cadbury, had given away her fortune to employees in the family's chocolate factory.

The Boekes lived in a simple country house surrounded by heather and pine trees, in an area where it was illegal to build outdoor fires. To Kees, any such prohibition was an invitation to resistance. One evening after the Arnolds arrived, he invited several hundred friends to a celebratory bonfire. By the time the police arrived, the fire was burning high, and the whole party was dancing around it. Heiner watched with delight as Kees took the astonished policeman by the arm and firmly planted him inside the circle. Then they all cheered and leaped around him. Heiner had never enjoyed a dance so much.

Halfway through their vacation, Eberhard received a telegram from Sannerz notifying him that a bank loan had been unexpectedly called in. Payment was due within days. As always, he refused to worry—he felt sure the needed money would appear. And it did: as the family was about to board the train home, a woman slipped up to Eberhard on the station platform. She was Maria Moojen, an Indonesian princess and a friend of the family. She pressed an envelope into his hands, saying, "For the cause."

The family's reception at home was icy. For Heiner and his siblings there was a small cake, but for their parents and Tata there was only watery soup. While they had been gone, several in the household had worked themselves into a panic over the loan. Now that the Arnolds were home, they were determined to speak their minds on the matter—and on the whole issue of "financial responsibility." Eberhard remained calm and would not budge. A man's faith, he said, is worthless unless it penetrates the material course of his life as well as the spiritual.

Furious, his critics called a meeting to take place the same night. As the session began, accusations began to fly, and a crowd of curious guests gathered to observe it through the open windows. All but a handful of members were openly hostile. They told Eberhard that he was a fanatic. "This whole place is built on dreams! You can't expect us to live on leaps of faith. We demand thorough planning, arrangements for financial backing, a dependable source of operating funds. You can't just talk about Jesus and his teachings: you have to take into account the realities of human nature." "Sannerz is a fraud," someone shouted in agreement. "You and Emmy are charlatans!"

Eberhard stood his ground and requested a chance to refute the accusations. "Miracles, too, are a basis for economic existence," he said, and told about the envelope he had received on the way home. Inside had been a wad of gulden which, when converted into marks, came to exactly the amount needed to pay off the loan.

But it was too late. "We've already begun liquidation proceedings," they told him. "Sannerz is dead. The experiment is over." One by one, they said they were leaving.

Christel was one of them, though Heiner could hardly bring himself to believe it. "We're still friends," he assured Heiner. And then, taking him on his knee: "It's not your fault. It's your parents who are guilty." Heiner was not consoled, especially when, the next day, he overheard the young man angrily criticizing his father.

Once during the unbearable weeks that followed, Hardy told Heiner that he had found his father in tears at the bottom of the staircase. How did you comfort a weeping parent? "I never, ever would have believed that people could hate like this," was all Eberhard said. Among those who slandered him most harshly were some whom he had loved and trusted for years. And as if that was not enough, they burned up precious firewood with the windows open, though it was summer, stripped the house and the outbuildings of anything valuable, and sold off the livestock, furniture, and farm implements. Someone even broke into the fruit preserves Emmy had set aside for next winter.

Eberhard, as if powerless to stop them, watched but did nothing. It was only when someone suggested dissolving the community that he came to life. Then, standing to his full height and speaking with his old vehemence, he reminded everyone in earshot that the community still had legal rights to the house, and would keep it as long as the legal quorum of seven members remained. And seven was exactly the number who stayed.

Christel left with the others. Heiner felt desolate. As he would later write in his diary: "He went away, and there was hurt and pain. I was scared of Papa and Mama. I didn't believe in God anymore, only Christel. At night I would still say my evening prayer. But then I would just fall asleep."

Heiner pined for Christel for the rest of his childhood, but not without a stab of guilt. Did missing him—loving him—mean hating his father? (Years later his father assured him it didn't—"You made a good choice in choosing him as a friend," he said. After his father's death, Heiner heard through a mutual friend that Christel often traveled to Hesse to pay his respects at Eberhard's grave.)

It was October before the last hostile faction left the house. (Many of them joined together to found a new commune, which disbanded within a few years.) Now, besides Eberhard, Emmy, Tata, and Moni, only Trudi, the children's teacher, and two other members—Suse and Paul—were left. The yellow villa seemed hollow and silent. Eberhard still romped and joked with the children, but otherwise he was withdrawn and sad. On occasion Heiner found his mother and her sisters wiping away tears.

Kees Boeke continued to fund the publishing house. There wasn't much left—those who had left Sannerz had taken the *Neuwerk* journal and most of the best-selling books with them. Just as bad for business was Sannerz's sudden isolation. In the aftermath of the split, rumors about the settlement flew in all directions, Eberhard was widely criticized, and many who had supported him earlier distanced themselves from him.

But despite Eberhard and Emmy's hurt, Heiner never heard them utter a nasty word about those who had abandoned them. "It is not that we who stayed are good, and the others bad," his mother explained. "It is just that they saw everything as an experiment, and we know it is a calling."

In November a strange young man arrived. He wore a brown tunic and sandals, and toted a knapsack and guitar on his back. His hair fell below his shoulders. He called himself Roland, after Charlemagne's legendary knight.

Heiner saw him coming and approached him right away. Within minutes Moni had assigned Karl Keiderling (his real name) to help get lunch ready by chopping wood for the kitchen fire. Heiner joined him, and soon they were chatting easily. Karl was relieved to have found the community, as on the way there from the train station he'd lost his way. He had met a policeman and asked directions.

"So you're going to the Jewish settlement?" the policeman had said.

"I've heard they are Christians."

"That may be. But who do you think they get their money from? Rich Jews! How else could they exist?" (In fact, an important benefactor for the Sannerz community was Max Wolf, the Jewish owner of a local factory, who admired Eberhard's commitment to justice and opposition to anti-Semitism.)

Karl, who was nineteen, told Heiner that his father had kicked him out of the house. He found a second father in Eberhard, though, and within days he decided to stay at Sannerz for good. He continued to supply the house with firewood, and Heiner helped him whenever he could get away from school. If he saw Karl through the classroom window setting out for the forest, he slipped away to join him. By the time Trudi noticed his empty seat, the two were usually out of sight, pushing their wooden handcart up the hill.

As winter turned to spring, Heiner and Karl spent hours on end watching deer in the forest or just lying in the grass talking. Most of the time neither thought of the ten years between them.

Heiner was about to get playmates his own age too, thanks to his parents' plan to rescue unwanted or orphaned children. That same year, no less than six new children moved to Sannerz. One of them was Sophie.

Fatherless since the war, Sophie Schwing was brought to Sannerz by a worn-looking woman who dropped her off in the children's playroom, and slipped stealthily away. Spotting a boy about her age on the rocking horse, and thinking him another foster child, the girl announced that she wanted a turn. Heiner refused. "It's my horse."

"They told me that everyone would share their things here," Sophie said, perplexed.

"I know. But it's *my* father who took you in," Heiner shot back. He stayed on the horse.

Sophie turned to enlist her mother's help, but no one was there. She started crying. The boy softened. "I know. You lost your Mama. But I don't have one either. I mean, I do—but she never has time for me. She has to clean and cook and weed the garden and be with guests—and she has to take care of the orphans. I guess we're even."

5

Conversion

AFTER HEINER TURNED ELEVEN, something began to take hold of him. An Indian sadhu, or holy man, was on a speaking tour of Germany, and he was making headlines everywhere he went. In the evening, as the family gathered around the kitchen table, Eberhard took out newspaper clippings and read them aloud.

The sadhu's name was Sundar Singh. As a fifteen-year-old Sikh growing up in the Punjab, he had desperately wanted to find out who God was. He read everything he could, starting with his own religion's scriptures, and then devouring the sacred books of Hinduism, Buddhism, and Islam. But he would have nothing to do with that hated imperialist religion, Christianity. At the Presbyterian missionary school where his parents sent him to prepare for university, he shredded and burned a Bible in front of his horrified classmates.

Sundar Singh's self-satisfaction with this deed was short-lived. One night not long afterward, he threw God a challenge: "Reveal yourself now, or I will kill myself to see what lies beyond." He refused to lie down, but stayed up praying.

According to his own account of what happened next, a glow filled the room at about 4:30. At first he thought there was a fire in the house. Then a figure emerged from the brightness and said to him in Urdu, "Sundar, how long will you mock me? I have come to save you because you have prayed to find the way of truth. Why, then, don't you accept it?" Seeing wounds on the figure's hands and feet, Sundar recognized him as Jesus.

When Sundar Singh told his parents next day, they dismissed it as a dream. As time went on, however, there was no denying it: the young man was changed. Relatives offered him all sorts of enticements if he would renounce his new faith, but to no avail. They disowned him, threatened him, and tried to poison him. Finally they banished him from his native region. Since then he had become sought after as few sadhus, wandering not only through India, but also Nepal and Tibet, spreading Jesus' message wherever he went. Now he was spreading it in Europe too.

Heiner was deeply stirred by what his father read, and over the next few weeks he often disappeared, taking long, solitary walks. One of his favorite destinations was a willow by a stream where he imagined himself living the life of a sadhu, leaving only to preach or to beg food from his listeners. He longed to meet Sundar Singh and talk to him. Perhaps he would come to Sannerz, and then he could ask all his questions. For one, had Jesus actually come into his room? Or had he shouted down to the boy from heaven? If he had shouted, the neighbors must have heard . . .

At the same time, other events were giving Heiner food for thought. Once as they were eating on the veranda, a disheveled man of about fifty lurched toward the house from the road, reeking of wine. On impulse, Heiner jumped up from his meal, grabbed the man's hand and invited him. When he asked his father if the man could stay the night, his father said, "Of course—that is, if he would like to."

Tears rolling down his face, the man then told them his story. His name was Karl Gail, and he was a murderer. A veteran of the military action to suppress the Chinese Boxer Rebellion, he had just been released after serving a long prison term. Now he was homeless. Everyone sat frozen, not knowing how to respond. But Eberhard stood up and wrapped his arms around the man. Then, turning his face toward the sun, he spoke to him about Jesus, who came for murderers and sinners of every kind. That night Heiner and the other children fetched blankets, and made up a bed for the man.

Then there was Oswald, who arrived in a skirt with a pink ribbon in his hair. Eberhard embraced him and offered him his study to sleep in. That evening at dinner Oswald stood up and proclaimed, "To the pure all things are pure," then disrobed.

Eberhard ordered Oswald to dress himself, and then confronted him: "Jesus wants to free you from the evil that is tormenting you. But you must choose whether you want to be freed, or not."

At this Oswald shrieked that the demons inside him would tear him to pieces, and ran from the room. At the table, no one spoke or moved. Heiner listened as the barking of the dogs marked Oswald's route through the village.

Heiner pondered why his father welcomed people like Oswald when even his little sister, Monika, seemed repelled by them. Why, after all, did such people flock to Sannerz, like moths to a candle? As he wondered, he found his own answer: it was the love that such broken spirits found there. Heiner noticed it when his father had turned Karl Gail's face toward the sun, and saw it also when he had thundered at Oswald – that was love, too. Then there was his father's authority: the way he spoke with a finality that seemed to come from beyond him.

Heiner never dared mention these things, but he sensed it had something to do with his father's closeness to Jesus. And so one day he shyly asked him, "How *does* one find Jesus?"

"If you seek, you will find," his father answered.

One evening at dinner, Eberhard told the household another remarkable story. Rachoff was a young man who had lived in the Russian port city of Archangelsk in the previous century. His wealth promised him a life of ease, and yet, like Sundar Singh, a strange vision had utterly changed him.

One night in his sleep Rachoff saw a man plowing as the sun rose above the field. Suddenly from a poor hut nearby came the sound of a violin. The man at the plow stopped and listened, and then went on. Soon the sound began again, though now it was the crying of a child. The man left his plow, went into the hut, and found a sick baby near to death. Bending over the child, he caressed it, and it was healed. Then Rachoff recognized the plowman. His heart bursting, he shouted, "Brother Jesus, I am coming!"

Leaving a note for his mother, he walked out of the city that same night. From then on, he wandered through Russia, aiding the downtrodden wherever he went. He rebuilt the houses of widows, exhorted high-living clergy, and stood up in a packed opera house to demand that the diamond-wearing patrons take responsibility for the slums at their doorstep. He told everyone he met about Jesus. Rachoff was loved by the poor, but loathed and feared by the powerful. After numerous arrests and banishments – from Kiev, Odessa, and elsewhere – he was imprisoned in solitary confinement. Starving and wracked by fevers, he grew emaciated and eventually lost his mind. In the end his guards took pity on him and let him out into a small enclosed garden. Rachoff spent the last days of his life sitting there, his eyes closed, a smile playing on his face, his stooped shoulders warmed by the sun. On occasion he circled or swayed with slow steps. "I am dancing," he explained, "for I shall soon see God." Then one evening, in the middle of such a dance, he was seen to stop suddenly. Opening his eyes wide, he cried loudly, "Jesus!" and slumped forward in death.

Heiner began to weep as his father finished speaking. In a daze, he left the table and stumbled to his room. He threw himself on his bed. Why did this good man have to suffer and end his life as a broken man? Why did Jesus have to die?

It was then that Heiner felt something he had never felt before: Jesus himself was in the room, addressing and summoning him. The power of his presence made Heiner tremble all over. Suddenly, the boy was possessed by a great love. He had an inkling of how God's heart must have melted as he watched the life of his son on earth – comforting children, healing the sick, pardoning sinners, and driving the money-changers from the temple; preaching to his followers, and finally dying in agony as a criminal on a cross.

In that moment Heiner received his life's task. He sensed it would mean suffering, just as Rachoff had had to suffer. Going out among people on Jesus' behalf meant going out among wolves.

Heiner could hardly wait for his father to come and say goodnight. But when at last Eberhard entered the room, Heiner was only able to mumble a few words through his tears. His father could not have understood, for he only rumpled Heiner's hair, murmured a kind word, and left again.

For a long time, Heiner lay staring at the ceiling. Although only eleven, he knew that what he had tasted was absolutely real. He imagined that his life might be something like Rachoff's. He would wander from village to village, calling nothing his own, and spreading the gospel to the poor.

6

The Sun Troop

DURING THE SEVEN YEARS that the Arnolds lived in Sannerz, the family never had a living room of their own. By 1925 – just three years after the split when Christel and the others had left – every corner held a bed, and the villa hummed with some fifty inhabitants, among them two young families and ten foster children.

The five Arnold children daydreamed about having their mother to themselves, but because Emmy had so many demands on her time, Tata and Moni mothered them just as often. If they were sick in bed, Tata sat with them for hours entertaining them with jokes and songs; if they came home starved, Moni would try to find something to hold them over until dinner. Sometimes guests would ask the von Hollander sisters how they could stand having the children's affection split three ways. Weren't they jealous of each other? "No," they said, "we are only richer this way, and the children are richer too."

Emmy did not neglect her children, though. Before bedtime she gathered them around her to tell them stories or sing with her lute. She let nothing keep her from these times. If community meetings went on too long, she would slip out through the kitchen to find them. It wasn't just a matter of having a cozy time: Emmy knew her children missed nothing of the goings on in the bustling house, and she made sure they had a place to air their observations and anxieties. Heiner's sensitivity was a special concern to her. As she wrote to a relative, "He is a child who flourishes only in the atmosphere of God."

Heiner and his brothers and sisters ate breakfast in their parents' bedroom each morning. During this quarter hour, Eberhard insisted that they should stick to topics that interested the children. Sometimes Emmy would forget and relate her worries—a troublesome visitor, the mounting debt at the grocer's. Then Eberhard would nudge her, "But Emmychen, now we are concentrating on the children." Sometimes there were clashes: Papa and Mama spoke frankly to each other no matter who was listening. This did not make Heiner insecure. Having often heard his father and mother saying to each other, "I wouldn't want to live one day longer than you," he never once doubted the unbreakable bond between them.

One morning the family had gathered for breakfast as usual when Eberhard noticed that Heiner, who usually lingered at the table, was eager to be on his way. So was seven-year-old Monika, who was edging toward the door. "Where are you two going?"

"I . . . can't tell you," Monika said.

That was the wrong thing to say to Papa, and he repeated his question. Still Monika refused to answer. Finally, she offered: "But Heiner has forbidden me to say what we are doing."

Eberhard turned to the boy. "Heiner, I want to hear all about this, immediately!"

Heiner shared everything, first hesitantly and then freely. How, one by one, he had told the other children what had happened in his bedroom the night their father had read them the story of Rachoff. How they had decided to follow Jesus as a group. How he had decorated the schoolroom for their first meeting with wildflowers, a candle, and a red cloth on the table. It had been a solemn occasion, he told his parents, and the children he had invited had entered the room in silence. This was not going to be a club—absolutely not. It was going to be a fighting unit, a squad always ready for action. They had argued about a fitting name and had finally settled on one. They would call themselves the Sun Troop.

Heiner finished, and Eberhard sipped his coffee. The bedroom was quiet. Then Heiner announced, "I have arranged to meet with some village children about the Sun Troop this morning. We've picked blackberries to eat with them at our meeting. If we stay here longer we're going to be late."

Eberhard gave his permission, and the children were gone. Later that day, Heiner met him again. His father said nothing. But that evening he entered the boy's room and kissed him over and over, saying, "I love you, I love you." From that time on, Heiner felt, his father was not just his father, but also his very best friend.

Heiner's conversion took Eberhard by surprise. He himself had had a similar experience as a sixteen-year-old, and had been similarly zealous in telling his peers about it. But since the war, he had begun to look beyond the revivalistic Christianity of his youth, and he was wary of pressing religion on his children. (Once he walked into the children's school room and found their governess, a former Salvation Army officer, in the middle of a lengthy lecture on a story from the Old Testament. Eberhard listened for a moment, then retreated without comment. The teacher never taught a Bible class again.)

Heiner told his father about his desire to take to the road, like Rachoff, in order to tell people about Jesus. "Heiner," Eberhard replied, "that is a wonderful idea. But why not focus first on the children right here, and the children in the village? Reach out to them, and help awaken in them what you have experienced." The boy agreed.

From the start, Eberhard advised Heiner not to let adults interfere in the Sun Troop—not even Karl. He himself came to the children's meetings only rarely. Yet somehow he was always familiar with how the little group was doing. He often invited Heiner to his study, and the two talked over the boy's newest ideas. Eberhard could read his son's emotions like a barometer, and when his enthusiasm flagged, he encouraged him.

After Eberhard, Tata was the Sun Troop's biggest supporter. Her bedroom was next to Heiner's, and almost every evening he visited her to talk. Everyone in the family knew that Tata's bond with Heiner went back to his birth, and that it was something special—on her birthday, for instance, they celebrated as if it were his birthday too. Now he confided all his plans to her. The sharing went both ways. One night she woke him, saying she had been unable to sleep because of a bad conscience: "Today I said an unkind word to one of the other women. It was a mean thing to do, and I need to tell someone." That was all—she said goodnight and went back to bed.

Apart from Heiner, the two other core members of the Sun Troop were Sophie and another foster child, Luise Kolb. Sophie was a year younger than Heiner. One day he had come up to her and talked to her about Sundar Singh, Francis of Assisi, and Rachoff. The way he talked made her pay attention: he was totally unselfconscious, his heart wholly on fire with the importance of what he wanted to relate. Then, in closest confidence, he told her of how Jesus had come to him.

"Doesn't Jesus expect something of me too?" Sophie wondered. Heiner talked to Luise as well, and she found herself asking the same question. That was how the Sun Troop had come into being.

The first thing they decided was to make a flag. Before Sophie came to Sannerz she had learned to sew from her mother, a seamstress. Heiner found a perfect length of red cloth. He stood behind Sophie and directed her as she cut out a circle of yellow flames, then watched as she sewed the two pieces together on Emmy's old treadle machine. Heiner tied the finished banner to a pole, and the same afternoon they carried it through the village, marching up and down the main road and singing lustily.

Heiner was outspoken when he thought a fellow Sun Trooper was not behaving as a Sun Trooper should. One day during class Sophie was caught reading a novel under her desk. Trudi noticed and asked her for the book. When she saw what it was—a popular romance—she said, "Sophie, this is not the best book for a girl your age."

Heiner jumped up. "What? You're reading a bad book? I would never have thought it. Sophie, how could you!"

"Heiner, have you even seen this book?" Sophie retorted.

"Me? No. I'd never read a bad book."

The two of them met after school to finish the argument.

On occasion he confessed a misdeed to her. Once he'd made a play for his mother's attention—he was tired of her constant focus on Hans-Hermann (he was always in bed with something) and Emy-Margret, who had tuberculosis. Faking a violent fit of coughing, he managed to scare her into having him checked for the same disease. It was a plausible ruse: aside from Emy-Margret, Eberhard had an active case, and Emmy's sister Olga had recently died of it.

It didn't take long for Heiner's conscience to strike him: "Sophie, I have to tell you something. I lied to my mother." And then, tears streaming down his face: "Sophie, I am the greatest sinner in the world."

He sat next to her in school. When Trudi gave them an arithmetic assignment, he passed his notebook to Sophie. "Here, write down the solutions for me," he'd whisper. "I need to think up what we can do next with the Sun Troop."

Trudi wrung her hands at his complete lack of interest in learning—and then at his heartfelt attempts to soothe her. "Why do you make such efforts for me, Trudi?" he said. And then, probably quoting Christel: "Fools remain fools, no medicine can help them." Understandably, Trudi was nervous when the school inspector made his visit. But whereas most of her pupils sat tongue-tied as he examined them, Heiner surprised everyone by answering one question after the other—correctly.

Sophie loved to listen to Heiner talk. His imagination was constantly active, and he was always planning something new. One day, she and Luise were working with Heiner in the potato field. So was a homeless man then staying at the villa, and Alfred Gneiting, a gardener who had recently joined the household.

After an hour or so the children got tired of working and climbed up into a plum tree, where they ate their fill of fruit. Alfred worked on, but the homeless man complained that he was tired, too, and stretched out beneath the tree and fell asleep.

Looking down on the man, Heiner suddenly noticed something terrible. His blue and white shirt had what looked like dark bloodstains on it. His mind racing, Heiner pointed out the stains to Sophie and Luise, and reminded them that the woods beyond the field were known to be haunted. Hadn't several villagers told their parents that people had disappeared there?

"This man must be a murderer," Heiner declared emphatically. "Think what crimes he may have on his conscience! We have to try to save him. We have to convert him!"

The girls agreed, climbed down the tree, and waited next to the man until he woke up. Then, though they didn't tell him why, they set to trying to convert him.

The Sun Troop took special care of Karl Gail, the ex-convict that Heiner had invited in from the road. He had since joined the household and been baptized by Eberhard, who, in order to give him responsibility, appointed him as the scheduler for the community's single bathtub. (One night he woke Eberhard with loud pounding on his bedroom door at 2:30 in the morning, calling out "Eberhard, Eberhard! The bathtub's ready!" Eberhard obediently went.) Now the children wanted to give Karl Gail a room to call his own. They set it up with a lantern, a New Testament, and a magnifying glass for him to read with—he had told them he could not afford to buy glasses. One evening Heiner, Sophie, and Luise dressed up as angels and visited him. Karl Gail was sitting at his table. The children sang, and he began to sob violently. Afterward he told them about the bad life he had led.

The children reminded him that "Jesus came especially for people like you." The old man straightened, and thanked them over and over. Heiner looked straight at him. "Karl, follow Jesus."

It was a Sunday morning, and Heiner met Luise as he was going down the stairs to the dining room. He was heading for the prayer meeting his father held each week. Somehow they got into a quarrel, and Luise slapped him in the face. A moment later Eberhard appeared, his New Testament under his arm. He saw that something was amiss.

"What is going on?"

"Heiner is being mean to me again," Luise whined.

Eberhard put his hand under the boy's chin and lifted it. "Heiner, why can't you be more loving?"

This was too much for Heiner, and he shouted: "You love all the children in this house, just not your own!"

With a slap, Eberhard's Bible came down on Heiner's head—not once, but twice—and he found himself being pushed into the store-room at the bottom of the stairs. The key turned in the lock. Heiner was furious. He listened through the wall as the service began with a song.

Then the door opened and his father came in. "What really happened?" he asked gently. Heiner told him.

"I acted wrongly. I ask you to forgive me," Eberhard said.

Heiner's heart melted like wax.

"Luise and the other foster children have no real parents," his father explained. "Even if I seem to treat them with more love than I treat you, you must remember they still miss what you have—and will never have it."

At that moment Heiner loved his father more than ever.

It wasn't long before the Sun Troop's first fire began to grow cold. Heiner was depressed. Papa had assured him that the calling he had received was real. And that confidence was a constant security for the boy, especially when others in the house sneered at him. One said his conversion was "awfully pious" and unhealthy; another had implied that it was put on. Most wounding of all, someone he thought he was close to had disparaged the Sun Troop to his father, not knowing that Heiner was listening in on the conversation. Papa had defended the children vigorously. But still Heiner was devastated by what he had overheard.

Perhaps it was a punishment for being disobedient to the call he had received. After all, months had passed since his conversion, and yet he still had not set off like Rachoff or Sundar Singh had. One afternoon while weeding the carrot bed with Sophie and Luise, he talked over the problem with them. They were frittering away their lives. Wasn't it a waste of time to spend an entire day killing plants, just because someone had decided they were weeds? What if they were flowers? Why not let them grow alongside the carrots?

The girls agreed. Heiner said, "Let's go up the *Langeberg* ("Long Mountain"). At the top we'll separate, and each of us will consider in prayer what Jesus really wants us to do. Does he want us to take to the road, or does he want us to stay at Sannerz? If we all get the same answer, we go. If even one of us gets a different answer, we all stay. Agreed?" They shook hands and set off at once. Alfred, their supervisor, caught sight of them as they disappeared. "Come back!" he shouted. Heiner ignored the cries—he needed to focus on their mission. Alfred tried to pursue the children, but they could run faster than he, and soon lost him among the trees.

At a clearing on top of the *Langeberg* each of the children went off on their own to pray. After half an hour they regrouped. All three had received the same answer: leave Sannerz today.

Heiner grew serious. "It's not fun and games to preach the gospel," he warned the girls. "People won't like it; they'll hate what we have to say. We may be put into prison with iron collars around our necks and chains on our legs. They'll tighten the chains slowly, tighter and tighter." The girls shivered.

Somewhere below them, Alfred was still crashing through the brush, shouting, "Come back! Come back!" Heiner looked up. Sophie and Luise had their heads together. "What are you girls whispering about?" he demanded. "Are you scared? If so, stay here. I'll go alone."

"Oh no, we're not scared at all," Sophie said hastily. "It's just that we've decided to bring our dolls."

"What!" Heiner gasped with shock. "You're talking about dolls? How can you think of your dolls at such a serious moment?"

The Sun Troop set off toward the next village in the warmth of the afternoon sun. Finally Heiner's longing had become a reality. This was how Rachoff and Sundar Singh had lived!

Then twilight fell, and eerie shadows began to crisscross their path. It was chilly. Heiner began to think about home. What would his parents say when they discovered that their son had abandoned them without even saying goodbye? He walked slower and slower, and then stopped. They could not leave Papa and Mama and Tata like this.

Alfred finally caught up with the "lazy bunch" as they straggled back across the fields, and hurried them on with indignant reproaches. Heiner only pretended to listen. His mind was spinning with conflicting thoughts. If he had really been called to live like the sadhu, why had his conscience stopped him as soon as he had set out? He wanted so badly to talk to his father. But Eberhard was away on business and not expected back until late. The boy could not bear waiting for him in the crowded living room. He went out to the barn and leaned against a wall in the shadows.

He didn't hear the sound of galloping hooves until they were close. Suddenly Papa shot into the yard and slowed his horse. "What is it?" he asked, fixing his eyes on Heiner as he dismounted. "I felt I had to get home straight away; that you needed me."

Heiner told his father everything as he helped him unsaddle. Eberhard did not laugh. Nor did he admonish his son. Reflecting on the tale with great seriousness, he finally said, "Heiner, you certainly cannot leave home in the manner you tried to this afternoon. You do have a task from God. But I believe you must fulfill it here. To go out like Rachoff is wonderful. But it is even more wonderful when you have been sent."

Some days later, Eberhard spoke to Heiner again and told him something the boy was still pondering years afterward. "You cannot build your life on the basis of feelings. Sometimes you just won't have the intense feelings you wish for. But even then you must carry on. You must simply obey the call you have received."

Lotte

LOTTE MET EBERHARD IN 1923, at a public speaking engagement in her hometown, Nordhausen. An orphan who had grown up in a home where she was never truly welcomed, she was a deeply troubled young woman. In a letter to the Arnolds, she asked to join their community, and wrote, "I lack what you have, which is the core: Jesus. The waves are drowning me, and I could curse those who brought me into this world. They have poured their devilish intentions into my heart . . . and now no one can rescue me."

To the children at Sannerz, Lotte at first seemed like any other sixteen-year-old. She liked to dance with Emy-Margret on the meadow outside the house. Then she began to behave strangely, affecting a peculiar, dark mood. "You and your silly Sun Troop," she jeered at Heiner one day after hearing him in a childish argument. "Always bickering, aren't you!" Lotte seemed to enjoy seeing the look of pain that her words produced.

Then the convulsions began. Her body quivered and twisted as if exterior forces were shaking her. She shrieked grotesque blasphemies in a voice that was not her own. The fits could go on for hours. Lotte had to be watched constantly, since whenever they left her alone she would try to kill herself. Only Eberhard and Emmy and a handful of other adults seemed able to handle the responsibility of watching her, and they soon grew exhausted from lack of sleep.

Eberhard was determined to help Lotte to a complete recovery. But he believed her attacks were not only a sign of emotional imbalance. A deadly battle between good and evil was tearing her apart.

Strangely, as the intensity of Lotte's struggle wore everyone out, it also drew them together. Moni, who had at first come to Sannerz to support her sisters, said that through Eberhard's attempts to free Lotte of her burdens, she sensed a new power of God in the house. It overwhelmed her, and now she wanted to stay, not just as a relative but on her own convictions.

Another household member decided to stay, too: Georg Barth, a twenty-three-year-old architect from Breslau. "In this house, I felt the nearness of the kingdom of God so strongly that I could physically taste it and smell it," he wrote. Eberhard asked him to begin supervising the children after school – something no one had done up to now. He taught them ball games, took them on hikes, or oversaw their chores and garden work.

Lotte's struggle, which continued throughout autumn 1925, affected the Sun Troop deeply. No one who lived in the house could remain undecided with regard to her battle – or so they felt, and they were determined to help wherever they could. Most often they did this by meeting and singing or praying for her. Once they invited the younger children in the house to join them for a bonfire. When they tried to light the fire, it went out again and again. Heiner couldn't understand it: the wood was perfectly dry.

Then he noticed Friedrich, a boy who, whenever he came to one of their meetings, ridiculed whatever was happening. He had come tonight, and as usual, he was mimicking Sophie, Luise, and Heiner as they tried to light the fire. Sophie and Luise pleaded with him to be quiet, but his remarks only grew more biting and sarcastic. Finally Heiner asked him to go home. "Sure – if it makes a difference to you," he laughed, and left.

Suddenly the wood, which had only smoldered until now, broke into flame, and the fire flared up so brightly that it lit the surrounding bushes. The children, awed by a presence they couldn't explain, stood in a circle around it, singing one song after another until it had burned down to the last coals. Then Heiner, holding their banner, led them home through the village.

Lotte slept in the room right above the bedroom Heiner shared with Hardy. Night after night the brothers lay awake listening to her raving. They didn't have a choice; it was often impossible to sleep.

One night the din was more than Heiner could bear. At midnight he got out his accordion and played and sang the Sun Troop's favorite songs. After a while Hardy sat up and joined him. They kept singing for hours as Lotte's screams and wails continued.

At three o'clock she grew quiet. Eberhard came down and asked Heiner to get dressed. They went upstairs. Lotte was lying on the floor motionless. Eberhard told him to kneel down beside him. Heiner was surprised—he had never prayed just with his father. As they knelt together, derisive laughter burst from Lotte's unconscious body.

A few weeks later, in December, Karl was watching Lotte while Heiner kept him company. Karl had just finished his lunch plate but was still hungry. He asked Heiner to stay while he ran downstairs to the kitchen for more food. The girl seemed to be napping.

For a few seconds after Karl left, Lotte continued to lie still. Then, with lightning speed, she darted down the stairs and out the door, sprinting through the snow. She was wearing only a light summer dress. Heiner rushed to the kitchen to find Karl, and together they chased after her. Lotte ran for half a mile, until she reached the *Waldquelle,* a small, spring-fed pool surrounded by tall firs. As Heiner and Karl caught up with her, short of breath and panting, she was sitting on a rock next to the pool. When she saw them, she threw herself into the icy water. Karl splashed in after her and dragged her limp body onto the bank. "Wait here with her. I'll run home for help," he said.

Heiner sat by Lotte where she lay on the snow, wet and unconscious. He did not know how to help her and was terrified of what might happen next. He waited and waited. Finally Karl returned with Eberhard, and they lugged her home, where Emmy and Moni put her to bed.

From that day on, Lotte's attacks became milder and less frequent. After Christmas they abated altogether. She did not regain full health straightaway, and sometimes she still had sharp mood swings. But it seemed clear that the battle was over.

Around this time, Lotte asked Eberhard to baptize her. He agreed to fulfill her request on the last day of the year. Heiner and Karl were to be baptized at the same time. Shortly before midnight on New Year's Eve, a large party set out from the villa and hiked through the snow to the *Waldquelle*. As they stood around the pool, singing, Heiner waded in and his father immersed him in the frigid water. Then he baptized Karl. Finally it was Lotte's turn. Pausing on the bank, she called out in a clear voice, "Jesus! Jesus, you are the victor!" Then she entered the water.

8

Father and Son

No one who aims to spend his life as a tramp should risk becoming over-educated – Heiner was sure of that. Hadn't Christel warned him that "an intellectual can never become one of the working class, not even a well-meaning one like your Papa"?

When Heiner turned fourteen, the minimum legal age for leaving school, he begged his parents for permission to quit. He'd waited three years since Jesus had called him. But his father refused. Still, he never pushed Heiner to apply himself or pushed him to improve his abysmal grades. Hans-Hermann and Hardy were different – he rarely spared them. Hans-Hermann was to be prepared for the university by intensive study at home, while Hardy was dispatched to a boarding school at fifteen. But Heiner knew that his father's lenience was not a matter of permissiveness. It stemmed from a sensitivity to his son's deeply-felt calling.

When guests came to the villa, Hardy and Emy-Margret would cluster around them. How they loved the bold new ideas of visiting authors, reformers, and free-thinkers! Heiner tended to ignore such people, not because he disliked them but simply because he preferred the homeless men who came with ragged clothes, broken shoes, and dirty hair. They seemed so much more down-to-earth than other visitors. When he met these "brothers of the road," as his father called them, the boy would put his arm around their shoulders and ask, "Do you know about Jesus?" Many would weep and tell him about their past lives.

Heiner often took walks with Fräulein Rotkohl, a plain young woman who was a long-term houseguest. Fräulein Rotkohl had few social graces and, as if that wasn't enough, the misfortune of a name meaning "red cabbage." Heiner noticed how lonely she was, and spent hours talking with her. He did the same with two old peasant women who used to walk through the village. Often they stood at the hedge by the villa, simply gawking, as if yearning for company. Their chatter bored nearly everyone else to tears, but Heiner was a good listener. Whenever they met someone from Sannerz, they said, "Oh, you must know Heiner—we'll never forget him."

The Sun Troop sold radishes and carrots to guests at absurdly high prices, and used the proceeds to buy groceries for poor families in the village. They left their deliveries anonymously, on windowsills. They also continued their campaign to recruit other children from the neighborhood. Once they invited all the children in the village to a meeting in the barn behind the villa. They sent around the invitation by word of mouth, and decorated the barn with flowers and the red flag. On the appointed evening, the barn was full of noisy children. Heiner tried to speak, but a knot of twenty-year-olds stood at the back, taunting him and throwing stones. He tried to open the meeting again and again, and each time he was drowned out. Then the Sun Troop tried singing, and took the hands of the youngest children and danced. The ridicule from the back got even louder.

Finally Heiner shouted at the young men, "Only those who really want to be here should stay. The rest of you may go!" Gradually the mockers drifted off, and then a few others, and then still more. In the end only one little girl was left. But from that evening on she was with the Sun Troop heart and soul.

That year was the twilight of childhood for all of them. Hardy joined the Sun Troop, and he soon had as much say-so as Heiner. The knot Heiner felt inside when he noticed this took him by surprise.

How could he envy his very own brother? It was a desecration of everything the Sun Troop stood for. Hardy, for his part, noticed how his assertiveness had hurt Heiner, asked his forgiveness, and offered to withdraw from the group. Heiner was filled with deep shame. (Little did he know his father's role in the events: Eberhard had told Hardy to leave the Sun Troop alone. "You're older than everyone else in it. And you need to respect what God has given your brother.")

Around the same time, Heiner found that his body was changing. He felt unfamiliar, embarrassing urges. His father told him that every man had to learn to deal with such things: "The answer is to learn self-discipline right from the start. Then it will be easy to control yourself later." He recounted how, as a sixteen-year-old, he had once prayed all night as he struggled to conquer his own drives.

Heiner was incredulous. "But Papa, the women your age are all bulgy or wrinkled. They aren't nearly as attractive as girls are nowadays."

"You see them now, when they're forty or fifty," Eberhard said with a smile. "I saw them when they were fourteen or fifteen."

Adolescence robbed Heiner of earlier carefree friendships, especially with Sophie and Luise. His father noticed the chill, and inquired.

"I'm scared of what the girls might expect of me."

"Fine. But be sure that the Sun Troop stays alive! It cannot die just because of your self-consciousness. *That* you must never allow."

Still, the simple, bright happiness of childhood had vanished. "Dearest Sophie," Heiner wrote one day to her in a letter that he slipped under her door, "Even though I might be distasteful to you – so that you always seem to run away from me – I have to tell you something: I'm only trying to be genuine, with all my might. But I can't!"

He daydreamed. He was standing in front of a huge fire, wanting to jump into the flames so all the filth in him would burn. Just as he tensed his muscles to hurl himself in, a massive wall formed in front of him and he saw only blackness. He tried to find his way back to the fire, but everything was dark and he was lost. He kept running into the wall and hurting himself, until he got calloused and hardened. He met others who were looking for the fire too, but because he was so hard and blind he dashed against them until they, too, were injured and unable to find their way.

"I've been living without God, without light . . . without love and joy," he wrote to Sophie on another occasion. "We've been a Night Troop, a Quarrel Troop, a Stink Troop. Not a Sun Troop!"

Hope sometimes flared up in him: "It will be different! It will be like it was!" At moments he felt as if he could fly for joy. But then his spirits would fall, and a brooding fear would grip him.

He accused himself: he was proud. He agonized over having unwittingly sinned. He became a stickler about personal hygiene, and feared that if he didn't stay clean enough, he might poison someone he loved with germs. One morning he was resetting a mousetrap outside his parents' bedroom (a daily chore), when his father, who was at breakfast, called, "Heiner, would you bring me the sugar?" The boy was thrown into a quiet panic. He had just held a dead mouse in his hands! Yet washing would take several minutes. But his father was calling him again. "Heiner! The sugar?" He went and fetched it immediately.

Later that morning he began to accuse himself. What if the dead mouse had been carrying a disease? How could he have exposed his own father to the danger of contagion? The boy wrote him a confession and put it on his pillow, addressed in underlined capitals: "Only for you."

The next day at breakfast his father called him in. "Would you be kind enough to bring me a dead mouse to stir my coffee with?" He roared with laughter, and Heiner finally relaxed. "By the way," he added, "*Anyone* who saw your letter would have thought it was only for him."

The villa was creaking with too many inhabitants, and the community desperately needed a larger house. But further accommodations were not available in the village. In the summer of 1927, the Arnolds found the Sparhof, a rundown parcel of fields and farm buildings about seven miles away, in the high hills of the Rhön.

The seller required a down payment of 10,000 marks, and no one knew where it would come from. Eberhard was unconcerned. "We have always moved forward on the basis of faith, never with materialistic considerations," he said — and signed the purchase papers. Shortly before payment was due, an unexpected letter arrived. It was from the Prince of Schönburg-Waldenburg, a family friend, and contained an offer for an interest-free loan of 10,000 marks. The Sparhof was theirs. (A decade later, local Nazis would approach the prince and urge him to recall the loan. They knew this would bankrupt the settlement, and so relieve them of having to dissolve it forcibly. At this dangerous moment, the prince announced his intention to convert the loan to an endowment — and did so.)

The move to the Sparhof took place over six months. First the living quarters had to be renovated and extended, the fences mended, and the stalls cleaned and repaired. A school also had to be built. Previously the farm had housed one farming family; now it would be home to a community of about fifty. Half of these were children.

Georg supervised the building crew and, whenever he had a free hour or two, taught handcrafts to the boys. A romantic, he was devout in the style of the Middle Ages. On occasion he made solitary pilgrimages to a nearby shrine to the Virgin — sometimes during work hours, to his coworkers' chagrin. Or he would sit alone under the ancient beeches above the farm, plucking his lute and singing old ballads.

Georg would rouse Heiner, Hardy, and the other boys at six every morning to jog a half mile into the meadows for a workout. During gymnastics, the clunky ivory rosary he wore on his neck would jump and clack, and afterward, when he changed his shirt for a clean one before breakfast, he did it painstakingly, so that the large white beads never left his neck even for an instant.

Heiner didn't share Georg's enthusiasm for early-morning exercise, and sometimes turned to Wolf, his German shepherd, for help. The dog was fiercely protective of its master and would attack anyone who touched him, even in play. Before turning in, Heiner would tie Wolf to his bedpost. "Georg can shout for me till he's hoarse tomorrow – but with Wolf on guard, he won't come into my room."

That Christmas, Moni and Georg were married. New people kept coming. One was Fritz Kleiner, a bushy-bearded blacksmith whom Heiner was assigned to work with every day after school. Fritz was making the ironwork for the stairs and needed someone to pump the bellows for him. Heiner had never had to work so hard – Fritz demanded complete attention to the job. Praise was out of the question; Fritz only spoke to tell Heiner that he was lazy or doing the wrong thing. Either the metal wasn't hot enough, or it was too hot, and sometimes it took all Heiner had to keep from throwing up his hands in frustration. But after work, Fritz was a different man. Together they would take evening walks, and Fritz would tell his apprentice how hard his own childhood had been – and how the injustices he had suffered had set him on the path to find a place where people could live as brothers. A friendship developed between the two.

Life at the Sparhof that first winter was grueling. While the household had expanded, the settlement's income had not. The soil was a poor clay, riddled with rocks, and though Sannerz was only seven miles away, the elevation here was much higher and the climate considerably harsher. The diet consisted almost solely of potatoes. Bread was seen as a luxury, and Emmy took to warning prospective visitors to bring their own if they expected it at meals. By spring, the tubers were yellow, spongy, and sweetish from long storage. And when the first hog was finally butchered, the glory of the feast was all too fleeting. Unused to digesting meat, every person on the farm came down with diarrhea.

Conditions at the Sparhof were still primitive two years later, in the autumn of 1929. Worse, Heiner, now fifteen, felt that a silent disaster had taken place inside him. He felt he had betrayed the calling he had received by letting hateful thoughts into his heart. The knowledge of his evil nature weighed on him like a leaden yoke.

October inched by, and then November. Heiner tried to brush away the sense of guilt, but each time he failed. It perched above him like a dark bird as he sat at his desk in the mornings, and glided snake-like behind him in the afternoons as he hoed in the garden.

In December the newspapers went wild with a series of murders in the city of Düsseldorf. Day by day there were reports of new victims, all of them young children. The police had no leads. Eberhard discussed the crimes over the table one evening with Emmy and Tata, while Heiner listened on. A feeling of distant comradeship with the murderer rose within him. "I don't know him, but he must be suffering just like I am," he thought.

That evening, Heiner stopped in Tata's room to say goodnight. His mind was still with the murderer. "Tata, what a hard life he must have. He must have suffered all kinds of horrible things in his childhood. That can be the only reason that he acts like he does."

"That cold-blooded man!" Tata's indignation gave her voice a sharpness he had never heard. "Anyone who is capable of murdering one child after another surely has a heart of stone. Think of what he has done! He has completely cut himself off from God."

Tata's words fell like hammer blows. Each syllable condemned him. Now he knew what sin was. It meant being cut off from God, forever. He was frightened, not of damnation, but of the darkness. He feared it would crush him. And yet he was a part of that darkness. He felt he was a Judas, that he had betrayed Jesus. Later he would recall, "I cannot describe what a terrible thing it is to have had a childhood like mine, and to believe that you have lost it forever. I prayed: 'If only it were given back to me for a single day, I'd be grateful for eternity.'"

Hardest of all, he now had to avoid his father. He dared not face him; he felt the sin within him was too shameful.

Now Christmas was approaching – the highlight of the year, culminating with his mother's birthday on December 25. At moments Heiner dared to hope that the season's gladness was also for him. "No," a voice within him answered, "you have no right to it. You are in darkness; you are sunk in sin." His sixteenth birthday came and went, and then it was Christmas Day itself, a joyless day. His friend Alfred, newly engaged, invited Heiner to a celebration. Heiner went, but suddenly he could stand the tension no longer. He ran outside up the hill behind the farm and threw himself on the ground. He had to be alone.

He had never known that the torment of a guilty conscience could be so cruel. He got up and fell down again. His heart burst: "Help me! Help!" Alfred came running from the house to ask what the matter was – Heiner had not realized that he had been shouting out loud. So now it was over. He would go and spill everything to his father. Even as he went, the thought terrified him. What if it cost him their relationship? How could his father tolerate such a sinner under his roof?

At home, his father was meeting with a group of younger children. When he saw Heiner he said heartily, "Sit down, you old Sun Trooper. Perhaps you'd like to speak with the children too." Heiner was unable to say anything. Looking at his father, he remembered how close he had been to him as a child. He ached at the thought of how far apart they were now.

The children left, and Eberhard invited Heiner to his study. It was a small room lined with shelves that overflowed with books from floor to ceiling. It smelled of cigarette smoke. On one wall hung a plaster cast of Christ's head, crowned with thorns. Heiner broke down and blurted out his confession, expecting to be ejected from the Sparhof at once. But his father was silent. Then he said, "Heiner, that was a terrible sin. But this is why Jesus died – to free us from guilt." With that he knelt with his son on the floor, and they prayed. Heiner had never felt such a deep surge of joy.

In the days that followed, Heiner's ardor blazed more brightly than it had in years. Once again his old dream of living like the sadhu welled up, filling him with enthusiasm. Unable to conceal it, he talked to his father, and this time – the boy could hardly believe it – he agreed that Heiner was old enough to leave school. "Spend your summers here at home. We need help in the garden, and there is plenty for you to learn. In the winter, when the work is slack, you can take to the road."

9

Adolescence

Eberhard and emmy had never wanted to found a community of their own, much less a new sect. Even before moving to Sannerz, they had sought out like-minded seekers, first in Christian revival circles and after the war in the religious socialist movement associated with Karl Barth, Paul Tillich, Martin Buber, and especially Leonhard Ragaz, as well as in the peace movement of Friedrich Siegmund-Schultze and the Fellowship of Reconciliation. For years they had felt a kinship with the Quaker and Anabaptist traditions, and around 1920, they discovered the existence of modern-day Hutterites. The adherents of this radical communal offshoot of the Reformation share the same roots as the Mennonites and Amish, and had been practicing community of goods since the early sixteenth century. Their model, like that of Eberhard's own community, was the first Christian church in Jerusalem.

Originating in the Tyrol, and fleeing one wave of persecution and warfare after another, the Hutterites had settled in South Dakota in the late 1800s. Eberhard studied their history, then corresponded with them, and finally decided to visit them in the hopes of forging concrete ties. Fundraising was also an important incentive. Surely these people who had suffered so much for their faith would sympathize with the Sparhof and give what they could. In May 1930, he left on a ship from Bremerhaven to visit them. He didn't plan on it, but he would stay in North America for a whole year.

Before Eberhard left, he looked around for someone who, in conjunction with Emmy and Tata, could take responsibility for the well-being of the Sparhof while he was gone. He chose Hans Zumpe, Emy-Margret's fiancé for the past one-and-a-half years.

Hans was a young accountant who had first arrived around the time of Georg and Moni's wedding; the following year he had decided to stay. When he made his request to join the community, he had impressed Heiner by declaring, "I will go with you all through thick and thin."

Hans had proved himself capable and energetic, in particular as a leader of the Sannerz youth. Emy-Margret, especially, had grown to admire him, and in August 1929 they had been engaged. Now Hans was part of the Arnold family. Eberhard treated him like a son.

While Eberhard was away in America, Hans oversaw the community's finances. He worked hard, staying up till late to balance the books. The community was heavily in debt to local merchants, but Hans did his best to assure them that when Dr. Arnold came back from America, he would doubtless bring home large donations.

At twenty-two, Hans was six years older than Heiner–dashing and confident, and a trustworthy comrade. Heiner looked up to him almost as a hero, and was soon calling him one of his best friends. He knew that his father trusted Hans, and so trusted him too. He often visited Hans's office to talk over the things he might have shared with his father, had he been there.

It wasn't that Heiner was unsure of himself. But he had always held himself accountable for the smallest wrongdoings. And since he and Hans were so close, it seemed natural enough to confess a personal failing to him. Hans was quite willing to listen to these confidences.

Beyond these bonds, Hans shared little in common with Heiner's earlier friends, or for that matter, with Heiner himself. Since boyhood,

Heiner had admired blue-collar workers and long-haired anarchists, whereas Hans prized the soldier-like orderliness of the burgeoning nationalist movement. Heiner loved melancholy folk tunes; Hans, militaristic marching songs. And while Heiner was often hesitant to express himself, Hans brimmed with self-confidence.

On at least one occasion, Hans lost patience with Heiner's scruples. Heiner had read in the Gospel how "the Son of Man had nowhere to lay his head," and—no doubt inspired by the example of Francis of Assisi, whose order owned nothing either personally or collectively—began to question whether the community should give up title to its houses and fields. One morning he mentioned his question to Hans, who let loose an infuriated flood of obscenities.

Weeks stretched into months, and Heiner missed his father more than ever. So did his mother, especially after Eberhard's letters began to arrive. In them he repeatedly mentioned his left eye, injured many years ago in a skiing accident but now badly inflamed and so painful that some days he could hardly leave his room. Then there were his fundraising efforts, which were still not getting off the ground. His return date kept slipping further into the future.

Just then, on top of everything else, Tata's tuberculosis flared up again, worse than it ever had before. The doctor was insistent: if they wanted to save her, her lungs must be allowed to recuperate in fresh mountain air. "Do you have any friends in Switzerland? Send her to live with them!"

◆ ◆ ◆

Heiner pedaled hard behind Hardy's bike until the Sparhof was out of sight. It was April, and the beeches were just leafing out, and he swooped down the first hill with a heathen shout. Part way Hardy jammed his feet into the road and skidded to a stop. "The brakes don't work," he said as Heiner coasted up.

They had five hundred miles of cycling ahead of them before they got to Tata in Fidaz, Switzerland—more than was fair to expect from a couple of battered single-speeds. "You take my bike, it's better," Heiner said. But Hardy refused to accept his younger brother's generosity, and soon they were quarreling furiously. In the end, they agreed to stop at the next village and find a repairman to fix the brakes—a weighty decision, since they had twenty marks for the entire trip.

Outfitted with new brakes, the boys biked south for several days, toward Lake Constance and the Swiss border. In Darmstadt, they spent the night at the house of an old family friend, a surgeon by the name of Dr. Paul Zander. In Tübingen, they dropped in on the Jewish scholar Martin Buber, whom they remembered from his stay in Sannerz.

The peasants they met along the way were most hospitable, and when the brothers stopped at a house to ask for water, the farmer's wife was likely to bring out a mug of rough homemade wine instead. Neither Heiner nor Hardy was experienced at drinking, and when they mounted their bikes again they would teeter, fall down, and lie on the ground, laughing.

Across the Swiss border the cycling became more strenuous. The mountains towered almost two miles high as they approached Fidaz. Tired out, Heiner and Hardy entered the village and asked directions to the house where Fräulein von Hollander was staying.

Tata was jubilant, and showed the boys her room. It had a big window facing west, and she said she spent hours looking out at the mountains. The sun was setting, painting the summits. "The mountains pull me up, high above the earth," she said.

Probably Tata guessed that she was dying. How long ago was it that, after a fit of coughing, she had tasted blood and felt a flash of fear? Whenever it was, she had told no one, not wanting to spend scarce money on treatment. Heiner, who used to sleep next to her bedroom, had often heard her coughing. Surely Tata herself had recognized the signs. Eight years before, she had helped Emmy and Moni nurse their tubercular sister Olga through the final days of her life.

Then again, Tata had always been recklessly selfless. Her health had been poor since youth, but that had not deterred her. She went on begging trips in the open sulky even in the freezing rain, and although the long Rhön winters wore her down, she refused to slacken her efforts. Sometimes she left for weeks at a time, wearing her brown Franciscan-style habit. News would trickle in by telegram — "500 marks promised"; "2000 marks in the mail" — and then the whole household stopped their work to celebrate. What most never guessed was how she braced herself before each trip. For a woman of her upbringing it was excruciating to beg. But that was how she wanted it. She had freely chosen this life of privation — of humiliation, overwork, undernourishment, and cold. "If I demand a better standard of living than my neighbors, how can I claim to love them as myself?" she would ask.

For all that, Tata had loved the good things of life: good wine, flowers, a bowl of whipped cream in a café, and, of course, always art, from Albrecht Dürer to the new German Expressionists. But now, in the evenings, when Heiner and Hardy came to visit her in her room, she told them about Francis of Assisi and his Poor Brothers. Her favorite legend was about how the monk had taken "Lady Poverty" as his wife.

They did not speak about her illness much. In the mornings, when she felt strongest, she led them on hikes through the Alpine meadows, showing them the white and yellow crocuses and the purple soldanella, and pointing out the cuckoo that she could hear even indoors. Then, before they knew it, their vacation had run out, and the boys were cycling back to Germany and the Sparhof.

One day when they had been home about a month, the telephone rang. Emmy picked up the receiver, and the telegram clerk read her a message: Eberhard's ship would soon be arriving at Bremen. The news overwhelmed her, and she wept so loudly for joy that it took several minutes before anyone could make out what had happened.

Hans went with Emmy to the port to fetch him. The ship docked and Emmy could see a crowd milling on the deck. But Eberhard wasn't among them. As the ship disgorged its passengers and the last family groups came across the plank, Emmy became more and more frantic. Anyone who knew Eberhard would expect him to be the first one off the boat. She asked a man who had just disembarked if he had seen a Dr. Arnold. "Of course," he said. "He's in the smoking lounge, sitting by himself."

Emmy and Hans went aboard. A figure she recognized as her husband was standing behind a smokestack. Was he trying to hide? She rushed forward to embrace him. Though tender, he was strangely unresponsive.

"I come with empty hands," was the first thing he said.

Hans froze and bit his lip.

They went to a hotel. Emmy later told Heiner how all through that night, his father had wept. A whole year of begging—and he had failed to collect the funds they so badly needed to build up the community. It was enough to break him. In the past, each time he had needed a donation—to acquire the villa, to finance construction or publishing projects, to buy the Sparhof or a ticket for his journey—the money had usually arrived just when it was needed. Each time he had perceived God's hand confirming and blessing his work. Now God had denied him. Why?

Heiner met his father at the train station, and they drove home in silence, the wagon winding its way through the villages where the Sparhof's creditors lived. People opened their windows and waved cheerfully as the procession passed. Dr. Arnold was home from America! At last they would be paid!

The welcome dinner was uncomfortably quiet. Heiner had rarely seen his father so reserved. He seemed to take up such a little space. But then, at the end of the mealtime, he stood up abruptly. Speaking boldly and passionately, his face shining, he spoke of man's power-lessness—and the power of the Holy Spirit.

Eberhard didn't bring back money, but he brought back new ideas. And now, inspired by what he had seen among the Hutterite Bruderhofs ("place of brothers"), he began to shape the Sparhof in accordance with their time-tested structure, drawing on a centuries-old Anabaptist tradition.

The vision of the original settlement was to stay unaltered, he reassured everyone, but as the community's development had made clear, there was a need for at least some definite order. Soon the Sparhof was experimenting with a new daily schedule. Families now ate breakfasts in their apartments, and only midday and evening meals in the communal dining room. Meetings for worship and business matters were to be held on workday evenings. Membership was for-malized too: long-term guests who wished to join entered a novitiate, or time of testing. Later, by means of baptism, they could commit themselves to the community for life.

Previously Eberhard had shared responsibility for day-to-day leadership of the community with Emmy and Else, with other members such as Hans helping as needed. Now, specific members were named to take on various tasks: a business manager, a work dis-tributor, overseers for the farm and publishing work. Eberhard asked the community members if they were in agreement for him to con-tinue to have overall responsibility, both in pastoral and practical matters. But while he accepted this role—no one else had ever come into question—he warned that it should never be seen as a political office or position.

A few days after Eberhard's return home, he came up to Heiner as he worked in the fields. "Heiner, I have a question for you. Your judgment is of greatest importance to me. It will have weight for our future." He paused, then asked, "I need an assistant, someone to help me lead the community. What would you think about Hans?"

Memories of the past year flashed through Heiner's mind. Hans was certainly a good candidate. He made things happen. True, there were those times when he had been two-faced or domineering—even cruel. But it didn't seem right to complain about that now, especially not behind Hans's back. Heiner decided to suppress his misgivings.

"Yes, I feel he's the right one," he told his father. He would live to regret those words.

10

Tata

In JULY 1931 – just in time for Hans and Emy-Margret's wedding – Tata returned home from Switzerland. The cure had failed.

Tata lived in quarantine in a one-room hut set apart from the main buildings of the Sparhof. Her arms were implausibly thin, and at times it seemed her neck would no longer support the weight of her head. By December, she was so emaciated that she could no longer walk, and in order to bring her to the Christmas Day festivities, the men had to carry her into the dining room on a beach chair. There, despite her weakness, Tata radiated energy and cheer. She greeted every child that passed her, and smiled at the fuss being made over her. But afterward, on the way back to the hut, she grew sober. "I won't leave this room again with a living body," she remarked as she passed over the threshold of the hut. Heiner was devastated. It was impossible to imagine losing her.

It was at this time that Heiner decided to join the community for good, making a solemn vow of lifelong membership. He had long known that this was his vocation, ever since his experience of forgiveness at sixteen. He had seen then that he could not simply go out alone to preach the gospel – he needed to be sent by a body of believers. What was the point of telling people about Jesus, unless there was a place where they could see that his teaching was no impossible ideal, but rather could become reality in daily life?

All the same, before making his vow Heiner was filled with trepidation, knowing how little understanding some in the community had for his "overly subjective" ardor. Remembering their mocking comments, he grew afraid of the future. When he confided these fears to Tata, she understood him fully. But she also admonished him: "Following Jesus just *will* demand struggle. I could easily have gone a nice Christian way and simply avoided people who don't appeal to me. But that is not the way of Christ."

Tata, like her sisters, was known for her merry mood and the way she loved to tell stories, including her old favorites: "Once I went to a revival weekend. In the middle of the night I awoke to see a strange man standing at the foot of my bed. Of course I was surprised and asked him what he was doing. In a peculiar, slow voice he answered, 'I have come to bring you Jesus.' When I heard that, I shouted as loud as I could, 'Help! Help!' The rooms next to mine were full of Christian revivalists. But none of them moved an inch. They stayed in their rooms shouting 'Help! Help!' too."

"So what did you do?" her nephews and nieces would ask on cue.

"I shoved him out into the hall myself, and locked the door after him." The family would peal with laughter.

Now laughter was difficult for Tata—her disease was manifesting its true strength. She called it the Leviathan, after the huge and many-headed serpent mentioned in the Bible. "Oh, the agony! The Leviathan is eating me up inside." She sobbed violently, and gasped for air. There was no bottled oxygen. And there was no doctor—Lady Poverty had made sure of that. In any case, a doctor could have done little to change her fate. Moni was on hand to give injections for the pain, but relief lasted only a few hours. After December 31 she ate nothing.

And so the New Year began. Heiner spent all the time he could in Tata's hut or nearby. He could not get enough of being with her. He helped Hans-Hermann find logs for the stove by her bed. Dry fuel was beyond their means, so the young men found green wood and tried to dry it out the day before it was needed. But despite their efforts, the stove smoked badly. Tata would cough and cry until she was out of breath. Afterward she smiled and said very softly, "Even in the hour of my death I will laugh."

Tata tried valiantly to cheer up those who visited her, and when they doted on her, she deflected their attention. "I don't want you to take the trouble. Please, don't let the cause be held up by me."

"But Tata," Eberhard protested once, "You have sacrificed so much for it. Even this dangerous illness came from that—from all those begging journeys you made in bad weather."

Tata smiled. "That may be. But if it helped further the cause, it is good. In any case, it was only a small mousy effort."

"But a *living* mousy effort!"

"Yes, and it was so wonderful. It *is* so wonderful . . ." Her voice trailed off.

A week after New Year's—it was a Thursday—the Arnolds walked out to the hut in the evening. There was a harsh wind over the snow. Heiner noticed that the moon and a star seemed poised over the hut. When he told Tata about it, she was pleased, and said it was a sign of hope. Then she asked, "Please, could you open the door? I want to see out. I want to look at the sky."

Heiner thought it was a crazy request—even with the door closed, the woodstove was hardly keeping the room warm. But Tata insisted. Gazing upward intently, her eyes shining from her pale, tight face, she cried out happily, "Look at those stars! That's where I am going— to the most beautiful land!" She would not allow the door to be shut for a long time.

From that evening on, she seemed to see everything around her with new eyes. "The powers of eternity are very near! I am exactly the same weak human being as always. Nothing has changed there. But now I have left behind what is happening here and am quite near to what is happening beyond. Yes, I am still very near to everything here, but I see it as if from another star." She paused and labored to take in air, sometimes between each phrase, sometimes after every word. Her ruined lungs heaved with a gurgle that struck Heiner as awful. "Once I nearly flew away. Suddenly my hands and arms went up high—it seemed to me as if I had wings. But then my limbs grew heavy as before, and I was in bed again, and it was gone. To be yanked back to the earth like that—it is agonizing. The body holds too tightly to the soul.

"Sometimes I would like to ask God that I might pass away peacefully, dreaming and with no death pangs, and awaken in eternity. But that would be impertinent. When it is hard, you must always remember that the victory is *God's*. Life is struggle and strife, and it is hardest when you're dying. In normal times, people often do not notice the struggle, so they do not fight it seriously and vigorously enough."

On her nightstand Tata kept lighted candles and two picture postcards, one of a local landscape and the other showing the ship on which Eberhard had returned from America. She explained to Heiner, "Here is our beautiful Rhön countryside, where I will board the ship. The landing is in another country—the most beautiful country." Heiner waited as she panted and tried to catch her breath. Her forehead was pulled taut, like a skin stretched over a drum. Her hair was damp with sweat. Later she said, "I see a long procession, full of lights! I see them, and hear them. They are calling, 'Come with us!'" She sighed with contentment.

The next morning, Heiner visited her again. She told him, "I would like so much to be with the prophets, apostles, and martyrs. But I shall only be with the little children to begin with." From the way she spoke, it was clear that she had been somewhere and knew what it looked like. Heiner was bursting with inquisitiveness. "Tata, what did you see?" he blurted out.

Tata did not answer. She only turned and glanced at him, as if hurt by such curiosity. In the silence, Heiner felt he was being punished for his presumption. But some hours later she turned to him with a message: "You will go through hard times. But never forget that the last victory will be God's."

Saturday passed, long and drawn out. On Saturday evening, she whispered, "Now comes the painful passage."

"And the greatest joy," Heiner said, as much to comfort himself as to reassure her.

"Yes." She smiled. "I have always prayed that I might see another spring. I love the swallows, I love the warm May sun. But for me it's already spring, even if it's still winter for you."

On Sunday she gradually lost the ability to speak. The whole family gathered around her bed. The waiting continued for hours. At one point she exclaimed, "It is so wonderful—so wonderful. I am allowed to go into another world!" Her chest pumped feebly and she struggled to raise herself.

Before dawn she began to pray. She stretched out her arms and tried to hold them up. They sagged, and she signaled that she wanted help. All through the morning, they took turns supporting her arms while she gazed out of the window, her face radiant, as if expecting someone to appear and fetch her.

That afternoon, in the neighboring village of Neuhof, a young woman climbed out of the train and scanned the snow-covered platform anxiously. She wore no makeup, and her dark brown hair was plaited into braids. She was Annemarie Wächter, Emy-Margret's former college roommate and best friend. She had visited twice before, but now she was coming for a year. Emy-Margret's father had invited her to take on the Sparhof kindergarten, and she had accepted without quite knowing why. Now she was nervous. She was about to enter a *religious* order, even though she didn't believe in Christianity, or God, or really anything. "I only knew I wanted to live a genuine life," she would later recall. "To bind myself to a single worldview . . . I could never stomach that. That is, unless there really is something so true that it's impossible to doubt it."

Annemarie spotted her welcoming party, a sturdy young farmer and a tiny fair-haired woman, who waved. Annemarie recognized her as Emy-Margret's old teacher, Trudi. The man, Arno, had come as the driver. Both of them looked somber, and Annemarie thought Trudi had recently been crying. No sooner had they exchanged greetings than Trudi said, "There is something I must tell you right away. This morning at eleven, Else von Hollander passed away."

Annemarie could not think what to say. Through Emy-Margret, she knew that Tata was an important and beloved personage. She had met her once, when Tata had visited the college and spent an evening in the dorm. Annemarie remembered her expressive face and her manner, reserved yet warm.

"What a day for me to arrive," Annemarie thought as Arno helped load her luggage onto his sleigh. Suddenly, she dreaded the end of the journey. After this heavy loss, the Sparhof would be wallowing in tears for days. She set her face doggedly and climbed into the seat. Arno untied the horses and eased them into a run.

11

An Arrival

Sparhof, January 11, 1932

The runners rasped as the sleigh left the snowy road, then slid to a halt. The froth-flecked horses steamed in the cold. Annemarie looked around. They had stopped in a courtyard surrounded by two big farmhouses, a dilapidated barn, and a Hansel-and-Gretel-like cottage with a steep roof and a huge chimney. That was the bakery, she remembered. Beyond the enclosure nothing was visible; fog lapped against the buildings like a milky sea.

Annemarie wondered whether coming here was all a mistake, shuddering to think of the way the religious people she knew dealt with death. The way they tried to cover their grief with little platitudes; the way they simpered and affected hushed tones.

Though she had been here before, the Sparhof looked foreign, not at all like the place she had visited last summer. In her memory, those few June days still shone impossibly bright. How deeply she had been stirred then! She especially remembered one afternoon when she had gone on a long hike with Emy-Margret's brother Heiner. He had been asked to accompany her for the outing, and although the situation might have felt strange, somehow it hadn't. He was lanky and very tall, not yet twenty, with arms freckled and muscular from days of plowing and haying.

The two of them had set out along the *Weinstrasse,* an old Roman road that ran through the Fulda Forest. As they walked, Annemarie realized that she was enjoying herself, partly because Heiner was so full of humor. Earlier she had noticed how the people around him often seemed to be laughing. It was odd, since he was no great wit. His own exuberance might have had something to do with it; the way he laughed till tears flowed down his cheeks, without making any effort to cut short his mirth. The whole top half of his nose would crinkle. Occasionally he would sing—mostly folksongs or ballads with many verses, which he sang to the end without embarrassment. His voice was untrained, but easy and musical.

When she and Heiner had returned that evening, Eberhard had announced that everyone should gather in the courtyard. They found the others forming a circle around an unlit fire, several dozen people standing shoulder to shoulder. Karl lit the kindling, and someone started a song. Soon flames were licking the large logs. Meanwhile, Karl was handing each person a piece of firewood, and Eberhard began to speak. "We live in this community in order to give our lives to the cause of God's kingdom," he said. "Tonight we want to commit ourselves anew to the cause, so that we might burn away for it like these logs. All who want to do this should add their piece of wood to the fire."

Annemarie tensed. She was impressed, more than she dared admit. She wanted badly to add her log to the fire, to join this unity, to be part of it. But where would it land her? "Wait," she told herself. "If you commit yourself now, what will you do if you later want to change your mind? How do you know your present feelings are genuine?" Undecided, she watched while Emy-Margret, Heiner, Hardy, and others took their turns, the sparks spraying up each time a new piece of wood landed in the flames. "Now!" she thought. But at the last moment, instead of stepping up to the fire, she let the log slip down behind her, where it lay hidden by her shadow. She hoped that no one had noticed.

Now it was January, and that summer bonfire was no more than a memory, distant and a little fantastic. It was impossible that this visit to the Sparhof would hold another similar experience.

But there was no more time for reflection. Arno, who had her bags, was telling her to follow him, and a figure was striding across the frozen ruts of the yard, beaming. It was Emy-Margret's father, and he came up and grasped her hand, saying, "Welcome! Welcome!" so warmly that Annemarie felt as if she were his daughter. Her anxiety dissolving, they walked together into dinner.

The dining room looked cozy and outlandish at the same time. The walls were painted bright orange, so that the pools of light formed by the kerosene lamps were pure tangerine, and the tables, with green linoleum tops and crimson details, seemed to glow. The people sitting at them—there were about sixty, Annemarie guessed—sat on long benches, apparently waiting for the meal to begin. Annemarie scanned their faces for evidence of gloom. But while many looked exhausted, none were downcast. In fact, the atmosphere was almost festive.

Dinner began. Dishes of potatoes and winter spinach were passed from a hatch, and Annemarie's neighbors filled their earthenware bowls. When almost all the diners had laid down their tin spoons, Eberhard stood up. He said he wanted to speak about Tata's last hours. Eberhard told how, as Tata's death approached, her faculty of sight had changed. What she called "the other world" had appeared to her, not as a dream or vision, but as something she really saw. "It's just as alive there as here," she had said. "I almost said that when I get there I'll write you—but of course that's not how it works." Knowing she had only minutes more, she had exclaimed: "The gates and doors are all wide open! Only the roads there are poor."

As Eberhard continued, Annemarie listened intently, then hungrily. Here was something she had never contemplated before—the existence of an unknown world. "And to think that it has broken into everyday life, right here on this spot, among these people, just this morning!" Something new was taking hold of her. She was gripped and shaken. *"This* is reality!" she told herself. "The other world isn't just something you read about in books."

By now the kerosene lamps were sputtering out one by one. No one relit them—there was a strict daily allotment of fuel. But to Annemarie, the room seemed full of light: "This is the life I want," she felt. "This is what I will give myself to, forever."

Annemarie had always been suspicious of piety. As far as she could tell, lofty words like "salvation" and "grace" and "faith" were just part of a strenuous middle-class charade. Even people who insisted they believed in these things had nothing to show for it in their daily lives, whether they realized it or not. But now, at Emy-Margret's community, her skepticism was being shaken. "There is something here that I have never felt anywhere else," she wrote home. "It is so real. It makes me want to stay here." A few weeks into her visit, she announced that she wanted to become a member.

Annemarie grew quickly into her new home. The work was hard and the diet spartan, but she loved being with the children and thrived in their presence. And there was Emy-Margret's father, who was constantly giving her new things to read and to think about. She had never been so stimulated, so full of questions and ideas.

On weekends, when they could be spared from the work, the young men and women of the Sparhof liked to go hiking. One summer Sunday, a dozen of them set off, walking at a brisk pace. They had only just started when one member of the party began to complain about his feet. It was Ernst, a guest. Ernst, a city-bred seminarian, viewed himself as a ladies' man, and Annemarie was his current target. Seating himself by the road and tenderly peeling away his socks, he had just located a blister and was now soothing it in a nearby stream. Annemarie looked away in disgust.

They persuaded him to continue hiking, but had barely gone another mile when Ernst begged them to stop again. By the time they reached their destination—a gymnastics center run by a local branch of the youth movement—it was long after dark. During the final stretch of road, Ernst had been calling a halt every few hundred yards.

While the young women found lodging in the school itself, the men found a hayloft in a nearby barn. It was already time to sleep; a precious evening had been wasted. Around midnight Heiner was awakened by his sister Monika. "Annemarie and I want to speak with you." Heiner followed her outside, where Annemarie was waiting. "This is impossible," Annemarie whispered indignantly. "We can't go on another day like this with Ernst. I've never met someone so flabby! It's unbelievable."

"But what can I do if he keeps stopping for his blisters?" Heiner asked.

"Monika and I have thought it all out. He's sleeping now. Let's wake up the others and leave him here. When he wakes up, he'll easily find the way home."

"No. We can't do that," Heiner objected. But Annemarie and Monika kept at him until she had won the argument. Soon Heiner was prodding the other young men awake, and by one o'clock they were all hiking again—without Ernst.

Before dawn, the boisterous party was at the top of a mountain, building a bonfire and dancing around it. They returned home to the Sparhof in the early afternoon.

"Where is Ernst?" Eberhard asked.

Heiner tried to explain, but his father interrupted him. "Ernst is our guest! What have you done with him? Tonight you will give an account to the whole community."

All that afternoon Heiner hoped that Ernst would show up. But he never did. Heiner ate dinner glumly and walked into the evening meeting afterward with a racing pulse and weak knees. As the meeting began, he rose to explain himself. He was describing his midnight conversation with Annemarie and Monika when his father exploded. "So you take your orders from two girls?" Heiner stood silent, shamefaced. "What have you done with our guest?" Eberhard repeated.

Ernst appeared the next day, limping up the road and nursing his feet constantly. Heiner, remorseful, apologized for what had happened. Annemarie welcomed him home with an unrepentant smile.

That summer, 1932, Heiner supervised the farm crew, which was made up mostly of the many guests who showed up. Several were radicals of one stripe or another. One morning, a new guest joined them, a nationalist pastor. He wore Nazi brown, and greeted them with "Heil Hitler!"

Heiner answered him with a simple "Good morning," but another man on the crew, a fervent Marxist, shot back, "Heil Moscow!" The two guests glared at each other.

"How are we going to survive a whole week hoeing potatoes together?" Heiner wondered. He knew that in the cities, street battles between Communist and Nazi paramilitaries had already resulted in dozens of deaths, and both visitors were fiercely partisan. But though they clashed constantly for the first few days, the two enemies gradually softened their positions. By the end of the week they were sharing cigarettes.

To Heiner, it seemed remarkable, since such friendships were becoming so rare these days. Elsewhere in Germany, in this last year of the Weimar Republic, life was becoming frighteningly polarized. More than six million people were out of work, and several major banks had collapsed, wiping out the savings of thousands. Extremists were attracting a wide following on both ends of the political spectrum, and Hitler's feared Nazis were steadily gaining clout.

On the face of it, Fulda, where Heiner would begin agricultural school that fall, seemed largely unaffected by these trends. Yet by the time classes started, the public mood was changing, as Heiner realized when he quoted Dostoyevsky to an instructor during a classroom debate. The teacher was unexpectedly hostile. "What do you know about Dostoyevsky? Does your father know you read him?"

The man was an undercover Nazi activist, as he would proudly acknowledge several months later. But no one knew this yet, and his hostility dumbfounded Heiner. "I have read his novels at home," he answered weakly.

"Well then, Arnold, tomorrow you will give us a lecture about your great Russian author," his teacher said.

Heiner was still more astonished. His classmates were a rough crowd, mostly farm boys. Most had probably never heard of Dostoyevsky. Obviously the teacher wanted to make him a laughingstock. Nevertheless, he agreed, and took the lectern the next day.

Heiner began his presentation by reviewing Dostoyevsky's life. The novelist, he told the snickering class, had sympathized with left-wing movements working to overthrow the czar until he and his friends were caught and condemned to death. "He was already blindfolded and tied to the stake in front of the firing squad. Then a rider galloped up with a last-minute pardon. This brush with death transformed Dostoyevsky. He began to see the underclass—outcasts, cripples, and criminals—as those in whom the spark of God sometimes burns brightest. His novels show there is goodness even in the most depraved characters."

Criminals, cripples, and the underclass—these were exactly the kind of people the Nazis were vowing to eliminate when they came to power. By their lights, a young German should never be reading books about them in the first place.

But now the titters had ceased, and Heiner's peers were listening respectfully. Visibly furious, the instructor limited himself to one shot as Heiner re-took his seat: "Arnold, you should have been an artist, not a farmer."

On January 30, 1933, as soon as classes were over for the day, Heiner went to his boarding house for a quick bite and an evening of studying. While eating, he turned on the radio, as was his habit. About five o'clock, the program was interrupted by an announcement: "President von Hindenburg has appointed Adolf Hitler as the new chancellor of Germany."

Heiner stopped chewing. This was an astounding turn of events. Only months ago, Hitler had been defeated in the presidential elections, and Hindenburg had shut the Nazis out of the governing cabinet. He had even outlawed the SA, the elite organization of storm troopers. Now he was handing over the reins to his old foe? It didn't make sense. Heiner decided to call his father right away. The Sparhof had no radio, and they might not hear about this for hours.

There was a long silence after Heiner told his father the news. Then Eberhard spoke, his voice grave. "Hitler as chancellor? The president has no idea what demons he is conjuring up."

12

Nazis

Fulda, January 30, 1933

As night fell on the day Hitler took office, the quiet town of Fulda became feverish. Heiner, who had been watching a throng gathering in the street below his window, decided to go out and explore. He walked into the heart of the city, toward the main square that spread below the cathedral. Catholicism defined Fulda's whole character, as it had for hundreds of years, even through the Reformation, when the rest of this region turned Protestant. Since then, it had guarded against every heresy outside its gates, including Nazism. When Hitler first began his march to power, the people of Fulda had despised him as a demagogue and a washerwoman's son. Nazi uniforms had been banned from the streets.

But tonight squads of brown and black-shirted paramilitaries were marching, singing, and carrying torches like a triumphant army in enemy territory. Which is what they were—SA and SS troops from out of town. In Boniface Square, they rigged up a stage and sound system. "Repent!" the man at the podium was bellowing as Heiner approached. His voice ricocheted back and forth between the bishop's castle and the cathedral. "Repent and join the National Socialist Party now, while Hitler is still merciful! Have you opposed us? Now is your hour of grace! Watch out, because the day of judgment is near!"

Columns of Nazis screamed back their approval like amens and brandished their swastika-emblazoned flags.

They were winning converts. A stream of people was flowing into the town hall where a meeting was in progress. Heiner followed them, half repulsed, half fascinated. Inside, three rows of black-clad men were arrayed below the podium, wearing the skull-and-cross-bones of the Death's Head SS. The speaker behind it was employing the same revival-tent style as his comrade outside. "Repent! Come on your knees to Hitler! The Thousand-Year Kingdom is here!"

Except for the men in uniform, few in the hall were card-carrying Nazis. But they must have long shared a silent approval of Hitler's goals. Now they roared with enthusiasm as the speaker denounced Social Democracy, the humiliation of Versailles, and the evil of world Jewry. They stamped and clapped and sang and grew tearful. When the speaker had lashed the crowd into a frenzy, a cluster of men broke into song. It was the old hymn to the dishonored glories of imperial Germany: *Deutschland, Deutschland über Alles!* The people sobbed in ecstasy, rising to their feet as one body.

Only Heiner remained sitting. The oneness of the crowd, so raw and passionate, stirred him even as it filled him with horror. "Here are people ready to die for a cause," he thought. "Maybe they're more ready to sacrifice themselves than I am. If only they were on the side of love! The early Christian martyrs died for love. This crowd will die for hate."

"*Aufstehen!* Stand up!" someone behind him hissed as the anthem continued. Heiner refused to rise—he was not here to participate in this madness. But the murmur around him rose to a small commotion, and he spotted a gang of toughs thrusting purposefully through the crowd toward him. Realizing that he was in danger of a beating or worse, he slipped to the rear of the hall and fled out into the night.

When he told his father about it that weekend, Eberhard was aghast. "You could have been killed! You have absolutely no business attending a Nazi rally. I forbid you to attend such a meeting again." The two of them were standing together looking out of the living room window over the Rhön hills. Eberhard loved the German countryside with the fervor of a Romantic. But today the sight of it seemed to pain him.

Heiner understood his father's concern. Anyone could sense the change that was taking place in Germany. But how could they know how terrible and far-reaching that change would be? This was the land of the *Wandervögel*—a country of nature-worshipers and leftwing hotheads, Zionists, nudists, and tramps. No other city in the world quite paralleled its capital, free-wheeling Berlin. Even here in the villages of rural Hesse, a tolerant spirit thrived. Two synagogues stood within a few miles of Sannerz, and near the Sparhof was the Gehringhof, a Zionist farm for training young Jews wishing to settle in Palestine—the two communities had exchanged visits. Surely this easy-going world could not disappear just on the say-so of a new chancellor, Heiner thought.

But within the first two months of his term, Hitler had burned down the Reichstag, banned leftwing parties, instigated a boycott of Jewish businesses, legalized the violation of civil liberties, and deposed local governments, replacing them with obedient appointees. And right in Sterbfritz, a village one mile from Sannerz, local men linked to the SA had assaulted a Jew. Without provocation, they had torn off his trousers, beaten him, and thrown him in a ditch. He had had to walk home through the village naked, to the delight of his attackers.

Heiner wondered if his homeland was possessed. As he described it later, "It was as if the devil's army had been waiting for an opening—disciplined and organized for attack. And now that it had gotten in, it was overwhelming everything."

That summer the gypsies disappeared. They had been there as long as Heiner could remember—three or four brightly painted wagons encamped in Herolz Forest. The camp was full of children and dogs. As long as they could find work in the area, they stayed on, mending kettles, sharpening scissors, and doing similar small repairs. As boys, Heiner and Hardy loved to visit their camp and sit around the campfire with the men, feasting on roast hedgehog, listening to stories, or watching a fiddler as his fingers danced over the strings. When the boys went home, they often brought a gypsy child with them to get a hot bath and a fresh set of clothes.

But now the wagons had vanished from the roads and the camp was empty. And the gypsies were not the only ones missing. The tramps were gone too, the same people Heiner used to befriend. Ever since the end of the Great War, thousands of these men had lived on the highways. Now, like the gypsies, they were no longer to be seen.

Few Germans knew or cared exactly what the authorities had done with the tramps and gypsies. In general, they swung solidly behind Hitler and were suspicious of anyone who dissented. Including the Sparhof. Soon neighbors were gossiping about how the Sparhof people never returned the "Heil Hitler" greeting and did not fly the swastika on national holidays. Farther afield, rumors began to fly about a "communist nest" in the Rhön, probably because of Eberhard's participation in labor rallies years before, and because of his friends in radical circles.

In April, local police arrived to search for "material dangerous to the state." Then in late May, the Sparhof residents woke at five o'clock in the morning to the sound of rifle fire. Storm troopers were marching toward the houses, firing what turned out to be blanks.

One day Eberhard took Heiner aside and told him about several recent warnings he had surreptitiously received from contacts inside the government. They had revealed details about Hitler's secret campaign against "undesirable elements." Heiner knew the story in generalities: there had already been a spate of assassinations. But what his father told him next left him pale. Fifty new concentration camps were to be established within a year. "If you ever read in the papers that I have committed suicide, do not believe it," Eberhard warned.

"Who is it telling you all this?" Heiner wanted to know.

"The less you know, the less you can betray if you are ever arrested," his father said. But he hinted that his sources were old friends who talked to him at considerable risk.

From the start, Eberhard warned fellow members of the Sparhof that neither he nor they could assume they would survive the Nazi regime. "Hitler has erected the gallows again in Germany. We must consider whether we are prepared to be hanged on these gallows, right here or in Berlin, or wherever it may be – even this year."

Eberhard felt that the community should remain in the country until they were actually driven out. "We cannot flee. We must remain at our post. We must show with our lives what justice, love, and peace look like. We must give a witness that is indelibly branded in the books of history."

That July the community celebrated Eberhard's fiftieth birthday. In the evening, after dinner, Eberhard rose to speak. "On this day I have been especially conscious of my lack of abilities and of how unsuited my own nature is to the work I have been given, remembering how God called me and how I have stood in his way, with the result that so much of what God must have wanted to do has not been possible. When I look back on the years that Emmy and I have been seeking, it is a miracle that we are still allowed to be a part of this community. This is only possible because of God's infinite power and forgiveness.

"Another thing concerns me very much: the powerlessness of man, even of the man who has been entrusted with some task. Only God is mighty. Even for the work that has been given us, we are wholly without power. We cannot fit one single stone into the structure that is the community. We cannot protect the community once it has been built up. We cannot devote ourselves to the cause using only our own strength.

"But I believe that this is precisely why God has called us: we know we are powerless. It is hard to describe how all our own power must be stripped from us; how it must be dropped, dismantled, torn down, and put away. What I wish is that this dismantling of our own self-will might be carried out to its full extent. This is not attained easily and will not happen through a single heroic decision. God must do it in us. But when even a little of our own power rises up, the spirit and authority of God retreats at the same moment and to the same degree."

Heiner thought about it only later, but as his father spoke, Emy-Margret's face showed increasing disappointment. Perhaps she had hoped Papa would use the occasion for a fitting celebratory address, highlighting the success of the movement he had founded. What had begun as a ramshackle attempt in Sannerz was now an established and increasingly international community of some 150 members, with newcomers arriving from Scandinavia, Switzerland, and even Turkey. Although finances remained precarious and food scarce, they were now running a progressive boarding school and publishing house while laying the groundwork for a forward-looking farming operation. Surely Eberhard had much to be proud of. Yet here he was dwelling on his mistakes and failures and speaking of the need to dismantle one's personal power. Modesty was all very well, but why couldn't her father acknowledge that he was a charismatic and successful leader?

Haying season came, and from dawn to dusk the men put in long hours of backbreaking work mowing the fields and laying the stalks in windrows. For days the women labored too, turning the grass with wooden rakes until it was dry and ready to be taken to the barn. It was beautiful out in the fields, among the larks and hedge roses, and as Heiner swung his scythe or forked mounds of hay onto the wagons, he thought about Grete.

Grete had arrived that spring, leaving the university where she'd been studying philosophy, and had thrown in her lot with the Sparhof, despite the alarm of her family and friends. She shared Heiner's keenness for the medieval mystics, and the two of them could talk for hours about what they were reading: Suso, Thomas à Kempis, and most of all, Meister Eckhart.

One day Heiner, finding his father alone in his study, confided in him that he regarded his bond with Grete as a special friendship. Eberhard gave his approval, but warned him, "Don't talk to her about love, and see to it that there is no caressing or kissing. It's too early for you to think of marrying."

Heiner gave his word—but he was still sure that Grete was the one. On Sunday mornings he would get up early to walk with her down the *Weinstrasse* to a spot far from the farm where they could read and talk together. For a few weeks he was happy. But Grete—usually a modest girl—wanted more, and began to shed her caution. One day Heiner came late to lunch from his farm work, and was hardly sitting down when she coquettishly pushed her own plate and spoon in front of him. Heiner stared at her, embarrassed, but she was oblivious to having crossed a line.

After lunch he took her aside and told her that their friendship was over. "I'm sorry, Grete, but please understand. It's finished." Grete responded by throwing her arms around him. Heiner pushed her away and walked from the room. They didn't speak to each other for months.

◆ ◆ ◆

"It can no longer be tolerated that a German community exists whose aims are the very opposite of National Socialism, and which advertises these aims by the spoken and written word. Of these aims, I need but mention the Bruderhof's fundamental repudiation of private property, its repudiation of the laws on blood and race, and its refusal to bear arms." So the National Socialist District Magistrate would write to the German Secret Police in a 1936 report in which he pressed for the dissolution of the Sparhof. To him, these people were not only closet Communists, but Jew-lovers and pacifists to boot. These were the sort of people the concentration camps had been built for.

Already now in 1933 officials in the Nazi government were drawing similar conclusions about the Sparhof. It would not be long before they turned their attention to this nest of "idealistic communists."

In October 1933, Hitler yanked Germany out of the League of Nations and announced a national plebiscite that was to be held four weeks later, on November 12. Every eligible voter would be required to answer a question whose meaning was not so much political as religious: "Do you, as a German man, and do you, as a German woman, approve the policy of your Reich government, and are you ready to affirm and solemnly to pledge yourself to this policy as the expression of your own conviction and your own will?"

Officially, votes were to be cast by secret ballot. But Eberhard was worried that the Sparhof was being watched, and two weeks before the plebiscite, he visited the District Magistrate's office to ask him what would happen if community members refused to vote, or voted no. The Nazi official frowned. "Do you know what that means, Dr. Arnold?" he demanded. "It means concentration camp."

Eberhard left the government office in great agitation. Coming home, he had the taxi driver drop him off on the road. He often went on foot for the last few hundred yards, through the woods and down the hill to the farm. But it had been raining, and as he hurried over the grassy slope, he slipped. Alfred, who had gone out to fetch him with a storm lantern, found him moaning with a broken left leg, and ran home to call Moni. When she arrived, she blanched: the fracture had shattered the bone so badly that a piece protruded through the skin.

They carried him home. When Heiner saw him, he looked half-dead, and his leg was bloody and contorted. But Eberhard's thoughts were less on his leg than on his fear for the future. What would happen to the Sparhof, to all the souls in his care? He worried especially about the foster children. That same night he called a members' meeting, which he held from his bed. Despite his physical agony – it was too late at night to call a doctor – he spoke with confidence and conviction. "We must prepare ourselves to endure hardship," he said, "or even to die." He suggested that they try to buy time. Rather than provoking the Nazis by boycotting the plebiscite, they would vote, but with a twist. Each member would write the same statement on gummed paper—a carefully worded declaration that they respected the government's authority, but gave their allegiance only to God. At the polls, they would each stick the statement to their ballot.

And so it happened. On the day of the plebiscite, Heiner himself stayed home; at nineteen, he was too young to vote. All the same, he was nervous, especially when zealous local election officials arrived at his father's sickbed with a ballot box.

That evening, while the votes were being counted in a nearby village, Eberhard called the community together.

"It is a great thing when individual people are moved to stand firm in unity with Christ. It is greater still when a church is so firm that it can demonstrate to the whole world by its daily life and work the character of the kingdom of God.

"It is a great thing when people are found worthy to be thrown into prison or killed for the sake of the gospel. It is greater still when a church is found worthy to be called to abandon the place it has built up so laboriously and to venture into the unknown, when on the threshold between having and not having, it can grasp anew perfect unity, peace, justice, and brotherhood in the unity of Jesus Christ and the kingdom of God.

"It is greatest of all if it is given in such an hour to love one's enemies in the spirit of Jesus Christ, to embrace those who intend to drive out the members of the church into misery and oblivion. It is useless to fall on our knees, to sing hymns and fold our hands, to babble about the cross, if we are not ready—ready as Jesus was to take the cross upon himself—to tread his path to the very last step, to the last breath. That alone is true discipleship of Jesus Christ; all else is lying and deception.

"So we are joyful. Even though we do not yet know if we will be found worthy of experiencing that ultimate reality, this day's act brings that reality before our eyes as a real possibility. That makes us indescribably happy, for Jesus said: 'When they denounce and curse and lie about you, leap for joy!'"

Eberhard hoped that their stalling tactics might gain them some breathing space. And for three days nothing happened. The fourth dawned gray and dull. Around eight in the morning, Heiner went to the stable to hitch up the horses for the day's work. He had just finished harnessing one horse and was fetching the second when Alfred ran in, breathless. "Two SS men are here, and I'm afraid they're on their way to your father." Through the mist, Heiner made out the two black figures moving toward the main house. He rushed to secure his horse, and then turned back to follow them. By now the whole farm was ringed with armed men, the mist spewing them from all sides as if from the ground—"like a swarm of ants," as one of the schoolchildren would later say. He saw SS, Gestapo, and local police.

Heiner sprinted toward his father's study. "Stop!" the shouts rang out from all sides. An officer waved a revolver and ordered him over to join a group of men in one corner of the courtyard. Among them he saw Alfred and Arno, and Friedel Sondheimer. Friedel was the mentally disabled son of a local Jewish lawyer, and Eberhard had taken him into the community as a kindness. "Against the wall, all of you!" Two guards grabbed Heiner and pushed him against the side of the barn. His mind raced. Hadn't his father told him how the SS carried out secret executions?

Heiner noticed that Friedel was refusing to line up with the rest of them, and whispered to him that he must obey. "No!" Friedel insisted. "The work distributor asked me to fetch firewood. I've got to do my job." Only after much pleading from Heiner did he let himself be tugged into line. After letting his prisoners sweat for an eternal moment, the officer called for five of his men. They searched each man for weapons, turning out every pocket. Finding nothing, they railed at them, "Fine, but it will be all the worse for you later!" Heiner and the others were hustled into the woodworking shop. Two men with drawn revolvers stood outside the door, and another stood by each window. "Where have you buried the weapons?" they asked again and again. "If you tell us of your own accord, your punishment will be reduced."

"We are Christians," Heiner said. "We have no weapons." The SS men burst into laughter.

Hours passed. The troopers had come at dawn, and now the sun was high. "What will happen at the end of the day?" Heiner wondered. "Will it be concentration camp or a firing squad, after all?" Hardest was not knowing what was happening to his father or anybody else; many of the women worked in the kindergarten or the laundry, in buildings where they would now feel vulnerable and alone. Suddenly the chief Gestapo officer entered the workshop, greeted the prisoners, and began inspecting the room. Heiner went up to him and asked whether he might go to his father. The officer asked for his name. "Arnold," Heiner replied. The man smirked. "I have been looking for you." He ordered two of his men to escort Heiner to the main building, one walking in front, the other behind him.

In the dining room, Gestapo officers were interrogating the adults one by one, their typewriters clacking as they took down information. Heaps of books and papers spilled from the tables—having failed to uncover a cache of weapons, the secret police had seized what other evidence they could, especially books with red covers ("surely Communist"), and letters from abroad. Heiner hoped they contained nothing with political overtones. "Horror propaganda" against Germany was punishable as treason. At one table, two officers were entertaining themselves by reading someone's personal mail. And now Tata's old art folders were being carried in. "Pornography," one sneered, as he leafed through a portfolio on classical sculpture.

Heiner was taken to a corner where Sophie, Luise, and another young woman, Liesel Wegner, were standing under guard. An officer was holding up the red flag Sophie had sewed so many years before. "You made this?" he barked, and began questioning them about the Sun Troop, while another officer typed everything. "You're Communists, aren't you?" Sophie said they weren't. "Then why is your flag red?" he answered with contempt. "Don't tell me you don't know what red means!"

Liesel glanced at his armband—a swastika on a red field. "You have red too," she pointed out timidly. The officer did not reply, but called an abrupt end to the questioning.

Meanwhile, in the room where Eberhard was lying, another interrogation was in full swing. Heiner could hear shouting and scolding—and his father's voice, clear and calm in the midst of everything.

Inspector Hütteroth, the chief, was leading the proceedings. He seemed most interested in proving Eberhard guilty of "propaganda against the state." Every May Day, when the Communists and Socialists marched for the rights of workers in the regional capital, Eberhard had marched with them, wearing a red shirt and carrying a red flag. Though never a member of any party, he had always been given a speaking slot at the rally. Now Inspector Hütteroth pointed to one of the SS guards. "This man swears to it that you called for insurrection."

"That is a lie!" Eberhard thundered, rising as high as he could without moving his casted leg. "I dare you to tell it again to my face! I have never done such a thing!" The SS man shrank before Eberhard's gaze and offered no rebuttal. Inspector Hütteroth, too, was tongue-tied and closed his book.

Next the Gestapo chief began examining the Arnolds' living room. He noticed the inlaid coat of arms on the furniture. "Is there someone in the house by the name of von Hollander?" he asked, perplexed.

Emmy looked up, startled. "Yes. That was my name. My father was Johann Heinrich von Hollander, professor of law at Halle."

"Then I helped carry your father to his grave," the Inspector replied, suddenly pensive. "I was one of Professor von Hollander's students." He clicked his heels and left the room.

At five, as it grew dark, the intruders left. They had made no arrests. Emmy sighed. To think that her family furniture, though scratched and chipped from years of heavy use, might have saved them from arrest! The SS men marched four abreast, while a big car carried away Inspector Hütteroth. With him went several baskets full of books, manuscripts, official minutes, and financial records. The neighbors, who had gathered to see how many people would be taken away, looked disappointed and slipped away.

That night the household met in the Arnold's living room. Eberhard sat on his bed looking white and ill. The Sparhof community was so young and inexperienced! Apart from him and Emmy, most of its members were only in their twenties. He longed to reassure, strengthen, and encourage them. At this very moment the Gestapo would be poring through everything they had taken. During the first minutes of the raid, Moni had managed to stuff several politically dangerous papers into the stove. But it wouldn't take long for them to find the evidence they wanted. Though consistently careful to show respect to the state, he had never hidden his disapproval for Nazism. What would happen next?

From that day on Eberhard often spoke of his death. "I cannot die until everything is in order," he told Heiner and the others, no doubt wondering who would guide the movement when he was gone. "I have to hurry; I won't live long."

It was at the end of that fateful year that Heiner and Annemarie found each other as if for the first time. For the most part they simply enjoyed each other's company. But without speaking of it, both vaguely sensed a deepening friendship.

Heiner was cautious after what had happened with Grete. Occasionally she still tried to speak to him about it, though Heiner always refused. Now she decided to try one more time. Maybe she suspected Heiner's growing interest in Annemarie. In any case, late one night, when Heiner came into his room, he found her sitting on his bed. He was appalled. Grete knew that at the Sparhof, no unmarried woman entered a man's room.

"Please, Grete, go! You know you're not allowed to be here," he begged.

Grete seemed not to hear his request, and instead started pleading with Heiner to reaccept her as a friend. Just then the door opened. It was Eberhard on his crutches. "It's already eleven o'clock," he said levelly. "Bring your conversation to a close and go to bed."

"Yes, Papa." Heiner sounded unnaturally eager. Grete made no move to go. Half an hour later, Eberhard creaked back down the hall. "Heiner, I asked you two to stop. Go to bed." The door closed again, and Heiner commanded Grete in the most authoritative tone he could muster: "You must leave my room. Please!" She didn't budge.

She was still there at midnight, frantic now, and beginning to weep. At twelve-thirty Georg, the night watchman, appeared with a lantern. Eberhard had sent him. Ignoring Heiner, he planted himself in the room. "Grete, I will not leave until you let me take you home"—at which she finally yielded. As Georg escorted her out the door, he called back over his shoulder, "Heiner, go to the kitchen."

Heiner obeyed, and found the last thing he expected: a plate of fried eggs and fresh coffee, prepared for him at his father's request. Soon Georg was back. "When you've finished eating, go to your father's study. He's waiting for you."

It was almost one when Heiner opened his father's door. In the dark he could barely make out the figure lying on the cot. His father sat up and looked at him searchingly. There was no word of reproach. "Heiner, it was something you had to fight through yourself. I couldn't help you, and I couldn't interfere. But I was praying for you all the time."

Silum

Liechtenstein, April 1934

Heiner shivered as he lay in bed, despite the sunshine that poured through the window. At this elevation, April was chilly. There was wood stacked in the corner, but no fire was burning in the stove. Fuel was too valuable to use up casually—bought as standing timber on remote parts of the mountain, it had to be felled, cut into logs, and then hauled home by handcart. His six-foot-two frame stuck out from his blanket, and a draft ruffled its hem. But why complain? The hut had been built for summer use, when the cowherds brought their animals up from the valley.

It would be months before the herds came up. Now, snowdrifts still hugged the walls. Heiner was running a fever. He had been bed-ridden ever since arriving here from the Sparhof a few days ago. The last few days had been long, but life here had its beauties—the alpenglow at dawn and then again at sunset, the white peaks all around turning into glistening red steeples and domes. And there had been time to read—Saint Augustine and Meister Eckhart—or to simply lie and think back over the rush of events that had brought him here.

Below Heiner's hut stood a modest chalet, a summer hotel the Sparhof had leased after suddenly having to evacuate its children from Germany. The trouble had begun on the last day of 1933, with a government order to dissolve the Sparhof school. Earlier, a horrified inspector had found the children lacking, not in the three R's, but in their knowledge of patriotic marching songs and political ideology. A Nazi headmaster was imminent, but he never taught a single class. By the time the Christmas holidays were over, his hoped-for pupils had all been whisked out of the country.

They had regrouped at Silum, in the principality of Liechtenstein. Annemarie had accompanied them as a teacher, and other adults had gradually moved across the border too. Heiner had been sent to teach the boys gymnastics and crafts. More recently Eberhard had even traveled down from Germany to see them.

Heiner had been sick almost from the moment he had arrived at Silum. He rarely had visitors, so he was overjoyed to hear someone at the door. It was his father, and as he hobbled into the hut, Heiner tried to imagine how he had dragged himself up the slope. It was a steep climb, and the last year had aged Papa deeply. Ever since the SS raid, he had been working relentlessly, visiting government offices, sending out an avalanche of petitions, arranging for the children's evacuation, and reassuring the Sparhof's anxious creditors. The Nazis were trying to bankrupt the Sparhof and were nearly succeeding: they had cut off all subsidies for the farm and educational work and prohibited fundraising and the sale of books and other wares.

Under these pressures, Papa had taxed his body more than it could bear. It was half a year since he had broken his leg, and still the bone wasn't healing. The fracture caused him continuous pain, yet he had insisted that the doctors outfit him with a walking cast, and he walked constantly.

"You're shivering," Eberhard said. "It's freezing in here." Dragging his cast, he stooped for a hatchet and started to chop kindling for a fire. Then he crouched awkwardly and lit it as Heiner watched. The hut began to warm.

For a while they chatted about everyday things, his father resting his chin on top of his two walking canes, eyes peering at Heiner. Then he paused. "Tell me, Heiner—have you by chance decided on the girl you want to marry?"

"Yes, Papa. Annemarie."

A look of joy broke over his father's face. "Annemarie? If that is the case, be assured you have the blessing of both your parents." He was beaming. "But Heiner" — he was looking him straight in the eye — "promise me not to rush into this. Give Annemarie time. Certainty is not something that comes overnight. I advise you not to talk to her about marrying until you're at least twenty-one."

Heiner agreed. True, a doubt did flit across his mind — "It's a long time to wait — eight whole months." But he brushed it away. Father and son sat together in wordless happiness while the pine logs crackled and spit. Finally Eberhard heaved himself up on his canes and went out.

Eberhard returned to Germany shortly afterward, and Heiner recovered from the flu and started his new job. Aside from teaching, he was to oversee the children in the afternoons. It was May by now and the Alpine meadows bloomed wherever the snow left patches of open ground. There was heather, violets, tiny orchids, and millions of crocuses. Whenever Heiner and Annemarie could both get away — no easy task, since both had to be free of supervising the children at the same time — they went climbing in the surrounding mountains. On Helawang, a nearby peak, they would watch the moon rise and listen to the endless roar of the Samina rushing through the narrow valley below.

Every young couple guards the time they can spend together, but Heiner and Annemarie had another reason for wanting to flee Silum whenever they could: everyone seemed so downcast. Hannes Boller, a middle-aged former parson, played a big part in this. On leaving, Eberhard had made him responsible for the group, and though at first enthusiastic, he soon yielded to a tendency toward nervous moralism. Hannes supervised the mostly young members of Silum with undue vigilance. He chaperoned their excursions. He made lists of "unchristian" songs they were forbidden to sing. He even censored outgoing mail.

Hannes's stuffiness was merely an annoyance at first. But soon his admonitions were stifling the entire household, and a defeatist mood settled over them. It didn't help that each fresh piece of news from Germany seemed to mock their brave dreams of a better world. Most recently, in June, hundreds of Hitler's opponents had been assassinated in the Night of the Long Knives. "Europe is going to hell," some in Silum began to think, "Why waste energy solving a personality conflict? Better to just live with it and try to get along."

Not everyone felt this way. Annemarie, for one, bristled at the idea that she should have left her family just to toady up to a clergyman. She and the others loved to tweak Hannes. When he showed up for their outings, they sang the hiking songs he had outlawed. While he droned through a Sunday sermon, they tossed paper balls. After he ordered early curfews, they celebrated till long after midnight, with pranks, singing, and wading in the large water trough that stood in the pasture.

Heiner joined in the fun, but he was torn. Whatever Hannes's faults, he was Papa's representative. Shouldn't Heiner be supporting him? And maybe Hannes was right after all. Who could take issue with the virtues he never tired of preaching—discipline, respect, attention to duty, and sober Christian living?

Heiner argued with himself. His heart told him that Hannes was a pious busybody; his head insisted that someone who looked so good could not be wrong. Gradually nothing seemed certain any longer, and his chief desire was to stay out of the fray. Depressed, he retreated into himself, and grew nostalgic about the past. How simple and obvious it had seemed then, to go into the world to bring hope to the poor! Now those yearnings seemed presumptuous. They would never become a reality. Here in Silum he was finally learning to know himself for what he was. He was a failure.

Perhaps the best thing was to simply give up his old dreams and settle down with Annemarie. In a way, it seemed a betrayal. But given the madness all around, wasn't a quiet, righteous life enough? The vision beckoned him alluringly. "I'll ask Annemarie to marry me right away," he thought. "It makes no sense to wait till I'm twenty-one." A few days later, he told Hannes of his love for Annemarie, and his hopes for a speedy wedding. He said nothing about the promise he had made to his father.

Then a minor disaster intervened. One Sunday night, when everyone in Silum had gathered for a meeting, Hannes came in stiff and aggrieved, with Annemarie and her friend Marianne Zimmermann walking shamefaced behind him. Hannes said he had to report a shocking incident: Annemarie and Marianne had taken the children on a hike to Vaduz, the capital of the principality, and then had gone *swimming*. And that in the fountain of the prince's park. To Hannes, it was the height of irresponsibility—especially for a group of political refugees. There could be a public scandal! Who knew how the government would react? He added that he had phoned Eberhard, asking him and Emmy to come. They would be arriving in a couple of days.

Come he did, but with consequences Hannes did not intend: not many days later, Eberhard relieved Hannes of his responsibilities, to everyone else's relief. Still, in order to avoid any difficulties with the Liechtenstein authorities, Eberhard suggested that Annemarie and Marianne leave the principality and move back to the Sparhof.

After Annemarie left, Heiner was miserable, his world falling apart. He accused himself. How had he fallen so far from the faith of his childhood? Why had the fire that had flared in him at the time of his conversion died? For whole days at a time, he lost himself in morbid introspection. "I am a failure at everything. I can't be trusted with anything. I have no idea how to go on." He began to hate himself.

Eberhard, who had stayed on at Silum, noticed Heiner's gloom, and it disturbed him. His son seemed to believe that it was somehow meritorious to torment oneself. Perhaps he was trying to purge himself, or to prove his mettle. But it could not be allowed to go on—not if Heiner was his son. "When there is pus in the wound, it must be drawn out to heal." And so one evening during the course of a meeting, he prodded Heiner to tell everyone what was on his mind.

Heiner rose and made a statement he had long been preparing. "I am co-guilty for everything wrong that has happened here. Because of my many mistakes, I am not fit to be involved in educational work. I ask to resign from the school."

Eberhard rose to his full height. "Heiner, you suffer from being in love with yourself. Do you think you are scoring points with God by continually talking about your failures? Our failure is a certainty to us, and so we go forward from it and get down to business. Your humble playacting is not genuine. You are perverting your youthfulness. That's all your melancholy spirituality has done to you."

Heiner was stunned. But his father wasn't finished. "Heiner has completely lost his way. Why? Because he is fixated on getting married, no matter what. When I was here last, Heiner, you promised me you would not get engaged before you were twenty-one—and now you try to reverse our agreement. You broke your word. Hannes tells me you turned to him to move things forward!"

"But Papa," Heiner protested weakly, "I only told Hannes that I wished that —"

"You misled Hannes! You forgot the most important thing I said to you: that you should give Annemarie time. You have trodden my trust underfoot. And Heiner, tell me this: Why did you never confront Hannes when you knew he was acting like a tyrant?"

"It was cowardice."

"That's not possible. That kind of cowardice doesn't exist. It is because you are concerned about the image people have of you, because you don't want any unpleasant situations. You always want to be surrounded by a cloud of meekness and holiness, Heiner. That is your so-called cowardice."

Heiner stood staring at his father with blank despair—he had known his father to shout, but not like this. The circle of faces around him blurred, and only his father's remained clear.

"Heiner, go back to the starting point, just as if you were a child again. Is this the kind of person you wanted to be when you were eleven and so full of dreams for the future? Heiner and his little plans for a cozy marriage must disappear behind the big questions: What will become of the injustices all around us, which cry to heaven? What will become of Nazi Germany and Soviet Russia? What is your responsibility in the face of all this? You have a sound body and a sound soul; you have gifts and strength. Use them! With your melancholy attitude you are living in chronic suicide.

"Why does success mean so much to you? It's putting on make-up before God. You think you are not doing well enough. Then you analyze yourself to find the cause of your guilt. You think you have to make yourself still humbler, to evoke God's pity. That is egoism! You want to make the Creator into your packhorse!"

In the silence that followed, the only sounds were the clock ticking and Eberhard's quick breath. Eberhard seemed to be waiting for something. Then he said, "Heiner, you have to recognize how utterly lost you are. What you said tonight comes from the abyss."

The meeting ended. Heiner was numb. As if through thick glass, he saw his father hobbling toward him, asking him, "How is it possible, Heiner?" His face was no longer angry so much as bewildered. "How is it possible that you let things go so far? Is this all we can expect from you after your childhood, after the Sun Troop, and after all we have experienced together? Why didn't you tell me what was going on here?" Heiner stood abjectly, saying nothing. His father pressed him. "Heiner, why are you like this?"

"That's just the way I am."

"What?" Eberhard cried out, his energy back in a flash. "Do you know what you are saying? You are accusing God! You're accusing your mother! You're accusing me!" The anguish in his father's face would stay with Heiner for the rest of his life.

Heiner began to tremble during the pause that followed. Then Eberhard said quietly and with deep sorrow, "You are the son in whom I had the greatest hope. And now you say this to me?" Heiner could not answer. The two of them went out into the night, Eberhard on his crutches, along the footpath that ran from the chalet. Above the peaks stretched the vastness of a starry sky. Looking into the valley they could make out the faint line of the Rhine River three thousand feet below. The lights of the towns along its banks twinkled as if from another world. Suddenly Eberhard asked, "Have you ever thought of all the people who live down there, with all their loves and sufferings and sins? Have you ever asked yourself what meaning each of their lives ought to have? Have you ever thought of the day when God's rule will break over this earth, and each little house in the valley will be flooded with light? Has any of this ever concerned you or disturbed you? Or have you only thought of your own happiness with Annemarie?"

Heiner answered. No, he had never really thought about this.

"Then where is your Christianity?" his father said sharply.

They stood side by side, gazing down. Heiner felt cold ripples up and down his neck. Gradually it dawned on him what it was all about. His father was saving him from something far worse than a life of failure or misery or even wickedness. He was saving him from the sin of turning his back on the promise he had made as a child. From choosing the comfort of pious complacency over a daring adventure. From denying his calling. From apostasy.

As Heiner recognized all this, he was filled with gratefulness. The strength of his father's love overwhelmed him.

The two of them walked back home. As they parted to go to bed, Eberhard said: "Never forget tonight."

14

Annemarie

Zurich, December 21, 1934

Half a year passed. Heiner was now living in Zurich, where he was about to finish his first semester at the Strickhof School of Agriculture. Annemarie, having spent several months at the Sparhof, was back in Silum. Heiner often went on hikes with her on the weekends he was home. But much as they enjoyed each other's company, they shied far away from talking about their love for each other. They were just friends.

It was almost Christmas, and Heiner was still at school. In two days he would celebrate his twenty-first birthday. At noon, when mail was distributed to the students, Heiner received a letter from his father—a long one, to judge from the bulk of the envelope. Nervously he tore it open and skimmed it with mounting excitement.

"My dear Heiner," his father wrote. "First of all, you must for once and for all stop complaining about your weakness of character—it is something you should take for granted. Everything that was wrong in the past is forgiven. . . . You have your parents' blessing if you decide to ask Annemarie to marry you. My deepest wish is that you might found a family, and do so hand in hand, building it up so thoroughly and firmly on the rock of Christ's church that for generations to come no earthly storm can shake it."

Heiner was overjoyed. If he could have, he would have replied to his father immediately. But the few minutes he had at his disposal were already over. In general, free time did not exist at the Strickhof. With its grueling schedule and military discipline, the school more closely resembled an academy for cadets than a college.

Heiner's entry into this regimented life had been a rough one. On his first day, dragging his traveling trunk into his dormitory, he learned that it was not made up of rooms, but just one enormous hall filled with rows of metal beds. Heiner's dorm-mates – almost all sons of Swiss farmers – had noticed his discomfort and offered to coach him on survival skills. For starters, they said, he needed to learn the regulations on bed making. Every morning the foreman would enter the dorm to inspect each bed. If he found an incorrectly tucked blanket or a wrinkled pillow, he would fling the offender's bedding onto the floor and sentence him to Sunday cow-stall duty.

The following morning, with these warnings ringing in his ears, Heiner had carefully made his bed and followed the others into the dining hall. He had high hopes of meeting as many of his new class-mates as possible. Maybe he would even find enough interest to organize a sort of student-level Sun Troop. He received his portion of food, sat down, and introduced himself to the others at his table. The conversation he hoped for fell flat. "What do we have here? Another noisy German?" It was the voice of the foreman, booming from across the room. "He talks as much as Hitler. We'll have to muzzle them both." Heiner looked up. Everyone else was eating their porridge in silence. Evidently conversation at mealtimes, like so many other things at the Strickhof, was strictly verboten.

As the days passed, Heiner grew used to the many prohibitions – but not to the lack of privacy. He longed for the chance to be by himself, even for a few minutes. But it wasn't to be. Eating, dressing, studying, working, sleeping – it all took place as part of a herd. The students were genial, but crude – and, Heiner thought, inordinately patriotic. "The Swiss are so proud of their mountains, you'd think they'd made them," he liked to say.

Classes, which included practical training in the fields, began at 5:30 a.m., followed by breakfast, a formal lineup, and roll call—all in silence. They then ran continuously until seven at night, broken only by an hour for lunch. After dinner, there was a mandatory silent study hall until lights-out at 9:30. Apart from Sundays and three weeks of vacation, every day followed a similar pattern.

Heiner chafed at spending his days in a classroom. The agricultural subjects were for the most part enjoyable. But mastering the natural sciences, economics, and literature, plus the basics of business management and accounting, seemed an endless uphill battle. To Annemarie, he complained of the "soul-crushing" drill. He must have known to expect no sympathy from his father on this score. Radical as he might be in other ways, Eberhard resonated with the school's old-fashioned aim of turning out men with firm characters and a self-disciplined bearing.

On December 23, his father's letter in his pocket, Heiner took the morning train out of Zurich. As it wound eastward between the mountains toward Liechtenstein, he thought with excitement of what might happen next—maybe even as soon as tonight. The ride seemed interminable. Then there was the bus transfer, and the long hike up the mountain. The trip had never seemed so long. When at last he stomped up the final slope to Silum and opened the door of the chalet, nearly everyone was already in bed. Luckily for him, Annemarie was still up, wrapping Christmas gifts for the schoolchildren with Emy-Margret. Seeing him, she welcomed him—rather briskly, he thought—and then told him she'd be working till late. He ignored the hint, loitering by the door and trying to make conversation. But her answers were curt. Deflated, he went to bed.

Now it was Christmas Eve. By the time Heiner had dressed, Annemarie was long up, finishing her gift-wrapping in a back room.

She stayed there all day, busily chatting with Emy-Margret. Heiner dropped in frequently, eager to help, but each time she waved him off. "We're fine—almost done." He grew despondent. Soon it would be Christmas itself. When, amid all the bustle, would there be time to talk to her alone?

In the evening there was a party for the children to open their gifts: a lighted tree, carols, and chaos and excitement as dolls, books, hatchets, and sleds were admired. The room was noisy and hot. Heiner, noticing that Annemarie looked exhausted, suggested going out to get some fresh air. She accepted—happily—and they slipped out.

Earlier in the evening she had found a surprise in her room: two white candles burning on her dresser, and a card and chocolates by her bed. "The gifts I found in my room were wonderful!" she told him. He hardly acknowledged her thanks. "I don't care if it doesn't matter to you," she went on. "But you must let me tell you. Your surprise made me very happy." Still no response; he seemed preoccupied. "How strangely he is acting tonight," she thought.

After a few more minutes of climbing—the houses were out of sight now—Heiner turned and started downward on a new path, one that wound toward the base of the mountain. The snow was above their knees, and it was strenuous to walk. Suddenly, as if noticing for the first time that Annemarie was at his side, Heiner launched into a description of his friends at school. She told him about the previous weeks at Silum, but felt he wasn't paying attention again. "Heiner," she told him, "I have to go back now. It's time to put the children to bed."

"But our walk has been so short." He sounded so pained that she quickly added, "It's true. We still have a few more minutes."

The path narrowed. A sheer rock-face towered up on one side of them and plunged down on the other. Under their boots the snow crunched, but otherwise all was silent. They stopped talking. Far below, the river twisted between constellations of glittering lights. "It looks like Christmas," Annemarie thought.

They arrived at a little dell sheltered by firs. Annemarie had been feeling for some minutes that Heiner wanted to say something to her. She waited for it, both eager and anxious. "Whatever it is, let him say it," she thought. She sat down on a rock, while Heiner stayed standing, as if struck dumb. At last he spoke.

"I have something important to ask you." He spoke about the summer day when she had first visited the Sparhof and they had gone walking. "Time after time since then, we've been drawn together. Every event, happy or sad, has led us closer . . ." Annemarie didn't hear him. Inside her a storm had burst, and its din drowned out everything else. Now was the moment to decide. She wanted to postpone it, but couldn't. And why should she try? Everything in the last year — even that hard separation last summer — had drawn them closer together.

She realized that somehow she had just made a crucial decision. She began to hear Heiner's voice again. ". . . And so it is my deepest plea that we follow one path together, united for the rest of our lives, not for our own sakes but in service to the whole world.

"I would like to ask you whether you feel the same. You don't need to answer tonight."

Annemarie sat motionless. After a few moments, he said he would like to read her a letter from his father. She nodded mutely. Taking two candles from his pocket, one red and one white, he lit them with shaking hands, fumbling in the wind with match after match before he succeeded. Then he read the letter from his father.

They were silent again. Wind breathed through the firs, and the two candle flames flickered. Annemarie tried to speak, but couldn't. When at last she did her voice was barely audible. "I also believe that everything has been guided this way."

They prayed, and Heiner said he wanted to read her his father's letter one more time. The wind had blown out the candles, so he relit them. "They will be a symbol for us," he said. "The red one for love; the white one for purity."

When they arrived back at the chalet, they separated. Annemarie rushed to her room, overwhelmed with happiness. Then Hardy was at the door calling her, and Hans was beaming and shaking her hand, and Emy-Margret was pinning a Christmas rose to her dress. "Come! Heiner told us you're engaged! It's time to celebrate!"

15

The Farewell

Strickhof, January 3, 1935

Heiner skipped afternoon classes on the first day of the new term. He wanted to be alone and think about Annemarie. So much had happened since he had left Zurich ten days ago! Christmas, their engagement, and then their day together yesterday. They had spent it walking the shore of the Walensee, which began happily, in the company of Sophie and her fiancé Christian, who had also recently got engaged. But in the afternoon the sky had been gray, and the dark lake somehow melancholy, with its cold little waves slapping the shore. And then they had had to say goodbye. "Now the same soulless drill will start all over again," he thought glumly. "The Strickhof – in exchange for hikes with Annemarie."

But he couldn't sit here and stew. He made an effort to reflect on the goal of his training as a farmer, which his father repeatedly impressed on him: not merely to prepare for his own future, but to build for the kingdom of God. He often pondered his father's vision: "All the movements of the past decades will one day converge in a radical awakening of the masses that leads the way to social justice and to God's unity. And so we prepare ourselves to set our little community in the midst of this mighty awakening. We must be ready to sacrifice ourselves. We cannot cling to a time when, as now, we are a small circle of people who know each other intimately. We must be ready to be consumed in a mighty outpouring of the Holy Spirit!"

Papa, as Heiner knew, looked toward the day when thousands would turn from the spiritual emptiness of their lives and begin to live in community just as the first Christians did—as they were trying to do at Silum and the Sparhof. These future communities would need capable members in as many fields as possible. That was why he, Heiner, had been sent to the Strickhof; why Hardy was at Tübingen becoming a teacher, and Hans-Hermann preparing for medical school—all at a time when there was hardly enough money to put food on the table. With a renewed sense of purpose, Heiner got up to find his books. There was work to do.

Two months passed according to the Strickhof's mechanical rhythm. There was little to break the monotony except Annemarie's letters. She had already written him more than a dozen, and he answered each one as quickly as he could. Time was always scarce, but finding a private place to write was even harder. He could not use the dorm, since the other students, reading over his shoulder, would mock his letters mercilessly. Lately he had taken to stealing down to the school's furnace room after curfew, where he could write till early morning undisturbed.

Then, in mid-March, his father arrived in Zurich, limping off the train in his walking cast. Heiner had been looking forward eagerly to this visit—it would be the first opportunity to talk with his father since the engagement, and there were a hundred things to discuss. Father and son embraced boisterously. But Eberhard had little time to talk. Two other members of the Sparhof had come with him for an important meeting. The Nazis were turning the screws tighter every day, and it was urgent to spend every minute in Switzerland raising funds and soliciting the support of old friends such as Leonhard Ragaz, the godfather of religious socialism.

All afternoon and evening, Heiner waited impatiently for his father and the others to return to the apartment where they were to stay the night. It was nine when the trio finally arrived. They looked haggard. The Swiss friends they had been counting on had been cool, and then hostile. The six-hour meeting had been a disaster.

Eberhard was light-hearted during dinner, teasing Heiner about Annemarie, and ordering a cake for dessert. He encouraged Heiner to take his fiancée to visit her mother in Thuringia during the next recess from classes.

At the end of the meal, his cheerful mood passed. Hitler, his father told him, was said to be on the verge of bringing back compulsory military service.

Heiner had been hearing of the possibility for months. Political news filtered to his father from many sources, including Baron von Gagern, a government official, devout Catholic, and old family friend. In order to get news, Emmy would go to von Gagern's wife for *Kaffee und Kuchen*. According to Baroness von Gagern, a decree would be announced any day. Refusal would be punished as treason, with no exceptions made. The consequences would be death or life imprisonment – and in most cases, the former would be carried out immediately.

As his father talked, Heiner realized how heavy the weight of responsibility must feel to him. If Baron von Gagern's warning was true, then every young man at the Sparhof was in grave danger. To them, the commands "Thou shalt not kill" and "Love your enemies" held true in all circumstances, and because of this, none would ever serve in the military – in any of its branches, in any form.

The community's stubbornness with regard to this position had long been incomprehensible to other like-minded groups. Most Christian dissenters – such as those of the Pastors' Emergency League – saw it as their God-ordained obligation to serve in the armed forces. Martin Niemöller, the courageous anti-Nazi pastor who would later gain fame as a survivor of the concentration camps, was typical. When Bruderhof members traveled to his house to beg for solidarity, he refused even to shake their hands, declaring: "I am proud to have served as a U-boat commander in the last war. If Hitler calls me back to my post, I will go." To him, military service was a Christian duty, despite his disapproval of Nazi policies (he would later change his views). But Heiner and his military-age fellow members held to the same convictions on Jesus' teaching of nonviolence shared at that time by Dietrich Bonhoeffer, whom Hardy had got to know in London the previous year. They were determined to refuse to kill – not for Hitler, and not for anyone else.

The meal was over all too soon. Heiner hoped that the others would let him be alone with his father. But again there was no time, as Eberhard still had to finish working over his notes and correspondence with his assistants. He did not finish till one o'clock. When he got up to go to bed, he apologized to Heiner that they still had not had a proper talk. "Come here first thing tomorrow; we'll talk then." They said goodnight, and Heiner walked to the Strickhof.

The next morning he rose early, full of anticipation, and made his way back to where his father was staying. The rooms were empty. As Heiner learned later, urgent matters had forced his father to take an earlier train than planned. "Why am I never allowed to be with my father?" he thought bitterly. "Every chance seems to be snatched away at the last moment."

He was still disconsolate when, four days later, on March 16, 1935, he heard the fateful news: Hitler had introduced mandatory military conscription. Germany's announcement surprised Europe and the United States, and stirred up a storm of diplomatic wrangling. After all, the Versailles Treaty had expressly forbidden German rearmament. For Heiner, though, the issue was brutally simple. Once the new law took effect, he would not be able to go back to the Sparhof or anywhere else in Germany without risking arrest. He would become a man without a country, just at a time when Hitler's long arm was stretching even into the Bruderhof's temporary home of Liechtenstein. Only a mile from Silum was Gaflei, a mountain resort where German Nazis congregated. It was rumored that they sometimes captured Jews by night and dragged them, never to be seen again, up a trail to a cliff. They were busy by day as well, for the principality had its own active and growing Nazi party. One of its first campaigns was to rid the area of "foreigners" – including the small local Jewish population, and the pacifist refugees at Silum.

But as summer began, it was not the Nazis who posed the greatest test to Silum. There were internal problems, and they came to a head in June, while Eberhard and Emmy were visiting from the Sparhof.

Eberhard was dismayed at what he found. The community was imploding in the same way it had just the year before. This time the cover was efficiency – not piety – and it was not Hannes, but his replacement, Hans, who bore the main responsibility. Yet the basic issues were the same.

In a series of meetings, Eberhard took Hans and his assistants to task. "You act like civil servants!" he told them. "Is this what we're living together for – domination and bureaucracy and officialdom?" He suggested abolishing all formal titles for a year. "The idea of true leadership has been polluted. We have no fixed offices here, only services that grow out of the stream of love. I don't want a title for myself or anyone else. Up until now, you have seen me as elder of the community. But if that term is felt to be a title, I shall lay it down. If it is a social rank, I hereby renounce it as a work of the devil."

Eberhard's listeners grew ashamed as they realized how far their community had drifted from what it was meant to be. Many wept. Only Hans remained unmoved. Eberhard pleaded with his son-in-law to recognize what he had done. Yet he refused to admit any guilt.

Later, at another meeting, Eberhard spoke in great agitation, cut to the core by Hans's stubbornness. "Do you want me to tell you how I see it, then, Hans?" he said. "Your hard-heartedness is destroying the community. You are returning its love with a slap in the face. Even Emmy and I, who love you as your parents, cannot seem to win your heart. You rule here like a king! And there is something else too. I have noticed that you let yourself be worshiped by the women!"

At these words, Emy-Margret protested and then fainted. But the meeting continued. Hours later, Hans finally softened. He said he realized he had failed, and that he was sorry for where he had hurt his coworkers. Instantly, Eberhard embraced him and declared the matter closed.

Shortly afterward, Heiner went to Silum for a weekend to see his parents. He did not know details about his father's recent confrontation with Hans. Nor did he ask for any, now that the two had reconciled. But he was still insecure about his own relationship with Hans, which had grown strained over the last year. Hans knew Heiner's tendency to worry about his weaknesses, and often derided his "emotionalism." When he and his father were alone, Heiner remarked, "I wish I had no feelings at all, and that I was like Hans."

Eberhard shuddered. "Never say that! The community can bear one person like that, but no more. Thank God he gave you a heart with feelings. The main thing is they are directed toward an honest goal."

That September, the Nazis intensified their drive to expel all foreigners from Liechtenstein. They canvassed every house and collected an impressive list of signatures.

Heiner had a week of vacation just then, and so he was in Silum to welcome his parents when they came to deal with the emergency. The circumstances were unfortunate, but still he was delighted at the chance for a reunion.

As soon as Eberhard arrived in the country, he paid a visit to the prince's chief minister, Dr. Hoop, a Catholic priest and distrustful of Nazism. Dr. Hoop listened sympathetically and promised to do what he could to help. "But if they collect enough signatures," he said, "my hands are tied and I can do nothing to save you. You must go directly to the people." He arranged for Eberhard to speak in a village near Silum after Sunday Mass.

It was a freezing October day when Heiner and his brothers brought their father down the mountain for the speech. Eberhard could not manage the steep descent on his own, having forced his leg to do far more than it could bear. In the previous year he had undertaken numerous strenuous journeys to Nazi officials, traveling to Fulda, Kassel, and even Berlin to inform the Gestapo as to the stance of the Bruderhof. All those railway transfers and taxi rides had prevented his leg from healing. Now it was so crooked that the doctors warned it might break again at any time.

Today he sat on a two-wheeled cart that his sons maneuvered down the path. It was a steep grade down to Triesenberg, and the young men had to strain to keep from picking up speed. Their father winced with every jolt. They were just trundling into the village when Mass ended. Not wanting to miss the excitement, virtually the whole congregation stayed, thronging the little plaza outside the church. Eberhard limped over to a small rise and looked over his audience of a few hundred, leaning on his two canes. The villagers stared back at the strange speaker distrustfully.

"Honored citizens, dear brothers and sisters," he began. Instantly he was drowned out by whistling and derisive shouts – and even a volley of rocks. None hit him, and he tried again: "Honored citizens of Liechtenstein, brothers and sisters . . ." Another uproar and more flying rocks. Heiner could see that it was not the villagers who were heckling his father. They were standing quietly, their faces impassive. The disturbance came from the back of the crowd, where a gang of young Nazi sympathizers had gathered. Each time Eberhard began to speak, they let loose a din of whistling and yelling.

Heiner burned with indignation and kept his eyes on his father, nervous for his safety. Though calm at first, Eberhard had now had enough. He straightened himself and looked over the crowd. "Why are you hiding back there?" he boomed, so loudly that even the dullest-looking villagers jerked to life. "Why are you staying in the back, like cowards? If you are against me, at least have the decency to come up here and tell me to my face."

The hooligans only jeered, and for a moment no one seemed certain what would happen next. But Eberhard's forthrightness impressed the older villagers, and they turned angrily on the gang at the back, which included some of their sons. "Shut up! Get out of here!" they shouted. "We want to hear what Dr. Arnold has to say."

The young men sulkily obeyed—and now the rest of the crowd was doubly attentive. Eberhard began again. By the time he was finished, he had won Triesenberg over. In a local referendum held some days afterward, the campaign to oust the community failed.

Friday came, and Heiner wondered where the week had gone. Tomorrow his parents would be returning to Germany. That afternoon, a premonition gripped him, and though it was triggered by a small incident, it would not let him go. The schoolchildren were performing a play in the dining room. Partway through it, Heiner glanced over at his father. Eberhard, who had always taken delight in such performances, was sitting hunched in his chair. His eyes were closed, and his features seemed to sag. Heiner wondered what was troubling him. The thought flashed across his mind: "Does he think he won't see us again?" The next day's border crossing was a known danger— the Gestapo had been using checkpoints to make political arrests for more than two years. In recent months, increasing numbers of priests, pastors, and members of religious orders had been disappearing.

When Heiner saw his father again that evening, however, he felt he must have been mistaken. Eberhard was giving a farewell message, and as he spoke, his voice rang with conviction. In a vivid sequence of verbal pictures, he brought to life the Book of Revelation. At one point, he evoked the vision of the beast from the abyss: A terrifying monster crawling forth out of the sea brings disaster to humankind. It forces all peoples of the earth to worship it, and imprisons and then kills the small band that refuses to obey. He didn't need to mention the similarity of this monster to Hitler's state, which was plotting murder, building concentration camps, and demanding a form of worship.

"The whole world worships the predatory nature of the state, crying, 'Who is like unto this beast, and who is able to make war with him?' The beast receives a mouth full of pride and blasphemy. All people—rich and poor, freemen and proletarians—are forced to wear the sign of idolatry on their arm or on their forehead. If they do not, they are not permitted to buy or sell; they are not permitted to live. What is the sign of the beast? It is the idolization of the power of man, the sign of the power of the state, of its prisons and its war making.

"Here it is necessary to hold with constancy to faith in Jesus. But in the end the Lamb will win, for he is the Lord of all lords and King of all kings. Even if we die, the final victory belongs to God."

The next morning, Heiner met his father on the veranda of the chalet, where they waited for Emmy and chatted pleasantly. They were standing side by side, leaning on the railing and looking out over the wide sweep of the valley. It was a magnificent view, from the highest gleaming peaks to the tiny patchwork fields along the Rhine. Each detail stood out crisply in the dry autumn air. Suddenly Heiner's father grabbed him by the shoulders and impulsively embraced and kissed him—several times. Then Emmy came out of the house, and it was time to go.

16

Four O'Clock

Zurich, November 1935

The letter from his mother said that Papa had undergone an operation to reset his leg. For several weeks, Heiner had known that this was coming. He knew the surgeon too—it was Paul Zander, who had given him and Hardy lodging on their cycling excursion to visit Tata in Fidaz four years before.

After two years of wearing a cast, Heiner's father couldn't wait to regain the full use of his left leg. "This is no way to live," Eberhard often sighed. That he was supposed to spend three weeks recuperating at the hospital, which was in Darmstadt, might even prove to be a blessing, Heiner reflected. Perhaps this would be a chance for him to get some rest away from the stress of holding off creditors and visiting Nazi officials.

But reading on, he learned that what had been intended as a simple surgery to shorten the bone had gone badly. In fact, the bone had grown so hard from overuse while healing that Dr. Zander had broken ten chisels on it. He had had to make some two hundred blows instead of the usual six or eight. Eberhard had been conscious through it all (he was under local anesthesia), and because the procedure took so much longer than planned, the injection had worn off half an hour before the surgeon was finished. Afterward he told Emmy, "They hacked and sawed and cut me to pieces." He had looked very pale, she wrote, and was in extreme pain. Still, Dr. Zander said this was to be expected after the surgery.

Shortly after the letter came, Hardy made a surprise visit. He was also going to school in Zurich (his refusal to say "Heil Hitler" had landed him in trouble at Tübingen) but rarely came over from the university to the Strickhof. Hardy had married Edith Boecker, a theology student from Hamburg, the year before, and the young couple split their time between Silum and Zurich. Heiner wondered what had brought him now. Hardy told him right away: "A telegram came. Zander will have to amputate Papa's leg below the knee."

Hardy went on to say that, according to Dr. Zander, the surgery would take only fifteen minutes, and there was no danger whatever. The doctor even predicted their father would walk more easily with an artificial leg than he would have otherwise.

That evening, Heiner joined Hardy at his apartment. Hans-Hermann was there too. The three talked over the serious turn of events, and agreed to travel to their father's side as soon as possible. Of course, there was the danger posed by the conscription law. But surely, if there was ever a time to risk crossing the border it was now. Hardy phoned Silum. Hans and Emy-Margret were taking a taxi directly to Darmstadt, and he asked whether they might take the three of them along. "Your father gave me instructions that you are to stay in Zurich," Hans told him. "Under no circumstances are any of you to risk your lives by entering Germany." Though disappointed, they obeyed. It did not occur to Heiner that his father was in serious danger.

Heiner might have acted differently had he known what Hans knew: that from his father's point of view, there was little time left. The previous week Hans had received a last testament from Eberhard in the form of a long letter. Addressed to Hans and Emy-Margret, and written from the hospital in Darmstadt, this extraordinary document described the essence of his vision for the community and offered guidance on how to fulfill that vision "when I am no longer among you." It had obviously been composed by a man preparing for death.

On receiving the document, Hans told Emy-Margret, "Papa has written a farewell letter." Yet he said nothing to the rest of the family, even though Hardy, Heiner, and Hans-Hermann called him regularly through the week, inquiring for news about their father. Nor did he tell them that their mother and Moni had called him from the hospital, reporting that Eberhard's condition was critical.

The amputation was scheduled for the afternoon of Friday, November 22. In Zurich, Heiner, Hardy, and Hans-Hermann each attended their scheduled lectures as usual. Knowing of no reason to worry for their father, and confident of a good outcome, they made no arrangements for contacting each other in case of emergency. Heiner sat in a forestry class from two to four o'clock. Shortly before the end of the session, he fell asleep at his desk and began to dream. He sensed his father approaching him, saying something infinitely important. Just then he woke. The bell was ringing four o'clock. Later he learned that this was the hour of his father's death.

With an overpowering feeling of his father's closeness to him, Heiner got up and filed out of the classroom with the other students. Just then a flustered secretary came up to him and handed him a telegram: "Amputation completed. Extreme danger to life. Prayers needed."

Heiner could not believe what he was reading. It could not be true. He sent up a panicked prayer and ran out of the building and down the street. He had to find his brothers. Hans-Hermann's school was not far away, and as he panted up the stone steps of the main entry, he ran straight into him and gave him the telegram.

Next the two ran for the university, where they dashed crazily through several buildings, flinging open the doors of lecture halls, barking, "Has anyone seen Hardy or Edith Arnold?" Finally they found their brother and his wife in the back of the library, absorbed in study. Heiner thrust the telegram at them.

"Phone Silum," they agreed. They set off for Hardy and Edith's apartment. It did not enter any of their minds that their father was no longer alive. Hardy placed the call, and Alfred answered. They asked for news, but he wouldn't give them any. All he said was, "Come home right away. Don't worry about the expense – take a taxi."

All the way to Liechtenstein Heiner fought back his fear. All his life he had dreamed of living with Papa as a grown man, working side by side with him, supporting him as a fellow fighter for the cause. And now . . . it couldn't be. For the last two years he had hardly seen him. And now, in his father's hour of greatest need, he hadn't even been praying for him.

Now the car was pulling up to Silum, and they were getting out. Snow had fallen. Annemarie stood in the road with Alfred. For a moment, they were all strangers.

Then Alfred spoke. "I have to tell you that your father is no longer among us." That was all. Heiner could not think or speak. Hardy was quiet too. But Hans-Hermann turned on Alfred, his whole body trembling. "You're lying!" he shouted. "You're lying, you're lying!"

17

The Last Letter

Heiner's father was buried on a windswept hill above the Sparhof the following Monday—a day so dismal that for decades, no one in the family could bear to talk about it. Neither he nor Hardy nor Hans-Hermann were present. They obeyed their father even in death by remaining beyond German borders. Given the political circumstances, there was little else they could do. Privately, their anguish knew no bounds. Meanwhile, Emmy, brave but frail, had to face her husband's graveside—and the darkest hour of her life—without them.

At Silum they held a memorial service the same time the funeral was taking place. It was Hardy's idea. Six young men carried a pine trunk representing the casket, and the rest of the household followed behind. The procession moved up the mountain in silence, the only sound the tramping of shoes on the packed snow.

While in Liechtenstein, Heiner and his brothers learned of their father's last letter to Hans and Emy-Margret. Heiner read and reread the letter, and for days the words re-echoed in his mind: "Everyone must be won for the greatness of the cause!" "The important thing is faith in the greatness of God!"

Eberhard's letter did not name anyone else to take his place of leadership. But it did reflect his trust in Hans, and it spelled out Eberhard's concerns and suggestions for the short term. "For the immediate future I advise you to work closely together with Georg,

Hardy, Heiner, Hans-Hermann, and similar spiritual elements, so that there will not be a stunting of the inner life. And I ask you yourself to hold to a clear line, united with Mama and Emy-Margret, keeping to the unchanged direction of the Spirit and of faith."

Because Hans had been Eberhard's closest assistant, it seemed natural that he should now fill his shoes. "We want to support you completely and serve the cause with all our strength," Heiner declared in a letter to Hans. Hardy and Hans-Hermann felt the same. So did their mother.

That December Heiner kept remembering a dream he'd had several weeks before. He had seen a desolate desert landscape whipped by a huge storm. As he watched, a solitary figure approached from the horizon. Buffeted by the tempest, he fought his way slowly forward on two canes. He came nearer and nearer, and suddenly Heiner recognized him. It was his father. His expression struck Heiner as one of utter devastation: this was a man who was cut off and forsaken.

When the dream had come to him, his father was still alive – supervising work at the Sparhof, writing articles, filling his study with cigarette smoke. Now he was dead.

"Papa died with a broken heart," his mother told him when she arrived in Silum a few days after the funeral. "He was distressed past bearing, because every day the Sparhof seemed nearer to falling apart."

The root cause: the community's inorganic division between two countries, which had been forced on them by persecution. All schoolchildren and men of military age had fled to Silum, followed by their families, while non-German nationals who were exempt from conscription staffed the Sparhof. There too few men remained to carry on the heavy farm work, and inexperienced members had been given responsibilities they could not cope with. Food, fuel, and credit were scarcer than ever, and harassment was continual. Simply passing through nearby villages had become like walking a gauntlet – villager after villager would shout "Heil Hitler!" and then, on getting no response, hurl threats and curses. And how long would it be before the SS raided the community again?

Beaten down by all these things, the community had grown weary. An apathy born of despair had settled over the whole farm and hung there like a spell. And though some tried to rouse themselves, most floundered in pessimism and resignation.

It was this state of affairs, Emmy reported to her sons, that had broken Eberhard's heart. Throughout his stay at the hospital, he had agonized over how he might pull the community out of the morass. But nothing he tried had worked. And the worst was this: before being put under anesthesia for the amputation, he had spent his last conscious moments feeling forsaken and alone. After the surgery, he had never woken up.

Emmy was composed as she told her sons all this—perhaps she was strong; perhaps the immensity of her loss was still incomprehensible to her. But Heiner felt the force of his grief from the beginning. It was different from when Tata had died. Losing her had also saddened him deeply. But then, his sorrow had focused him and brought him new strength and purpose. He sensed nothing of that now. Troubled by the image of the lonely wanderer in the desert, he kept tormenting himself. Why hadn't he understood the dream? If he had really loved his father, wouldn't he have rushed to Darmstadt? It also pained Heiner that his father's death seemed so accidental. Brave and daring as his father was, his death had not come in the way Heiner had imagined, by the hand of an SS assassin or a concentration camp guard. That kind of death—martyrdom—would at least have made sense.

Emmy told her sons how two days before his death—on Repentance Day, a national holiday—Eberhard had asked her, "Have you read in the paper whether Dr. Goebbels has repented?"

"Ebbo," she had whispered worriedly, glancing around to see whether his roommates had heard him. One was a policeman. She would have to stop her husband before he said something dangerous.

But he went on. "Goebbels will have to give an account for every idle word he has spoken."

"Everyone must do that," she replied for the benefit of the policeman, who had rolled over and was obviously interested.

"Emmy!" Eberhard raised his voice sternly. "Let us call a spade a spade! Will Goebbels repent publicly for every idle word that has come out of his mouth? God will demand an account."

Now Emmy was visibly upset. What would he say next? But the policeman smiled and said, "Don't worry. We can learn a lot from Herr Doktor. He is a very good man."

◆ ◆ ◆

A week after the funeral, Heiner's leave of absence from school ran out, and he returned to Zurich. Mostly he grieved. "My very dearest Annemarie," he wrote from the Strickhof, "Just like you, I feel so powerless and tired. This experience, this fact, is too heavy for anyone to be able to get over it in his own strength. And even if it were possible, that would be only by means of hardening the heart, which is very dangerous. And yet there is a way: by looking toward Christ, by looking toward the future. For me there is actually only one of two extremes: either hours of pain and despair, or hours of strong faith in God's future and the future of the cause. It is extremely hard, of course, that it had to be the way it was; that he had to die in just that way, and that we actually had no idea. And how infinitely I loved him. He was my father, and yet he was much more to me than a father, however good, can be to his son. I am realizing this here at the Strickhof by the stupid things people say to me, which though lovingly meant are terribly far removed from what this means to me."

In fact, Silum was just as bleak, as Heiner found out through his mother, who had come to Zurich to be with her sons. Only a month had passed since Eberhard's death, yet already Hans was acting contrary to directions he had set in ways both small and large. Far from supporting his grieving mother-in-law, Hans was snubbing her and brushing her aside. And as if that wasn't enough, he was drawing on isolated sentences from Eberhard's farewell letter to back his claims to leadership, and clamping down on those who questioned him.

Several months earlier, Eberhard had cautioned Hans about his tendency to "rule like a king," and Hans had promised to take the warning to heart. Now it seemed he had forgotten it completely. He clearly regarded himself as his father-in-law's successor, a term Eberhard had not used, and had himself officially installed as the community's leader in a torch-lit ceremony held at the Sparhof one night.

His self-importance showed itself in more sinister ways too, as Heiner gathered from Annemarie's letters. In January, while bawling out a young member who had unwisely passed confidential information to the community's neighbors, he started cuffing him on the ears so forcefully that people in the next room heard the slaps. The young man did not dare defend himself, and yelped *"Jawohl!"* with every blow.

Emmy's attempts to bring up her concerns to Hans went nowhere, so Hardy, Heiner, and Hans-Hermann resolved to confront him. They felt they had no other choice: Hans opportunistically used their father's last letter to assert a claim to leadership, but cavalierly ignored what it said about pastoral matters, let alone Eberhard's direction that Hans should work closely together with Emmy and his fellow members. In a phone call with their sister Emy-Margret in Silum, the three brothers voiced their disagreement with the course she and Hans were taking. "You are treading our mother underfoot." She reacted indignantly, accusing them of "supporting Mama's weaknesses." Later they called again, and then – their anger rising – yet again. Hans now refused to come to the phone. But to those at Silum, he made his intention clear: he had no plans either to consult with Emmy or to follow Eberhard's wishes. As he put it, "The dead hand no longer rules."

After a further phone call between Zurich and Silum, one which ended in furious shouting, Hans informed members at Silum about the dispute. The three brothers, he said, had offended the unity of the brotherhood and must be reprimanded. Emy-Margret agreed, saying that as painful as it was for her, she had to agree with Hans: her brothers and mother were in the wrong. Neither said anything about the nature of the Zurich group's concerns. No one even asked what they were.

Georg was summoned from the Sparhof, where he and Moni had been entrusted with the community's leadership after Eberhard's death. At first Georg was dissatisfied with Hans's approach. "Shouldn't they at least be given a hearing?" Georg asked.

Hans exploded. "That's a stab in the back!" Georg backed down, and everyone agreed that Emmy and her three sons must drop their criticisms at once. Annemarie, Alfred, and Arno were dispatched to Zurich to deliver the community's decision. Neither Heiner nor the others could accept it. Annemarie told Heiner he was simply rebellious. Suddenly both were shouting at each other. "If you don't respect my father, I will have nothing to do with you." He yanked his engagement ring off his finger and threw it at her feet, then turned his back on her and walked away.

All four Arnolds in Zurich rushed to Silum, where Emmy requested a private meeting with Hans. He refused to see her or his brothers-in-law, and sent an ultimatum instead: Either you accept my leadership without question, or you are rebels. Heiner and Hardy were beside themselves, and went from person to person begging them to hear their side of the affair.

The standoff with Hans continued for five days, until Heiner and his brothers backed down. Still staggering under the blow of their father's death, they had lost the will to fight on alone. Besides, Heiner remembered the rash words he had let fly over the phone. What if, because of him, the entire community were to split? He decided to give in. Eventually, all three brothers retracted everything they had said, and apologized.

But Hans was not ready to forgive. Speaking in the name of the community – so he claimed – he ordered Hardy and Hans-Hermann to drop out of school, and sent Heiner back to Zurich in disgrace. Then, harping on the way that the three brothers had lost their tempers, he spread the word to watch out for them: "They are unstable and rebellious, especially Heiner." The concerns they had raised in good faith were cast as a blatant bid to take control of the community's leadership – something that had never occurred to them. From now on, the three were marked.

Heiner and Hardy submitted – what else could they do? Hans-Hermann, the youngest, was crushed. And Emmy, newly widowed, now bore a double grief. She had always cared for the community as for her own family, and till now she had been honored as a mother in return. After this, many no longer showed her the same warmth or respect.

18

Refugee Wedding

Heiner was behind in his academic work, and final exams were only weeks away. Numbly he set about studying. While his father was alive, Heiner's childhood vision—becoming an itinerant like Francis of Assisi or Rachoff—had been a steady, if vague, incentive. Now his father was dead, and Heiner's dreams seemed to have died with him.

Heiner and Annemarie had made peace before his return to Zurich—after trading apologies, both had broken down weeping, and everything between them had melted away. Later she wrote to him, "My beloved Heiner, I am so inexpressibly glad that we are again united. Everything is like new. Have you already put your ring back on? Heiner, don't think anymore of the old things; I won't either. . . . Not the tiniest thorn remains in my heart." She suggested a wedding date at the end of April.

Heiner wouldn't have to wait that long. Exams at the Strickhof were to be held in mid-March, and after that he planned to move back to Silum. Just in those days, however, Hitler handed down a new decree requiring all German men abroad to register for military service. Almost immediately, the government of Liechtenstein informed Silum that it could no longer harbor German draft evaders, and that violators would be arrested and extradited. After all, the principality had an armed force of only seven policemen and could not afford to resist its giant neighbor to the north. "The great Liechten-stein Army!" Heiner liked to joke. "Four generals and three privates."

The Silum community acted quickly, dispatching a team to England and Scotland to search for a suitable property. (In 1934, the community had welcomed its first English members, and there was growing interest among pacifist circles throughout Great Britain.) Soon they found Ashton Fields, a farm of several hundred acres near Cirencester, in the Cotswolds.

Heiner, meanwhile, graduated from school and returned to Silum. The deadline for leaving the country was two weeks away. In the interim, he and Annemarie agreed, there would be time for an expe-dited wedding on March 24, a Tuesday.

Hedwig Wächter, Annemarie's mother, was among the wedding guests. No one took it for granted. A cultured widow who had devoted her life to the cause of progressive education, Frau Wächter ran the Keilhau boarding school. A landmark institution, Keilhau had been founded a century before by a relative, Friedrich Fröbel – the inventor of the kindergarten – and the previous three directors had all been Wächters. Annemarie, it was hoped, would help carry on the torch. Then, disastrously (so her family saw it) the girl had lost her head and joined an obscure commune.

Frau Wächter had found the rupture exceedingly painful, for she had always been close to her daughter. During a last visit home, Annemarie had found relations so strained that she fled the house, secretly packing up her personal belongings and sneaking to the train station. More recently, her mother had begun to warm to her daugh-ter's fiancé. Right after the engagement, Heiner had written to ask her blessing, and though she hadn't really answered him, she had reconciled with Annemarie and accepted her decisions. Now she put up well with the unorthodox wedding, even if it was not exactly the sort of ceremony she would have planned for her youngest daugh-ter. But there was no time for further arguments. The need for haste trumped everything – not even Heiner's brothers managed to attend.

On a bright spring day high above the Rhine, the bridal procession wound its way through the meadows around Silum, and Georg Barth married the couple. Right after the ceremony they left for Zurich, from where they planned to travel on to the community's new farm in England, via France.

In Zurich they ran into trouble immediately: Heiner was denied a visa to France. The French consul, seeing that his passport was about to expire, refused to do anything unless it was extended. But Heiner did not dare enter the German consulate to ask for an extension. The officials there were sure to notice that he had not registered for military service, and it was easy to imagine what the consequences would be. People had been arrested at the consulate by the Gestapo and shipped across the border to concentration camps.

The two of them went to a café outside the consulate and reviewed their options. Should they try to cross the French border illegally? It wouldn't be hard to get into France, but since they would surely be caught in Calais or Dieppe when they tried to board the ferry to England, it still might not save them from deportation to Germany. They talked and argued for several hours. All of a sudden Annemarie stood up, grabbed Heiner's passport from the café table, and—as he watched with anxiety and pride—marched boldly into the consulate by herself. Ten minutes later she emerged, glowing and waving the passport.

"How did you extend it?" he demanded admiringly. "Simple," she said. She had walked straight to the consular official and laid the passport under his nose—a risk, since he could have confiscated it. Knowing this, she had come straight to the point: "We are newly married and on our honeymoon. Here's our marriage certificate to prove it. We wanted to visit friends in England. Would you please extend my husband's passport?" The official, noting that Heiner had failed to register, had begun to refuse, but then wavered. This no-nonsense young lady was such an *echt deutsche Grete*—such a genuine German sweetheart. "It's against all the rules," he had murmured as he flipped through the passport. "But for a honeymoon . . ." And then, with a gallant grin, he had banged down his stamp.

The Zurich–Paris train brought them to the French capital by nightfall. The following day they made the Channel crossing without incident, and found their way to Ashton Fields Farm. Alfred welcomed them. Like Heiner (and the community's other Germans of military age), he had also devised an escape route from the Continent, and was now here to help build up the new English settlement.

Ashton Fields Farm looked partly like a dilapidated medieval manor and partly like a pioneer's homestead. Coming from the road, Heiner and Annemarie had driven past endless hedged fields. Next, they passed through a complex of muddy yards—hen yard, duck yard, stockyard, and piggery—and mounds of straw and manure untidily interspersed with the rusting farm machinery. In the middle stood a cluster of rundown buildings, all of stone, their steep gray roofs tiled with slate. Now Alfred was showing them the cottage where they were to stay. Heiner noticed broken windows, unhinged doors, and a fireplace in every room. Annemarie noticed the overgrown gardens, bright with daffodils and yellow primroses.

Heiner loved the place instantly. Here he could put his Strickhof training to work. What did it matter that in the barn, he and Hans-Hermann had to stretch tarpaulins over the cows to protect them from crumbling masonry? For six weeks, he worked fourteen-hour days to prepare the fields for spring planting, using an antiquated tractor that took forever to start.

Finally, when May came, they took a week for a real honeymoon on the seacoast near Minehead. There were cliffs that dropped straight into the surf and isolated villages of white stone houses with thatched roofs. While out walking, they spoke for hours about Heiner's father and about Tata. Perhaps Annemarie relived for Heiner her arrival on the Sparhof the day of Tata's death, and perhaps Heiner reminded her about a dream he had had.

"It was a few weeks after Papa died. I saw a white tower as if from a great distance. Within it I found Papa and Tata, sitting side by side. She was showing him a book, and they were both absorbed in it. The pages were not covered with print but with living pictures. Although I tried to look at them I could see only a little. I could make out a southern landscape with palms; it seemed to me that the two of them were looking at the life of Jesus and how he walked on earth. Papa was marveling to see the true story of how God had guided the course of history. 'All these connections! All these wonderful connections!' he kept exclaiming."

Heiner looked at Annemarie and was overcome with love for her. Here they were, safe from the clutches of the Nazis, with a lifetime together before them. Here, they would let nothing divide them. In this beautiful new country, in May, the world seemed full of promise again.

19

Emmy Maria

England, July 1938

Heiner was on the train home coming back from Birmingham. It had been a hectic four weeks, and he had been busy from dawn to dusk at the new outreach center the community had got going. But now his mind was on the farm. Through the train window, he watched as steep-roofed stone barns sped by, the pastures around them spreading like patchwork. They bore a resemblance to Ashton Fields. He wondered what the farm crew had managed while he was away.

In just two years, they had transformed the property into a model of progressive agriculture. Two hundred people were living off what had been a family farm. Even the neighbors, generally wary of newcomers, admitted that the cash-strapped Germans had done an amazing job.

But the farm was not the reason for Heiner's homecoming. He fumbled in his shirt pocket and pulled out a letter. It was dated a week ago, July 17, in Annemarie's hand. "Dearest Heiner," she wrote. "How is your work going in Birmingham? How absolutely happy I shall be when you're home again. As for me, I'm doing well, though finding it harder to get around. The midwife came and examined me today—I believe she thinks it's going to be a small baby. But if so, it will be all the sweeter! I can feel the baby kicking energetically. That comforts me, since it reminds me of you."

For the past month, Heiner had been waking each morning nervous that he'd miss the birth, although the baby was due only in August. He had even requested the installation of a telephone in the center—no easy task, since the caretakers were pacifists sold on simple living. Now there was a phone, and no call had come. He decided to take a sabbatical and wait for the baby at home.

Heiner got off the train at Kemble, a village five miles from Ashton Fields, where a horse-drawn trap was waiting for him. As he pulled onto the grounds he scanned the farm with excitement. No less than three new buildings were going up.

It was hard to grasp how much had happened here in two years. As of the past spring, Silum was no more. The last members had fled Liechtenstein the same day that German troops marched into Austria, just over the mountain.

Already the previous spring, in April 1937, the Sparhof had been shut down. Dozens of Gestapo and SS men had swooped down on the community, forbidden everyone to leave, and secured all the buildings. Then a Gestapo commander had read out an official order: the Sparhof was hereby dissolved on account of its hostility to the National Socialist state. All of the community's assets were confiscated—land, buildings, documents, and personal valuables.

As for the fate of the inhabitants themselves, they were saved by a hairsbreadth. Two North American guests—Hutterite ministers whom Eberhard had befriended in 1930—had traveled to Europe to return the visit and chanced to be at the Sparhof on the day of the raid, and their presence unnerved the Gestapo intruders. Instead of arresting—or shooting—their prisoners, the raiders ordered them to vacate the country within forty-eight hours. (Two days later, armed guards escorted the refugees to the border.) Three of the Sparhof's directors had been arrested and imprisoned, though ten weeks later, under circumstances that seemed miraculous, they were released.

Not long afterward, Hans's leadership had collapsed after he made an underhanded attempt to stop the community from naming Georg and Hardy to the pastoral team. (Up till then he had been calling the shots without consulting anyone.) When confronted, he had tried to banter his way out of trouble, and had been caught lying. The more he had dodged and argued and explained, the more glaring his dishonesty and highhandedness had become. Finally, to the relief of most, the community had decided to relieve him of his responsibilities.

The two Hutterite ministers, when informed by letter of Hans's removal, firmly endorsed the decision: "He has been an unwise and unworthy leader, and should not be reaccepted into the community without serious repentance," the two experienced pastors wrote. They added that in their judgment, "because he has misused his office so very much," Hans should not serve in the community's leadership in the future either.

Now Ashton Fields was blossoming. Crowds of mostly young guests swarmed the farm. With the clouds of a new conflict looming over Europe, veterans of the Great War were calling for peace with an unprecedented urgency, and tens of thousands were joining a vibrant peace movement. The more radical among them, dissatisfied with mere activism, were looking for a whole new mode of living, and new cooperatives and communes were springing up all over England.

Apart from those who were seriously interested in community living, busloads of tourists arrived on the weekends at Ashton Fields. Students and members of the Workers' Education Association, the Peace Pledge Union, and the Fellowship of Reconciliation poured in, sometimes hundreds at a time. So did communists, socialists, agnostics, atheists, and others who were fed up with the empty promises of "churchianity." Hearing their heated discussions reminded Heiner of his boyhood in the villa at Sannerz.

Now it was his turn to serve these people just as his father had done. Just a few weeks previously, the community had asked him to serve as one of its pastors, together with Hardy, Georg, and others. In the discussion leading up to this decision, Sophie had recalled his gift since childhood in caring for people, stating simply, "I always thought this is what he was meant for." Heiner's mother Emmy had been far less enthusiastic. Knowing all too well the burdens that leadership brings, she had begged the community to find someone older – after all, Heiner was only twenty-five. In the end, though, she had acceded to the unanimous sense of the other members, and Heiner had been appointed.

Heiner had never sought this responsibility, and it weighed on him. He wrote to Hardy, "It often horrifies me when I see myself as I am and what the church has laid upon me, the service of the Word of God. Sometimes I can hardly grasp the grace that I am allowed to serve Jesus so. He is my comfort and my hope, and he gives the strength. This faith is our support. It is pure grace."

Emmy was blissful to have her family united again at last. She was also happy to see Heiner back home from Birmingham in time for the new baby. Now that they were all together, there was nothing to do but wait.

The baby refused to hurry. July dragged by and August began. In the hot evenings they sat up late speculating. Where should it happen? At home, Annemarie decided. Boy or girl? "Before I wasn't sure," Annemarie said, "but now I have the feeling it's a girl." At the end of July, Frau Wächter joined them from Germany. She planned to nurse Annemarie after the birth.

On the night of August 14, Annemarie told Heiner that she had seen two shooting stars sail majestically across the sky, "like a child's soul with its guardian angel," she said as they went to bed. Hours before dawn she woke him. "My contractions have started. Not often yet, but regular as a clock." Heiner pulled on his trousers and ran to wake his mother and Moni.

When day came, the public nurse was summoned, as required by British law. The moment she arrived, she took command. Her first edict was No Fathers Allowed, and she lost no time in banishing this one from the house. Heiner was crestfallen – this was not how he had imagined the birth of his first child – and crept outside, where he seated himself on a bench below Annemarie's second-story window. Frau Wächter was sitting there, and side by side they listened as the labor pains grew ever more intense. Frau Wächter was wringing her hands. Struck to the heart with something like guilt, Heiner made a silent vow to love Annemarie much more tenderly for the rest of his life. He knew with sudden clarity that she would be a wonderful mother.

The morning wore on. Finally Heiner could bear it no longer, sprang up from the bench, and dashed upstairs. The nurse tolerated him for a few minutes before ordering him out again, but he soon reappeared. Their quiet duel lasted all day and into that evening. When it became clear that the labor wasn't going well, Dr. Winter was summoned from Cirencester; he told Heiner they would have to use forceps. Then, at 9:40 p.m., Annemarie's agony was over.

Heiner was at her side when the baby came. It was a girl, and they named her Emmy Maria. Heiner stood openmouthed and unbelieving and joyful all at once. He was a father!

The baby was tiny, barely five pounds. But from the start she was immensely curious about the world. Her large, dark eyes were constantly moving, and Annemarie was laughing because the baby kept sticking out her tongue and then drawing it in again.

Annemarie's mother was to sleep next to the baby and take care of Annemarie, so Heiner roomed alone the next two weeks. He was very glad to move back in when his mother-in-law went, and to be able to talk alone, just with Annemarie. His favorite times were the evenings, when they sat together with the baby. If Annemarie drifted off, he stayed awake to make sure Emmy Maria wasn't too hot or too cold. Every day brought new joys. One Sunday afternoon they picked bunches of forget-me-nots, and Annemarie twisted the pale blue blossoms into a crown. "Your first garland!" she told the baby proudly.

Heiner's sabbatical lasted five weeks. In mid-September, the community asked him to return to Birmingham to establish contacts among like-minded seekers and to raise funds for the development of the settlement in England.

Heiner loved his work and was absorbed by it. And the people he met loved him in return: his unselfconscious manner, his heavily accented, broken English, and most of all, his genuine interest in whatever they had to say. He was busy with an endless round of public addresses, church socials, and garden parties. He relished meeting each new circle: Quakers, social workers, vegetarians, Tolstoyans, disciples of Gandhi, and members of the Peace Pledge Union. This last organization boasted a membership of hundreds of thousands, each of whom had signed a promise to renounce war.

But at times the enlightened middle-class idealism became too much, and Heiner yearned to meet more ordinary people. Then he would retreat to the working-class pub around the corner from his room. Most of the regulars were socialists, and when they saw he had no money to spend, they chipped in to get him a pint.

Other nights took Heiner to a place that reminded him of his childhood, when his father had brought him along to evangelism meetings at the Salvation Army. The Citadel, as Birmingham's Salvation Army hall was called, was famous for its brass band. Heiner made many friends there, from the officers who ran it to the homeless people, ex-cons, and alcoholics who congregated there. He reveled in their singing, and soon knew the words to their socialist-tinged hymns. At the climax of the service, as the trombones bellowed and the tubas went oompah, he joined in lustily. "I am not under law but under grace!" "Salvation for all!"

Every two weeks—or every week, if he could—Heiner went down to Ashton Fields to see Annemarie and Emmy Maria. Emmy claimed that father and daughter shared a resemblance. "With her snub nose she looks just like you did as a baby." Annemarie shared their joy, but often glanced at Emmy Maria with a secret anxiety as well. If only she would get stronger! For his part too, Heiner had been worried ever since he had seen Moni's expression as she examined the baby two days after the birth. She had consulted the doctor, who was reassuring, though he mentioned corrective surgery later on. For the first six weeks, the baby seemed to be gaining well.

But in early October, Emmy Maria came down with a fever and stopped nursing, and Annemarie begged Heiner to come home right away. Heiner was perplexed at seeing his daughter; to him, she seemed livelier than ever, even doing little push-ups in her crib. But there was no doubt that she was also losing weight.

When she cried, Heiner would take her next to him in bed to quieten her. Mostly it worked. "Look how she responds to any sign of love!" he exclaimed. "She must have such a tender soul." Often he sat by her crib looking into her face and talking to her.

When Heiner was not in the house, Annemarie sang to her, or wound up the music box he had bought in Birmingham. Often the baby stopped crying with the first chiming note.

In November, Emmy Maria developed bronchitis and a serious internal infection. She vomited up her milk and no longer laughed or gurgled. Moni called Dr. Winter from Cirencester. After examining the baby, the doctor looked grave. "Get her to the hospital so we can watch her."

Heiner slumped in the uncomfortable hospital chair, unable to believe the matron's words. "Your baby probably won't last until tomorrow. As you know, there's nothing more we can do." And then, quite matter-of-factly: "The baby's mother needn't come to visit it anymore. We shall inform you when everything is over."

He tried to control his panic. "She's only the matron; the doctor will know better," he reassured himself. Aloud, he asked to see his daughter.

"It might distress you, Mr. Arnold. But . . . all right then. Follow me."

The first thing he saw on approaching her crib was the gleaming saline apparatus that stood at her head. Emmy Maria was crying hard, but when she recognized her father she grew quiet, fixed her eyes on his, and held his gaze. Heiner noticed that her skin seemed translucent—like white wax—and that a latticework of tiny blue veins could be seen through it. She was so thin! Suddenly it struck him: she might really die. Wiping away a tear, he went to call Annemarie from the waiting room where she was resting. As he walked away, Emmy Maria's bright eyes followed him, huge and beseeching. She looked so forlorn, he thought—a tiny body lost in a white expanse of sheets.

In the afternoon, Dr. Winter confirmed their worst fears: the infection had spread, and there was nothing more to be done. Heiner told him that in that case they would take Emmy Maria home. The doctor asked for one more day. But the following day, he released the baby, and Heiner called a taxi. Two nurses bundled the baby and helped them to the car, then laid Emmy Maria in Annemarie's lap. "But she's still so warm and alive!" Annemarie exclaimed. The nurses looked uncomfortable. One whispered to Heiner, "You'll be lucky if she survives the ride home."

When they arrived at Ashton Fields, Moni carried the baby up to Heiner and Annemarie's room. Emmy and the rest of the family followed, and so did others. Soon the little room was packed with people. They lit candles and sang Christmas carols, and Heiner said a prayer. They sang late into the evening, until one by one, people said good night and went to bed. Heiner and Annemarie stayed awake with the baby.

For the next four days, the three of them never separated. Now and then, Heiner or Annemarie would doze while the other watched Emmy Maria. Emmy and Moni dropped in regularly, and Hardy and Hans-Hermann sat up with them during the night. Others in the community came by with food, bouquets of wildflowers, or offers to help with the housework. Schoolchildren brought pictures they had drawn. Marianne Zimmerman, a close friend from Silum days, stood in the corridor all night, just in case she might be needed. An atmosphere of compassion and caring surrounded the baby—and not only that: it seemed to emanate from her and unite the whole community.

As time passed Emmy Maria grew so weak that she sometimes did not react at all when her parents caressed her, but only lay there, her eyes half-open, her breathing shallow. Then she would suddenly rally, crying and – when Annemarie fed her from a dropper – smacking her lips with pleasure.

Sometimes she smiled as she slept. Dr. Winter, who came on a house call (now only as a friend), was amazed by her endurance, remarking, "She must have a powerful will to live."

She grew worse. Her face had grown terribly thin, and the only sign of life was in her eyes. "The weaker her body gets, the more it expresses her soul," Annemarie thought. Emmy Maria could not cough up the mucus that collected in her windpipe, and each breath was labored and rattling. Moni tried to stimulate breathing with mentholated steam, but even the most concentrated doses did not help.

In the evening she lost consciousness, and for the next eighteen hours only her lungs fought on. Heiner sat by her throughout it all, moistening her lips with water. Her hands grew cold to Heiner's touch. Annemarie picked her up and held her in her arms for a long time.

On November 21 – it was eight in the evening – Emmy Maria suddenly woke from her coma and opened her eyes wide. Afterward everyone who saw it said how extraordinary it was: how she gazed without wavering first at her mother, who was holding her, and then at her father, and then at her mother again, back and forth. Her eyes, bright and unclouded, had no suffering or sorrow in them. They shone with an unearthly radiance – as if bearing a message of joy from another world, her mother thought. Then she raised her arms high and lifted her head, and the light in her eyes went out. Her breathing stopped a minute or two later, and Emmy reached over to close her eyelids.

Heiner carried the elmwood coffin (Fritz had made it) at the head of the burial procession, with Annemarie at his side. His grief came in immense, overpowering waves. Inside this box was their firstborn child. She had loved life so much, and they had prayed so hard for her, begging God to save her, and refusing to believe that he would take her. And yet he had.

After the funeral, they went for a week to a cottage on the sea—a haven of solitude and silence between horizons of water and heather. Though exhausted, Annemarie simply could not sleep. Heiner sought to comfort her, but his anguish tormented him. Why hadn't God answered their prayers and saved their baby?

And yet, in their pain, the two grew closer together than ever before. It was as if the light in their daughter's last gaze had welded them together. The vastness of the ocean reminded them of eternity— and wasn't it eternity that they had glimpsed through her eyes?

As they walked or sat or talked—or wept—they began to see her last moments as a call to renewed faith. In his diary, Heiner wrote, "When you were taken from us, my Emmy, I made a vow, which you should tell Jesus for me. I will never serve darkness, never serve death. And then your shining eyes, filled with light from beyond, gazed into ours. What did you say to us? For you were no more a child of earth, but already a child of heaven."

20

Heliopher

In December, when Heiner and Annemarie had been home from the sea for three weeks, he fell sick with a kidney infection. It was the third recurrence of the disease in the past three years. On Christmas Day, the familiar fever and back pain forced Heiner to bed for several days. Facing the ceiling with nothing but his grief to occupy him, he spent hours thinking. Losing Emmy Maria hurt more than he could believe. And beyond his own pain, he knew, was that of the millions suffering under Hitler's regime. He wrote to Hans-Hermann: "The question of the refugees and the persecution of the Jews is just terrible — one has to think of them constantly. . . . May we never become insensible or without pity toward their cruel fate. And we know that we come across only a tiny part of what is happening to these people. There is so little we can do. What will become of it all?"

Often he felt tense and surrounded by temptations. If only it were possible to have even one word with his father; to be able, just once more, to knock on the door of his study. "Come in!" his father would shout, glancing up from his desk, and Heiner would sit down in the smoky blueness, and tell him everything, and his father would say . . . What would he say? Heiner would never know.

The closest he could get to his father's study now was by reading. He turned to a volume he knew his father had set great value on, the biography of a certain Johann Christoph Blumhardt. Heiner had heard his father speak of Blumhardt all through his childhood – and years later he would hear others speak of his influence on Karl Barth and Dietrich Bonhoeffer. But he had never read much about him.

As told by his biographer Friedrich Zündel, the story of Blumhardt begins drowsily, detailing the early years of an unknown, straitlaced young Lutheran pastor who lives happily with his wife, a missionary's daughter, in a village in southern Germany. In 1842, this country parson's life takes a startling turn. Ever since arriving in the village of Möttlingen four years before, Blumhardt has sensed that there is something odd and unhealthy about Gottliebin Dittus, a parishioner. Lately, however, unsettling tales are making the rounds concerning the young woman. Uncanny things are happening at her house, it is whispered: strange noises and lights, apparitions, and other manifestations of the supernatural. At first Blumhardt tries to ignore the rumors. He is a down-to-earth man who detests sensationalism, and his main worry is about declining church attendance. He refuses to investigate or even visit Gottliebin. "These things are best left to a doctor," he maintains.

But not long afterward, it is the local doctor who is reproaching Blumhardt for his excessive caution. "From the way that girl is left to suffer," he tells him, "you would think that this is a village without a pastor." The affair is becoming a public scandal; curiosity seekers start booking rooms in the inn across from Gottliebin's house. Finally Blumhardt begins visiting the young woman – and comes to believe that it is a case of demon-possession. Blumhardt has no idea how to help. One day, as Gottliebin lies senseless after one of her frequent inexplicable fits, he impulsively exclaims, "Lord Jesus, help me. We have seen enough what the devil can do. Now let us see what God can do!" With these words, he begins a campaign of prayer that, within the next two years, involves the entire parish and sends reverberations even further afield.

The battle drags on for months, with blasphemous outbursts, grotesque seizures, violent rampages, and suicide attempts. Finally, in

December 1843, it climaxes. The turning point comes when the young woman cries out in a strange voice, "Jesus is victor!"–and is cured.

Within days, a change comes over Möttlingen: village drunks sober up (and stay sober), swindlers pay back their victims, unhappy marriages are transformed. Adulterers even beg their cheated spouses for forgiveness, and a murder case is solved. From miles around come reports of cripples, epileptics, and mentally ill people being healed. Blumhardt, who is credited with all this, is as awestruck as the next man but rejects any connection to himself and sternly discourages sensationalism. The remarkable events are widely publicized nonetheless and are soon being known as the Möttlingen Awakening.

At this point in the story, Heiner was only halfway through the biography. But it was beginning to work on him like few books he had read. He felt a little as if he were reading about his father. He was stirred, not just by the story itself, but by an inkling of the great historical sweep that connected it with his own. So much of what had happened in Möttlingen had happened in Sannerz too. And who was to say it couldn't happen again?

For the third time in his life, he felt overwhelmed by a power that he could not explain, but which was real–deeper and truer and more engulfing than anything set off by nerves or emotions. It was as if dawn was breaking over his soul. And in its light he could see and feel the compassion of the man of Golgotha–and his fathomless heartbreak and loneliness too. Heiner wept.

In the weeks that followed, Heiner was gripped by another story connected to his father, a story by the Russian author Maxim Gorky that he remembered from his childhood in Sannerz. That month, Hardy had published a folktale-style retelling of Gorky's story in the December 1938 issue of the community's periodical, *The Plough*. The story had long fascinated Heiner, in the same way the tales of Rachoff and the sadhu had, but now it struck him like some kind of prophecy.

Once upon a time–so the legend ran–there lived a people who were lost in a vast, dark forest. The trees stood so close that the light of the sun could not penetrate their entwined branches, and wild animals used to prey on the inhabitants—especially those who strayed too far from the protection of others, or from their homes. All of them lived in constant fear of death, and over time the ever-present darkness began to settle in their hearts and strangle them from within. Soon they could no longer love but began to hate and murder each other instead. Yet they were forced to remain together, as it was impossible for any one of them to survive on his own. Years passed, and they lost all hope of ever finding their way out of the forest. Now and then a last weak gleam would brighten the eyes of the eldest as they remembered their happy, sun-filled youth. But younger generations mocked these memories as tall tales. They could not believe in a light they had never seen.

Among this people, however, was a young man called Heliopher who grieved over the misery of his people and pondered how they could be saved from it. One day he set out on his own to seek the sun. He wandered through the trackless forest, torn by brambles, attacked by beasts, and fighting despair. Often he thought he could no longer go on, and feared he would fall exhausted—and forever forgotten.

One day he caught sight of an unfamiliar glimmer. Breaking into a run, he raced toward it. It grew brighter and brighter. Suddenly he burst out from the trees into a magical land full of color, and lifting his eyes he saw the sun for the first time. He fell unconscious, overcome. When he woke, he found himself in a green meadow, being watched over by people unlike any he had ever seen. They were strong, but gentle, and not only lived together, but truly loved one another. Among them, his heart filled with lightness and joy.

Yet Heliopher's happiness was not complete: he was tormented every time he thought of his own people in the dark forest. Finally he went back to find them. "Come, brothers and sisters," he told them, "I will lead you to the light." At first the people murmured and frowned, and the young laughed, incredulous. Yet as he told them more, their curiosity grew, and a strong desire to see the sun awoke in them. At last they agreed to follow him.

The way through the forest was long and difficult and demanded selflessness and perseverance. People began to murmur, and some of them muttered, "He has misled us; let us kill him."

Heliopher knew their thoughts and reminded them of what lay ahead: the land of the sun, which was full of light and love. But they answered, "You liar! There is no light, there is no sun. Let us return to our homes. We will be murkier than the forest, and crueler than the wildest beast. Let us at least be masters of the forest!" Heliopher begged them to continue, but they would not listen to him, flinging their arms about, raging in despair and shouting, "There is no light! There is no sun!"

Then, as they moved in to attack him, Heliopher cried out, "Follow me!" and tore open his chest with his nails. He grasped his heart, which burned with love so brightly that it lit the gloom, and held it high over his head in both hands. Then, striding forward, he led the amazed people out of the forest.

As they entered the country of the sun, the people danced in its rays and loved one another. But Heliopher, as he came to the edge of the forest, stumbled and sprawled on the ground, broken. Even in death, he still clutched his radiant, pulsing heart.

Images from the story kept appearing to Heiner. When lying awake at night he pondered what it meant. Here was a parable of Jesus' way of sacrifice. What would it mean for his own life?

21

Primavera

Ashton Fields Farm, October 1940

Heiner heard the bomber coming. By now, after three months of air raids, everyone could recognize that distinctive ominous drone. Recently the bombers had been coming every two or three nights. Usually they would veer east toward London, where, by the end of the year, they would kill 23,000 civilians. But sometimes they headed north, to the factories of the English Midlands. And though Ashton Fields was far enough from the nighttime glow they left on the horizon, it was far from a safe haven. Right in the vicinity were no less than five Royal Air Force bases.

Then it came, right over the roof: a long hiss that ended in a nearby field with a blinding flash. An incendiary bomb. Thankfully it did no harm. Still, it took Heiner's breath. In the neighboring village, a bomb just like this had recently killed a man.

The air raids frightened the children, but Heiner and the other adults had a worse fear: invasion. In the previous months, German troops had overrun one country after another: France, Luxembourg, Belgium, Denmark, Norway, and the Netherlands. Britain seemed to be next on the list. As Heiner lay awake that night listening to passing bombers and far-off explosions, a scenario kept playing across his mind. The *Reichswehr* advancing across the Channel into Wiltshire and Ashton Fields. Annemarie and he, with all the other Germans in the community, captured and shipped to a concentration camp, or shot as traitors. Roswith—one-year-old Roswith, whose birth had brought so much happiness back into their lives—an orphan . . .

It was hardly a groundless fantasy. After the war, documents obtained by the Allies would show Hitler's plans for occupying Britain. They showed that the SS had prepared six commando teams to comb Britain immediately after the planned invasion and round up all opponents to Nazism, including German émigrés.

Such nightmares vanished by day, if only because there was so much work to do. Guests continued to flock to the farm, and every month, dozens announced their intention to stay. The community had also taken in twenty Jewish refugees from Austria, including three children evacuated by the *Kindertransport* rescue mission, and was searching for patrons who would sponsor more. Thirty members of Hashomer Hatsa'ir, a Zionist youth group, had come for one year of agricultural training before traveling on to Palestine to found a kibbutz. Housing had to be built for all these new residents, and rations stretched. Heiner was constantly busy training new field hands. It seemed that every new addition to the community had come straight from the city, or from the university.

Not everyone who visited took to the rugged life. Guests who had no skill at farming or building were usually assigned to work in the vegetable kitchen, a cold little room where a never-ending supply of parsnips, turnips, and carrots had to be washed. Once Hardy asked a guest who was about to return home if she could share what she thought about her visit. She answered, "Yes, in one word: *Carrots!*"

Bigger challenges occupied the community, too. Since spring, the threat of internment had hung over them. As enemy nationals, there was always the chance that they would be rounded up and sent off to a detainment camp. Most Germans in England had already been interned months ago, and Heiner and Annemarie and their fellow German members had been spared only because of a passport stamp that certified them as "Refugees from Nazi Oppression." But still they were subject to a 9:30 p.m. curfew, and they knew such exemptions could be withdrawn and were liable to vanish any day.

At any event, they were being watched, as Freda Bridgwater, a young Englishwoman, had found out the previous May. Eight days after marrying a German Bruderhof member, she had been arrested and interned on the Isle of Man as an enemy alien.

Then, as the bombing raids increased in frequency throughout the summer and suspicion and fear of foreigners grew, several neighbors had turned hostile. Local newspapers regularly printed letters attacking "the German Peace Community." Fantastic rumors spread quickly. "The Germans at Ashton Fields are spying on the airbases," it was said. "They're buying fields for paratroopers to land on! They're planning to help the invaders!"

The rumors spread as far as Westminster. The House of Lords discussed billeting a guard at Ashton Fields, and in the House of Commons a certain Captain Alan Graham took the floor, demanding to know why the "German Peace Community" had not yet been interned. His questions were prompted by several local rumors, including one inspired by a treehouse the Ashton Fields schoolchildren had built; "they are building observation towers," the story went.

To Captain Graham's bewilderment, someone rose to the defense. It was Lady Astor, the American-born viscountess who had made history a decade before by becoming the first female Member of Parliament. "Is it not true," she said, "that this is a community set up after the last war whose sole concern is Christianity, and that the members of it are a great asset to the country instead of a liability?" Captain Graham was not in a position to press his point, and there the subject was left. (Unbeknownst to her fellow MPs, Lady Astor had sympathized with the Bruderhof ever since hearing about their expulsion from Nazi Germany. But until now, she had championed their cause only in private.)

Ashton Fields had a harder time finding advocates in its immediate neighborhood. Drunken soldiers of the Home Guard arrived one night, searching farm sheds and dwellings—and ordering a fruit tree to put its hands up or be shot. Regional newspapers printed calls for a boycott of the community's milk and eggs, after which most of the customers vanished. Once two ruffians were overheard in the local pub planning to set fire to the farm buildings (their plans were thwarted). "Isn't it time to leave Britain?" Heiner and others wondered.

In June, the community wrote to the House of Lords requesting permission to emigrate to Canada, and over the next months they also looked into the possibility of finding refuge in other countries, including Jamaica, New Zealand, Australia, and South Africa. In August they sent two representatives to New York to see if the United States might accept them. Eleanor Roosevelt put in a word for the group, but it went nowhere, and meanwhile one prospective country after another turned the would-be immigrants down. At the height of this war, no one wanted to touch a pacifist group of mixed nationalities.

Finally, in the fall, they found a nation that was willing to adopt them. It was Paraguay, a country so obscure that many found themselves looking up exactly where in South America it was located. And Paraguay was more than just willing to take them. It also promised three unheard-of privileges: freedom of religion, freedom of education, and exemption from military service.

The British Home Office issued the required exit permits. Coming at a time when the country was besieged and desperately fighting off an air force ten times the size of its own, it was a remarkable act of generosity. Over the next year, the government would allow 350 people from Ashton Fields to leave the country, among them three doctors and a high proportion of able-bodied young men.

On the night of November 10, German aircraft razed Coventry, sixty miles to the north. Flashes from the explosions were visible throughout the night. Three days later, while Coventry continued to burn, Annemarie went into labor. The baby was a boy, and they named him Johann Christoph in honor of Blumhardt. He would be called Christoph. Throughout the first days of the baby's life, the bombs kept falling. They hit so close that the walls of the clinic trembled.

Ashton Fields was in a flurry when Annemarie brought Christoph home. Huge packing crates were being filled with everything from bedding and kitchen utensils to books, printing equipment, and farm machinery. In one cramped office, a team of typists was working feverishly to complete a dwindling pile of paperwork. The first group of travelers were to set sail for South America in ten days, and among those leaving for the docks were Emmy, Hardy and Edith; Hans-Hermann and his wife, Gertrud; and Alfred and Fritz and their families – eighty in all.

The refugees had little money, no knowledge of the country that was to be their new home, and no living arrangements in place for when they arrived. And to get there, they faced a transatlantic crossing filled with dangers. The Blue Star Line, which was to take them, had been specifically targeted by the German navy, and British losses to U-boat torpedoes were on the rise. But if the moment of farewell was solemn, it was not tearful. As Emmy put it, "We have always lived by faith. Why shouldn't we believe that God will guide us now?"

Other groups set sail for South America in the weeks that followed, so that by February, only sixty-odd people were left. In the community, everything was topsy-turvy. It was Heiner's job to sort it all out; he had been left responsible for the orderly closing of the location in England. And yet it was hardly possible to close it down. New people were still arriving daily and several begged to join, although the place looked a wreck after the mass departures. The school, the communal kitchen, and the business office were barely functioning for lack of staff.

Neither was the farm, which was becoming a headache for Heiner. Though Ashton Fields had already been sold to finance the move to South America, the contract was clear: the farm work must not fall behind during the course of the sale, and if it did, there would be a stiff penalty. But the fields had not been plowed, much less seeded. Heiner could not work the farm himself, as he was constantly in London for meetings with the Home Office, the Blue Star Line, and the contract lawyers. But who else could do it? He had no illusions about the abilities of the newcomers.

Take Gwynn Evans, the new wagon driver. From the way he stood uneasily in the wagon, holding the reins with arms outstretched as if in supplication, it was plain he was no farmer and no horseman. His horse ambled as slowly as it could without actually stopping, while Gwynn called out gentle reproofs in a cultivated accent—he was a Cambridge-educated minister of religion. Guy Johnson, a lawyer, was learning to repair shoes; Charles Headland, the pig man, was a chartered accountant; and Ruth Cassell and Margaret Stern, the two young women paddling vats of clothes in the laundry, had just graduated from medical school.

In later years, many of these people would remember their time at Ashton Fields as the best chapter of their lives. Their enthusiasm was never so glowing, their vision never so clear, their courage never so fresh as then. They were leaving the gray compromises of the old world to help bring a new one into being. "We are off to build up Zion," they liked to repeat. That this meant leaving family and friends for the South American jungle only heightened the sense of adventure.

Humor helped to defuse the tensions that inevitably arose in tight quarters. One morning Heiner was drinking coffee in his office—and noticed water coming through a crack between the boards in the ceiling. A guest was scrubbing the floor above. Heiner shouted up, "Your water is about to drip into my coffee."

"You shut up!" the guest shouted back defensively. "Be glad you've got coffee for the water to go in." Heiner teased the guest about the story for days. The guest stayed on.

Heiner knew that enthusiasm alone would not plow the fields or plant fifty acres of seed potatoes, as the buyer's contract required, so he was thrilled to discover that one of the new arrivals was an experienced farmer. Johnny Robinson had appeared in mid-February on a shiny new motorcycle, with his wife clutching his shoulders. Both were socialists and firm agnostics. So were many of the other guests, but something about Johnny made him stick out. For one thing, he made it clear that he had no intention of being converted. Yet he also claimed to be convinced that the Bruderhof was where he wanted to spend the rest of his life. A man of fiery temperament, Johnny meant business, and soon added all his cash and property to the community's common purse.

A week or so after Johnny's coming, Heiner approached him and told him everything that needed doing on the farm. Johnny raised his eyebrows, but nevertheless agreed to take on the job, especially when Heiner promised him paid labor.

The paid labor never appeared – every penny was needed to pay for the next passage to South America. Johnny would simply have to get on with the job himself, together with one of the white-collar newcomers. By some miracle, they got fields ready for planting.

Now the next obstacle emerged: there was no money to buy seed. When Heiner and his right-hand man, Stanley Fletcher, came to Johnny to discuss this problem, Johnny looked perplexed. "Well, I've given you all my money," he offered. Which was true – Johnny had even turned in his collection of phonograph records. But Heiner was grinning and looking at Stanley.

Stanley slapped his forehead with mock spontaneity, as if he had just had a wonderful idea. "You know, Heiner," he exclaimed, "Johnny has a lovely motorbike."

There was a short silence as Johnny struggled to master himself. Then he pulled himself together: "If you must, you must." The next day he sold the bike and bought seed with the proceeds. By the end of April, as the last large group left for Paraguay, the fields were shimmering with new green.

Amidst the tumult of closing down Ashton Fields, Heiner depended heavily on his brother-in-law Hans, and their relationship warmed. Over the past three years, Hans seemed to have changed. Admitting that he had acted wrongly ever since Eberhard's death, he had expressed remorse to Emmy and to the whole community, clearing up individual incidents of past arrogance. Seeing his earnestness and new humility, the community had solemnly reconciled with him, assuring him that the past was now forgiven and forgotten. At Emmy's and Heiner's urging, he had been appointed financial manager, a role in which he was charged to work closely with Hardy, Georg, Heiner, and the rest of the leadership team.

The *Avila Star*, which was painted in wartime camouflage, gave a grim first impression, and as Heiner helped his family up the steep gangway stairs he blanched momentarily. For all his fears of bombs and an invasion, England was safety compared to sailing to South America at the height of the Battle of the Atlantic. Just in the last days there had been another report in the paper about the spread of Germany's submarine "wolf packs" and the use of its new magnetic mines. He looked down at five-month-old Christoph, fast asleep in a large wicker basket, oblivious to the very notion of fear.

For the four weeks of the voyage, the *Avila Star* followed an erratic course, zigzagging across the Atlantic to throw off the enemy. After living on wartime rations—and in poverty for all of his life so far—Heiner found the mealtimes unbelievably lavish. The leisurely pace was unfamiliar too. To while away the time, there were lessons in Spanish and deck tennis, chess matches were held, and a small choral group was organized.

In the evenings, Heiner would gather the group of would-be pioneers on the deck under the stars to keep their courage up. Often he read aloud from the biography of Blumhardt that had come to mean so much to him. Or he would tell them about the fellow members they were about to meet in Paraguay—many in the group were young Britons who had only joined the community after the first group had departed Ashton Fields the previous November. To much laughter, he would affectionately tell of each one—Edith, Hardy, Moni, Georg, Alfred, Sophie, his mother Emmy. To those who had just joined the group, such as Peter Cavanna, a twenty-one-year-old who had been training as a solicitor, Heiner's anecdotes gave crucial reassurance—he could hardly wait to meet these unknown brothers and sisters.

Still, nothing could erase the constant specter of an attack. The crew practiced firing the ship's guns for an hour each day and led repeated lifeboat drills in case the ship was torpedoed. Passengers were instructed to stay dressed even in bed. At night, the blackout orders were so strict that it was forbidden even to smoke on deck for fear of being seen by the U-boats. "My heart sank," Captain Fisher confided in the cigar lounge one evening, "when at the start of the voyage I saw all your children coming on board. I thought of the danger, and wondered if I could bear such a heavy responsibility." (As it happened, all four of the Blue Star vessels that carried Bruderhof travelers, including Captain Fisher's, got them safely to South America but were later torpedoed and sunk.)

It was mid-May when Heiner first spotted land: the coast of Brazil. He was standing on the deck with Annemarie waiting for dawn to break. At first sight the new continent looked lush with promise. All that morning they stood leaning over the rail. As they entered the harbor for a temporary stop at Rio de Janeiro, spotted porpoises swam alongside the ship, and huge, gaudy butterflies fluttered around the rigging. Planes flew out toward them across the bay like noisy toys. At the foot of the mountains along the beach spread the city itself, an expanse of white houses and domes. Here and there a skyscraper jabbed the horizon.

Rio was even more magical by night. After a year and a half of strict blackout in England—and on the ship—the galaxy of lights struck the travelers as a promise. Here there were no bombers or submarines to fear. The city was mirrored in the water of the bay, and high on Corcovado, beneath a full moon, gleamed its most famous landmark, the huge and radiant statue of Christ. "As beautiful as a fairy tale," Emy-Margret exclaimed.

"New land! New life! New everything!" That's how Johnny Robinson described the feeling of the pioneers, and Heiner felt the same. But he was deflated when at the ship's next port of call, Buenos Aires, restrictions prohibited anyone from going ashore. There was one consolation: mail from Hardy. As part of the first group, Hardy had been in South America since January, and his letter described how, after weeks of strenuous deliberations, they had settled on a suitable property and purchased it. Conditions were primitive – it was a remote location surrounded by swamps and jungle – but everyone was in good spirits and determined to make a go of it. Unfortunately there was also painful news to report. Dysentery had broken out, and most of the children were sick. Two babies had already died.

Heiner put down the letter as fresh memories of Emmy Maria surged up in him. So the new venture had begun with a rash of deaths? He winced when he pictured the stricken parents and when he thought of Roswith and Christoph. Had they escaped the Nazis and risked an Atlantic crossing only to see their children die in the jungle?

In a daze, Heiner looked for Johnny. During the voyage, the two of them had become close friends, spending hours talking on the deck. Johnny would talk of farming, Tolstoy, the socialist cause; Heiner, in return, would tell him stories about his father. "How I wish I could have known him!" Johnny had exclaimed. Now Heiner pulled his friend aside and told him about the two babies.

"Well, Heiner, I'm very sorry to hear that," said Johnny. Silently, he felt that Heiner's grief was rather out of proportion. Were these people made of such soft stuff that they weren't prepared to take a few losses? Pioneering life had only just begun, and these deaths would hardly be the last. And so he added, rather too cheerfully, "We're going to have to expect a struggle of that nature in this foreign climate, you know. We'll take it on. Buck up, Heiner!"

Heiner stared at him, then abruptly turned and walked away.

For days afterward, Heiner avoided Johnny, while Johnny, who was hurt at being shunned after weeks of growing so close, was forced to contemplate the incident. Eventually he came to realize what lay behind Heiner's emotions, and the two found a renewed understanding for each other. "There is a mystery of love which is involved here," Johnny wrote later. "Most people who see a great deal of human suffering—especially socialists like me—tend to toughen themselves so they will not have to feel the pain of each individual. That way they can keep up their courage to work on the big problems. By contrast, Heiner does the opposite, for he cannot callous himself. His kind of love goes right to the heart of the individual grief; it is pure sacrifice."

◆ ◆ ◆

For three days the riverboat plied its way upstream toward Paraguay, and in it Heiner encountered his countrymen-to-be for the first time, in close quarters. In the third-class cabin he found himself pressed from all sides by onions, oranges, mosquitoes, and cigar-smoking passengers of both sexes who spat tobacco juice with a virtuosity that astonished and disturbed him. (None of the books he had been reading about Paraguay had mentioned this national pastime.) The air was stifling and motionless, and as the portholes were close to the water, they had to be closed whenever the vessel was in motion. The latrines were broken, though constantly in use. They emptied straight into the muddy water, just feet from the hatch where the proprietor of the canteen let down her produce to be washed.

Heiner watched the passing landscape eagerly. Rolling down to the banks of the mile-wide river stretched the grassy pampas of Argentina. He saw grazing cattle and the gauchos who tended them, cocky men with spurs and a springing step. Then, as the boat neared Paraguay, the vegetation on the banks changed to palms and tall bamboo and then to dense jungle.

In Asunción, the grimy, humid capital, they found Emmy and Hardy and Edith waiting to welcome them. After receiving customs clearance, they traveled another two days upstream by riverboat. During the voyage, Heiner tried to persuade his brother that Hans should be reappointed as a pastor in the community. "If he is really forgiven shouldn't he be shown full trust again? Can't we suggest this to the other members?" Hardy disagreed vehemently, pointing out that Hans was already fully forgiven and trusted, but that a leadership role was a separate question. Heiner let the matter drop.

They disembarked at Puerto Rosario. It was a port in name, but other than that there was little to distinguish it from the rest of the shore, unless you counted the uneven planks that someone had pegged into the high bank to make steps. The prospect of unloading several tons of luggage here seemed daunting, to say the least, especially in pouring rain. But they had reached their destination, and it needed to be done.

Now they were tying the first heavy crate with ropes and straining to move it. They heaved to the rhythm of the Paraguayan captain: *"Tumba! tumba! tumba! tumba!"* He stood over them with a smile, relishing the sight of Europeans toiling at a job usually left to natives.

The men *tumba*-ed and sweated for hours. A handful of Paraguayans came and helped them, letting off shrill hoots whenever a crate reached the top of the bank. Johnny began to hoot too, and soon the rest of the men were joining in. It kept their spirits up. Though soaked to the skin and caked with mud, they laughed as they worked. Hours later, the empty boat pulled away and headed upstream.

In the meantime a small train of wagons had stopped nearby and the drivers were getting out. Gaunt and barefoot, and speaking German (they were Mennonite refugees who had come to Paraguay a few years before), they shivered as rain dripped from their ragged clothes. Perhaps a little money could be earned by transporting these immigrants to their new homes.

Estancia Primavera—"Spring Estate"—consisted of a neglected cattle ranch surrounded by twenty thousand acres of swampy grassland and virgin forest. Stands of sweet orange trees grew in the jungle, perhaps planted by Jesuit missionaries long ago, but mostly the place was an untouched wilderness inhabited by howler monkeys, tapirs, pumas, ostriches, parrots—and boa constrictors. Now an entire village of Europeans with not much more than the clothes on their backs had arrived to tame it into a livable home.

By the time Heiner and Annemarie's party arrived in late May, Fritz and his building team had thrown up the first primitive shelters, nicknamed the "gallop huts" for the speed of their construction—long, narrow sheds with hewn tree trunks for uprights and thatched roofs made of mud and colorado grass. There were no walls.

Privacy was impossible. Each family simply set up house in a section partitioned off with improvised hangings, using the travelling trunks as furniture and laying down their bedding cheek by jowl wherever there was space. Evenings were marked by a regular choreography: first the women and children changed while the men and boys waited outside; then, after the candles were snuffed out, it was the men's turn to get ready for bed.

That was a mere inconvenience. Far worse were the diseases that had struck the first large group of settlers. They had not traveled straight to Primavera but had spent three months at a temporary encampment in the Gran Chaco, Paraguay's infamous "green hell." There, all the children had caught a disease which left their eyes so swollen with pus that sometimes their eyelids turned inside out, attracting flies. (For several weeks they had feared it was trachoma, which causes blindness. Luckily it turned out to be conjunctivitis instead.) And because bites from mosquitoes, ants, and tiny flies tended to become infected, many suffered from huge sores, especially on their legs. Even strong men hobbled in pain, and at one point Moni was bandaging around a hundred sores, and treating 150 pairs of eyes.

Also common were scorpions, parasitic worms and the *ura*, a maggot that tunneled beneath the skin.

The food consisted of yams, "goulash" (really a thin, gristle-flecked gravy), and manioca, a starchy tuber which was the local staple. Many lost weight, but no one starved.

Hygiene was a problem. Water had to be carted in drums on a wagon from a spring more than a mile away, and there was never enough for bathing. Luckily a stream bed not far away was found to fill up after every rain, so at least there was somewhere to go after a long day to wash off the sweat and the caked dirt and sand.

But despite the starkness of daily life, the lush new land was putting its spell on them—"a unique effect, somewhat like that of wine," in Edith's words. Nothing here was tepid: the day was sweltering, the night frosty. And the vigor and luxuriance of the tropical plant life made the place seem like paradise. It filled Heiner with awe, especially when he walked to work at daybreak. As a giant red sun bobbed up over the horizon, the low mist covering the grasslands shimmered like a sea, and birds, frogs, and insects filled the air with a deafening dawn chorus.

Heiner's heart sang with them as he thought of everything that had already been accomplished. Plowing with a team of oxen, the men had already turned over seventy-five acres of new ground. A team of members was erecting a sawmill, using an ancient but still functional steam engine they had bought in Asunción. Fritz was overseeing the construction of a fourth dormitory, and a three-room cabin that would serve as the midwife's delivery room was almost finished. So was a new bakery. In a year or two, Primavera would be a full-fledged church community. But it would be more than that. However isolated, it must be built up as a new beacon for the cause of brotherhood and love.

And then, two weeks after Heiner and Annemarie had arrived, their baby boy fell ill, first with German measles, and then with whooping cough and bronchitis to boot. Christoph's coughing bouts lasted for hours, so that he became blue-faced from suffocation. Annemarie was frantic, yet here in the jungle there was little anyone could do to treat him. For them, as for so many other families in Primavera, hard times had begun.

22

Repentance

Primavera, summer 1941

A third baby died at the end of June 1941 – Fritz's eighteen-month-old daughter, Christine, exhausted by croup. Heiner held the funeral service. As he watched Fritz carrying her little white coffin to the cemetery at the edge of the jungle, he shuddered. How many more babies would this land demand of them?

It was, in retrospect, a turning point for the community, one that marked the beginning of what would be its grimmest years. Though the previous year had been far from easy, their hardships had always faded before their vision of the future. They were leaving Europe to establish an outpost for the peaceable kingdom; they were a remnant, snatched from the chaos of war. Transplanted in a new land, they would flourish as never before. Now that future was here and, seen from up close, it no longer looked so rosy.

Their pioneering enthusiasm did not disappear all at once. It still showed itself in many ways: Trudi holding classes at a makeshift blackboard in a shack; Adolf and Wilfred, the surveyors, trekking miles through snake-infested swamps; Fritz spurring on the building team at a breakneck pace; Emmy and Moni making their endless rounds, tirelessly nursing the sick and making sure everyone was fed and cared for. The young men in the dairy crew were in high spirits too as they struggled to build up a herd that would actually produce milk—there was just enough for each child to receive a small ration. Two thousand head of cattle had come with the ranch, but they were wild. And by the time a cow was lassoed, dragged to the milking post, and trussed, the subsequent milking session often yielded no more than a pint.

Yet as the weeks went on, morale began to drop. Death dealt by far the harshest blows, but hunger ground them down as well. Aside from the occasional orange, breakfasts still consisted of manioca or flour paste (the same sour stuff used for sticking up street posters), and lunch and supper menus were just as simple: more manioca. Meat was rare.

So far, the garden crew's attempts to grow additional food had failed. One of their first projects had been to plant one thousand banana suckers, an arduous project that took many days. The bananas had grown beautifully at first, but then a single heavy frost had wiped out the entire plantation. Dozens of cattle were escaping, or being stolen, for lack of fencing.

In general, Paraguayan temperatures were far colder than anyone had expected, especially at night, when wind gusted through the wall-less shelters. Winter bedding had been blithely left behind in England, so there were never enough blankets. And those that there were grew damp from the heavy dews or were drenched during downpours, when the rain blew across the sleepers in horizontal sheets.

Some, like Emmy, made the most of such situations. "One night the wind was so strong that I thought we would be blown right away!" she reported in her notebook. "In London, during the air raids, thousands have to sleep side by side in the underground stations. Here we are at least sleeping in comparative safety." But others found themselves unable to muster such gratitude.

Meanwhile dozens, primarily children, continued to suffer from parasites and sores—and from dysentery, jaundice, malaria, whooping cough, and croup. No wonder several mothers were on the verge of breaking down.

All of these shared hardships might have drawn them together — that was how the community had weathered trying times in the past. But now the opposite threatened to happen. The shoulder-to-shoulder solidarity of the first months was fraying fast. Tensions at work flared into quarrels, and differences in opinion turned into entrenched divisions.

Many who had joined at Ashton Fields fought secret feelings of discouragement. Back there, in England, they had known why they wanted to live in community. They had caught a life-changing glimpse of what it could mean. And so, while the rest of England succumbed to the spirit of war, they had given up everything to live for peace. A few had even left spouses and children behind.

That zeal was now flagging. As Ruth, the young doctor, said to herself, "This isn't the life I thought I was coming to."

Emmy and other older members dug in their heels. "We have to face this struggle together," she told a group of women that she had called together. "We have gone through many hard things, and it may become even harder. Let us stand together and have faith that God knows what he is doing and has his hand over us."

Words like Emmy's lifted flagging spirits, but those who voiced them were few and far between. By July, evening members' meetings — previously a time of inner gathering and common prayer — were becoming the scene of heated arguments, bickering, and traded accusations. Sometimes angry shouts echoed across the compound, unnerving newcomers and novices, who did not attend. In the meantime, by day, the work did not slacken but went on just as frantically as before. Clearly, something would have to give.

Hardy was one of the first casualties. While away in Asunción on business, he was accused of overspending, and he returned to a clamor of bitter complaints. In a series of meetings that left him embarrassed and discredited, he was grilled about real and imagined blunders — and asked to step down as a leader of Primavera. For his part, Heiner agreed that his older brother had too often been high-handed in pushing through his own ideas, and had confronted him for it. Yet he shuddered at some of the spiteful accusations that were now being aired, often enough based only on old grudges. In this atmosphere of mistrust, how long would the community hold together?

In the previous half year, two other leaders of the community had been similarly removed. (Georg had been asked to step down earlier, before leaving England.) Now only Heiner remained at the helm, burdened with duties he had never expected or sought, and responsible for the welfare and survival of more than three hundred people. He was just twenty-seven and felt terribly inadequate. And as if all his other worries weren't enough, his kidney troubles had come back, confining him to bed.

Nor would the infection go away. In mid-August, Cyril Davies, an Englishman fresh from medical school who was Primavera's main doctor, started him on several medications for chronic pain and restlessness. Among them was a sedative, potassium bromide, which was then in common medical use, though it was known to be toxic, especially when taken at high doses for long periods.

Heiner found his illness easier to bear than his realization that the community was disintegrating before his eyes. How could Primavera have fallen into such chaos? Papa, Mama, and Tata had founded Sannerz in order to realize a vision of brotherhood and justice—a vision that was all the more vital now, when a second world war was claiming millions of victims all over the globe. Yet here they were squabbling. Was it for this that they and their children had risked crossing the submarine-infested Atlantic? Was it for this that his father had sacrificed so much?

His father—Heiner longed for him constantly. How much had gone wrong since his death! His last letter followed Heiner's thoughts everywhere. If only the community would return to the course it laid out for them! But how? The people his father had named to help hold the community true to its origins – Hans, Georg, Hardy, Hans-Hermann, and himself, as well as his mother and Emy-Margret – almost all had failed in fulfilling this task. And now, everywhere he looked, including in himself, he saw only suffering, misery, and failure. At times he despaired so deeply that he no longer desired to live. "It has been too terrible since Papa died," he thought.

By the end of that summer Heiner had become too sick to remain with his family and was moved to a special hut, where he lived alone. Annemarie, now six months pregnant, stayed in the dormitory building with Roswith, while nine-month-old Christoph, still critically ill with whooping cough and bronchitis, was entrusted to Phyllis Rabbitts, a nurse.

The hut was simple: one twelve-by-twelve-foot room, with drafty plank walls. Its three windows were rigged with mosquito netting (there was no glass) and there were shutters to close them at night. Compared to the communal sheds, it was palatial.

Heiner kept getting sicker – and weaker. In mid-September, he developed papilledema, a swelling of the nerve at the back of the eyeball. Papilledema, then as now, was known to be a serious warning sign. It indicated end-stage disease, or a brain tumor, or severe poisoning – poisoning from too much bromide, for example. Cyril noticed it with alarm, and tracked its progress in his medical notes. But apparently he did not recognize what it meant. Indeed, he kept prescribing heavy doses of the drug.

On September 29, Heiner took another turn for the worse. Not only was organ after organ failing, but he was also short of oxygen and had difficulty breathing. In the afternoon Cyril came into his hut, visibly shaken. "There cannot be much more time left," he said.

The nearness of death transformed Heiner. His spirits rallied as if preparing for a momentous event. And he was. Life was running out, and before it was gone he must accomplish his mission. This was no time for caution: from now on, every moment had to count; every thread of his life must be reexamined and brought together. Above all, every task that had ever been placed on his shoulders must be taken up one final time – and fulfilled.

One of these stood out above all the rest: the community's restoration to its early vigor and health. God would certainly require him to account for this. So would his father. But how could the people in Primavera find their way back to it? In a sense, he knew the answer. He knew that all of them desperately needed personal renewal – himself as well. They needed to rediscover the joy of their first love. Nothing less would be enough to save them. But how could such a renewal come about?

Heiner asked for the community to gather and had himself carried out of his hut on a stretcher. "Brothers and sisters," he began, "I am not worthy of speaking to you. But because this hour is critical, I want to beg you: Repent. Each of us bears a guilt for what has gone wrong; I know I do. But let us turn away from all this evil! Only remorse for the past can give us courage to face the future."

Heiner grew short of breath as he spoke but pulled himself together: "We have a promise – 'Behold, I make all things new!' Everything can become new! Let us return to the calling that brought us here in the first place. Let us change our lives and love one another so that everything can become new!"

As the meeting broke up, joy swept the gathering; many embraced and asked each other's pardon. "This is the gospel – this is what we need now!" "I have grown callous and cold. Forgive me." "I have been far too wrapped up in my work."

Faces streamed with tears. Karl, who had been weeping openly throughout the meeting, was now so deeply moved that he fainted. The hope they had lost in the bleakness of the last months was returning with double strength. At last their course had been reset.

For the rest of that week, the community was in upheaval. People met to set relationships straight and to rid themselves of longstanding

grudges. Heiner heard a dozen, and then at least a dozen more confessions. Faces were cheerful and frank, and eyes shone. Exhaustion
vanished.

Heiner hoped that the new mood would make it possible to tackle
the urgent question of leadership. What Primavera needed was
people with humility, people who saw leadership as a service, not a
rank. Rereading his father's last letter, as he did often, Heiner decided
it was time to reinstate Hans, Georg, and Hardy. All three had served
the community as leaders before, and more to the point, all three had
been chosen by his father. Here, at long last, was an opportunity to
bring Papa's last wishes to fulfillment.

Six years ago Hans had betrayed those wishes; now he seemed
a changed man. Then, it was true, he had revealed a capacity for
cruelty. But in the intervening years he had shown a new humility.
And didn't the Gospel say one should forgive "seventy times seven"?
"After everything that's happened since Papa's death," Heiner said
to himself, "this would be the perfect opportunity for a fresh start.
The slate must be wiped clean. Hans and Hardy and Georg and I will
work as a team."

The matter was now settled in Heiner's mind, yet he still hesitated
to share it with anyone. He feared that many would balk at supporting Hans; that the memories of the past would still be too fresh.

At the same time, his condition was worsening every day. On
October 3, his breathing pattern became harsh and irregular. He
gasped and convulsed as he fought for air. Cyril was called, and after
a brief examination, he announced, "Cheynes-Stokes breathing."
The death struggle had begun.

"How much longer do I have?" Heiner wanted to know. Though
his body was near giving up, his mind remained clear.

"At most, forty-eight hours," Cyril said.

Annemarie was sitting beside Heiner, holding his hand. He looked
at her with a rush of love. She seemed so exhausted; her mouth set,
her eyes dull. She was expecting a baby in three months, and besides

worrying about Heiner, she was also looking after Christoph. After many months, the little boy was still battling fevers and bronchitis.

Outside the window a group was singing to him. He saw Alfred, Sophie, Karl, and Johnny, Ruth, Phyllis and many others. There were children singing too. He told Annemarie he wanted to speak to them, and she called them to come to the window.

"I have a question for the community," Heiner began. He paused to gather his thoughts, and then plunged in. "Isn't it time to reinstate Hans, Georg, and Hardy? Each has failed in the past. But we all need to be forgiven. Couldn't we give them our full trust again?"

A murmur of assent ran through the group, and several hurried off to fetch the three men. They soon arrived and entered the hut. Meanwhile someone ran to the sawmill to pull the engine whistle — the signal for a meeting. Within minutes the whole community had gathered, the adults in a semicircle around the front of the hut, the children's faces pressed against the mosquito netting. Heiner looked out at them and repeated his suggestion.

Then: "You have all heard me now. Does anyone have an objection?" There was only silence. "Then does everyone agree?"

"Yes," they answered as one voice.

Heiner went on. He was still lying on his back; he was much too weak to sit. But he spoke deliberately, with a long pause between each sentence. "Among us none should lord it over the others; rather, we should all serve one another in love. We have experienced the bad fruits of following a human being as the masses follow a so-called great leader." (That was Hitler's term for himself, as Heiner's listeners knew.) "This attitude must be rejected. When we ask a person to take on such a responsibility, let us not see him as a great leader; let us focus on the spark of God living in him. Everything depends on mutual forgiveness."

Heiner was fighting for air; his chest heaved. His voice climbed and then dropped and then climbed again erratically. Yet to those outside, each word was audible. And they remembered them clearly many years later.

"What a mighty thing it is to live for God's kingdom! Do not shrink back. Live for it; look for it. It is so powerful that it will completely overwhelm you—it will solve every problem in your life, and on earth. Everything will be new, and each person will love the next in Christ. All separation and sin, all suffering and darkness and death will be overcome, and love alone will rule."

When Heiner had finished, he beckoned for Hans, Hardy, and Georg to kneel by his bed, and asked them three times, in the same way that Jesus once asked Peter, "Do you love Christ?"

"Yes," they answered.

"Then take care of the flock."

Finally, laying his hands on each head in turn, Heiner commissioned them and wished them strength, compassion, and humility.

Nightmares

October 1941

Heiner noticed that his breathing had become easier and more even. He was less often in pain. Would he live after all? After examining him, Cyril declared that the immediate threat of death had passed. And he seemed to be right. During the next two weeks Heiner received a stream of visitors, and almost every day, people met for spontaneous gatherings outside his hut. Often he spoke to those who had come. "Let's not slacken! We must keep on searching. We cannot stop until the promise has come true for us: *All* things new!"

If the change in Heiner's outlook was unexpected, so was the change in Hans. Up until the moment he knelt for Heiner's blessing, Hans had acted as a loyal and intimate friend. He had volunteered to stay up several nights a week as his nurse. Now, overnight, he seemed to have grown cool. At first Heiner did not want to believe this to be so. Was it possible that his brother-in-law's friendship had all been an act? "If that is true," Heiner thought, "then by trusting him again I have made the biggest mistake of my life."

What Heiner would only learn decades later, through Georg, was how deeply Hans resented losing the position he had carved out for himself after Eberhard's death. Now, having regained the trust of the community—through Heiner, no less—he set about building a base of support. Usually it was as simple as buttering someone up: "We need efficient men like you," he told the building foreman. "Your musical gifts are such an asset!" he murmured to the woman who directed Primavera's choir.

Heiner knew none of this. Nor was he aware that Hans sometimes stationed himself outside the door of the hut in order to buttonhole visitors as they came out. "That was rather emotional, wasn't it?" he might comment snidely. "It seems to me that Heiner's old weakness for exaggeration is returning." To others he added, "We have to stop this swindle!"

Georg, who tended to be easily swayed, gave ear to Hans's whisperings, and bolstered them with his own. "You're right. I wonder if it isn't just pious hysteria. And all these ecstatic gatherings outside his hut—it's high time we became sober and objective again." Soon the two of them were secretly discussing how they might reverse the new direction the community was taking.

In late October something happened that took everyone by surprise: Heiner began to have hallucinations. One day, snakes twisted themselves around his limbs. Another day his throat was pierced as if by jabbing needles, and shards of jagged glass embedded themselves all over his body. Still another time, an evil beast descended on his hut and entered it, stalking him in the darkness as if waiting to kill him. Each time these sensations came, he cried out for help. But his nurses seemed powerless to do anything but look to him with pity and disbelief.

Sometimes Heiner wondered if the nightmares had something to do with Cyril's drugs, and resisted taking the bromide, only to have it forced into his throat as two men held him down. At other times he tormented himself with self-accusations. Maybe it didn't have anything to do with the medicines; maybe he was going mad. Feelings of guilt pursued him. Was he being punished for some heavy sin? Even when he slept his dreams were hideous and dark.

At first, few knew what was happening to him, except his family, Cyril, and Hans. But someone must have spread the word, for rumors of Heiner's abnormal behavior seeped out. To Gwynn, the minister-turned-wagon-driver, Hans intimated that Heiner's strange behavior at night was hardly consistent with his calls to repentance during the day. Many didn't know quite what to think of what they had heard. Even his friends took to avoiding his hut.

The bright hopes of early October were gone; by the end of November, they had almost been forgotten. Many were confused, especially the new British members—people like Johnny and Ruth and Gwynn. In England Heiner had been a counselor and friend. And here in Primavera, he had been the only voice to call for unity amid a Babel of conflicting opinions. Then why did Hans and Georg seem so cold to all they had experienced around his hut? Why were they and their friends now openly ridiculing Karl and others for having responded "too emotionally" in those meetings? And why had Hans announced that there would be no more gatherings—or even visits—at Heiner's hut? He claimed this was Annemarie's request, though many felt that could hardly be true. (In fact, it wasn't.)

By December, it was clear that Heiner had escaped death. But he still looked skeletal and could not get out of bed. An American guest happened to hear of his condition and arranged for him to be flown to the capital for treatment. Cyril, Georg, and Moni accompanied him. Here, in Asunción, Heiner's recovery began, in the private hospital of Dr. Juan Boettner, a specialist in internal medicine.

Shortly after admitting the new patient, Dr. Boettner took him off the bromide. Heiner's hallucinations soon ceased, never to return. Cyril noticed the remarkable change in his mental state and drew the inescapable conclusion. He diagnosed bromide intoxication, and added in his notes, "Perhaps I gave too much of the drug in the past."

It was December 20 when Cyril made that entry; he had first recorded symptoms indicating an overdose on September 15. Yet during those three months he had never wavered in administering the bromide. And now, though the effects of his prescription could not have been any clearer, he recorded his findings privately in a medical file—and left it at that. He never told Heiner or Annemarie what he had determined, nor did he inform the community at large. They were all left to assume that Heiner had a psychotic streak and suffered (as he himself wondered) from *Verdunklung*—a "darkening" of the spirit.

Heiner spent a few weeks in Dr. Boettner's care and then returned home for further recuperation. His kidneys improved, he put on weight, and after some weeks he could walk again. A month after his return, in January 1942, Annemarie gave birth to the baby they had been waiting for. Heiner named the newborn, a girl, after her, but they called her Anneli for short.

In April, Dr. Boettner saw Heiner again. "You are as good as cured," he told him, "but you must continue to be careful. Sleep enough, and eat all you can. You're still much too thin. You can work, but I'd advise resting half-days."

Heiner was overjoyed and kept thanking the doctor until he realized he was repeating himself. After months of enforced idleness and isolation, he was eager to get back to work. He knew that there would be plenty for him to do. Beneath the bustle of daily life, he noticed that many were unhappy. It was not (as it had been during those first months in Paraguay), a matter of open chaos or complete deprivation. People were adjusting to the climate and the rough conditions, and day-to-day life was settling into a rhythm. But inwardly, so many seemed cramped and weary. Were they numb? Were they suffering for lack of spiritual care? Three more children had died during his illness, and yet so little time had been set aside to mourn them. And what had happened to those he had felt so close to last October?

When Heiner arrived home from Asunción, Primavera celebrated with him. "It's a miracle," many said. "He has been restored, from death to life." This joy was genuine, but it was not shared by all.

As it happened, Hans was away from Primavera just then, having taken Emy-Margret to Asunción to see a tuberculosis specialist.

The Zumpes—and Cyril, who traveled with them as Emy-Margret's doctor—had overlapped a few days with Heiner in the capital, and they had all stayed at the same hotel. It had not been a happy time. Hans had reacted impassively to news of Heiner's recovery, and when Heiner had taken leave of them to return home, they had seemed relieved.

Two weeks after Heiner's homecoming, the Zumpes and Cyril arrived back in Primavera, and shortly after that, Hans called the community together. He opened the meeting by announcing he had news about Heiner's medical condition. While in Asunción, he and Cyril had discussed the matter with Dr. Boettner, and the doctor had given important guidance: he had forbidden Heiner to do any spiritual or pastoral work.

Heiner, who had come to the meeting suspecting nothing, was stunned. When he had left Hans and Cyril in Asunción, neither had told him they planned to discuss his case with Dr. Boettner, much less asked his permission. What on earth were they trying to prove by this? And why did Hans's report contradict what Dr. Boettner had said to his face just fourteen days ago?

Most people in the meeting were equally bewildered. What right did a doctor in Asunción have to dictate who could do pastoral work in their community and who could not? Heiner was someone they had come to trust. Whether healthy or sick, he was someone you could count on. All the same, despite their astonishment, none of them questioned Hans. Heiner sensed they feared his brother-in-law.

◆ ◆ ◆

Fritz was the one who had asked for the meeting of Primavera's leadership. Two months ago, in May, he and his wife, Martha, had lost another daughter—their second child to die in less than a year. Grief had softened Fritz. Though still known as one of the community's most energetic workers, it was Primavera's spiritual health that concerned him now, even more than his many concurrent building projects. Like Heiner and Hardy and their wives, he worried that the community was growing callous, lacking in tenderness and compassion. Not surprisingly, the three couples had grown increasingly close.

Today Fritz spoke forthrightly to his coworkers in the leadership. "Primavera needs to change from the ground up. We have become cold and official. What Eberhard Arnold started has been lost through power seeking. It has been replaced by a dictatorship. The mob-like spirit in some of our meetings is the exact opposite of brotherhood! Each of us must be the first to admit that we have gone wrong, and turn around. We need to become humble. We must find the love and joy that first brought us together. We must . . ."

Georg cut him short. "We have heard more than enough about repentance! Who do you think you are anyway, to call the community a mob? How dare you talk of dictatorship!" Fritz looked crushed, and confusion ensued. But by the time they all parted, it became clear that he had backers: Hardy, Heiner, and one or two others.

Georg was triumphant when he reported back to Hans, who had stayed away: "We finally have them in a trap." That same day, they called an emergency meeting. All Primavera was to attend, except the newer English members, who were assigned to babysit the children. "We plan to discuss matters that go back to before you joined us," Hans explained to them.

As the meeting began, Georg had the chair. He described what he felt had led to the morning's clash. "Heiner, Fritz, and Hardy have been heading in a worrying direction for a long time now. They talk about 'renewal,' and everyone is supposed to fall into line behind them. But isn't this just a clique with a private agenda? Look how they are trying to bring division!"

Murmurs of approval answered Georg from all sides.

"And this morning," he continued, "Fritz slandered the community. He described it as dictatorship run by a mob." Cries of outrage rose from all sides. The accused attempted to explain themselves but were roundly shouted down. Then, without further ado, they were ejected from the meeting.

Over the next weeks, the three men's supporters were systematically neutralized. Suspected sympathizers, including their wives, Emmy, and a handful of others, were interrogated and silenced. As for Fritz and Heiner and Hardy, Hans and Georg were determined to make an example of them. They suggested that the three be excluded from the community and put in isolation at the edge of the settlement. This would be a form of church discipline, based on the sixteenth-century Anabaptist church orders that Eberhard had brought back with him from the Hutterites in North America.

Most members of Primavera agreed to the proposal—some with conviction, others out of fear. Who wanted to be lumped with "the clique"? (The newer English members had no say in the matter but were informed only after the fact.)

In theory, Fritz, Heiner, and Hardy were each to live alone for a time of self-examination, after which they would be welcomed home and reconciled. In practice, Hans and Georg made sure the time was as punitive as possible. Each of the three was placed in a small hut in the jungle outside Primavera. Separated from wife and children, and forbidden to talk with anyone, they were to work full days in the fields. The arrangement was to last indefinitely, until Hans and Georg were assured their attitude had changed.

Over the next weeks, loneliness ate at all three men. But Heiner, who was still underweight from his deathly illness the year before, was hungry as well—so hungry he could hardly stand it. Part of it was that Cyril had put him on a no-protein diet for his kidneys—a recognized therapy at the time, even if it was hardly suited to the realities of life in Primavera. After removing meat from a diet of manioca and goulash, what was left? And how did such a regimen harmonize with Dr. Boettner's order that Heiner should eat everything he could to gain weight?

Perhaps Cyril thought out a solution to these objections, but if he did, Heiner never knew. At all events it was Hans and Georg who supervised his daily schedule. Heiner got his meals by fetching a plate of food from where it was left for him outside his hut — a small platform that looked like a birdfeeder. The plate typically held a small portion of cooked squash or manioca. And nothing else.

Soon he was starving. Some evenings he walked far into the jungle looking for wild oranges, though their season was over. He even picked through garbage pails looking for scraps. When Hans found out about this, he raked him over the coals. "How could you disobey Cyril's orders?"

But by now Heiner's hunger had taken over. It had grown so intense that he risked going right into the community kitchen. He knew it was siesta; the place would be quiet. Entering, he found some leftover scraps in a bowl. He ate a little quickly, and stuffed the rest into his pocket.

Suddenly Georg was at the door. "Thief!" he shouted. "How dare you steal!" After scolding Heiner, he ordered him back to his hut — and made sure that in the next days, the story of his theft made the rounds.

Despite their interest in Heiner's diet, Hans and Georg did not take his poor health into account when it came to work. He was assigned the most strenuous tasks, digging postholes or hoeing manioca for hours in the burning sun.

Some who noticed the harshness of Heiner's treatment complained on his behalf. The cook who prepared his plate, for instance, took it to Emy-Margret in distress. She knew that Hans, not the doctor, oversaw such things. "Can a man really live on this?" she asked. Emy-Margret looked frightened, and said that she would look into it. But she didn't, and after a few days, when questioned a second time, the cook got the point, and stopped asking.

Others might have wondered about Emy-Margret's relationship with her mother and brothers. Not Heiner. Like her aunt and her father before her, Emy-Margret suffered from tuberculosis, which had taken a serious turn in Ashton Fields and had become still worse in Paraguay. She was currently in a seven-year quarantine, living separately from her husband and children. Spending her days largely alone, and often lost in fairy-tale reveries, she was somewhat aloof from goings on in the community.

Yet Heiner knew that, despite her isolation, she was deeply involved in everything she wanted to be involved in: organizing the women's work teams and overseeing the kindergarten. And she was hardly ignorant of Hans's doings—he kept her up to date, and she attended community meetings. Though Cyril was currently treating her for what he called "nerve illness," she still found the energy to summon her mother Emmy to her room to berate her for supporting Fritz and thus "stabbing Hans in the back." (Meanwhile, Hans told her brothers that she was on the verge of death, and claimed it was their fault.) In short, Emy-Margret lived under her husband's shadow and in his thrall.

Hans and Georg stopped by to check on Heiner every few days. Their visits were the only times he had contact with other human beings. But there were no friendly conversations. Instead Hans would grill him about his past, harping again and again on the time of his illness. "Don't you see what a hypocrite you were when you preached to us about renewal? What was going on when you had your hallucinations? Were you mentally ill? Are you perhaps still unstable?"

Heiner began to doubt himself. "How can you be so certain that you were right?" he wondered. "Perhaps everyone else is right, and it is you who are in the wrong." One day, he told Hans he wanted to humble himself. Later, his turmoil turning into desperation, he confessed every sin he'd ever committed.

Hans listened eagerly to all Heiner had to tell him. But unlike a priest, he did not offer absolution. On the contrary, using his precise memory of Heiner's weaknesses—after all, Heiner had confessed his failings to him before, at the Sparhof—Hans effectively cowed him into submission. Visit after visit, he gave Heiner no hope of returning to his family. After a while, Heiner came to see that no amount of humility would be sufficient. Hans wanted him to repudiate his whole life up till now—the Sun Troop, his dreams of mission, his relationship with his father.

Heiner could not bring himself to do this. In his lowest moments he sometimes questioned everything, including the genuineness of his conversion. He began to feel he was going mad. Two decades later he could still point out the trees that he banged his head against during those agonizing days and nights. But still he refused to give in to Hans.

In mid-November, Hans and Georg finally let him rejoin his family, though not because anything had been resolved. In their eyes, Heiner was pitiful—a tormented soul. They announced that he was returning to the community as if on probation.

Heiner returned to an altered landscape. While he was away, it had become bad manners in Primavera to speak of anything that might encourage "religious exaggeration." Blumhardt's writings, for instance, were suddenly frowned on, and so was talk of Sannerz and the Sparhof. Women were now formally excluded from decision-making—perhaps in order to silence Emmy. Unbelievably, even Eberhard—whom Hans derisively referred to in his diary as "the big father"—was suspect.

Signs of the new order were visible on all sides, even in the outhouse. Half a year earlier, Hardy had asked Fritz to print a collection of his father's poems—verses that expressed Eberhard's most intimate thoughts. The pages had not yet been bound into books when the two brothers had been separated from their families. Now Heiner found the unbound galleys set out for use as toilet paper.

Deep within, something snapped. But he said nothing aloud. He was tired of fighting. He was the father of a growing family, and he could not face being separated from them again. For the time being he would simply say nothing about his pangs of conscience—not to Hardy, Fritz, or his mother, and not even to Annemarie. He forbade himself to oppose Hans even in his thoughts.

24

Among Children

WORK CREWS were replacing the hung sacking on Primavera's dormitories with real walls, and a second settlement was going up a few miles from the first. The lathe shop hummed from dawn to dusk, and its products – turned bowls, plates, and candlesticks – were beginning to make a name for themselves in Asunción. Meanwhile, more than a hundred acres were under cultivation, bearing manioca and squash and a few other vegetables, maize and sorghum for animal feed, and citrus fruit. Aside from these operations, a hospital was being built to serve the impoverished local population.

Primavera's members worked and sweated like heroes. Their achievements were the fruit of ingenuity and perseverance. They made do with little and bore setbacks stoically. They celebrated weddings, births, and school graduations in creatively organized communal festivals. They urged each other onward in dedication to their life together, with countless acts of generosity and self-sacrifice, especially by the mothers. Many of their children would look back on these years in Primavera as "the most wonderful childhood."

Yet despite the camaraderie, it was not the life of brotherhood that many had known in earlier years. Hans's iron fist was growing tighter and tighter. On the surface, the trappings of equality were carefully preserved, at least as far as the men were concerned. In the all-male decision-making meetings, the most trivial practical questions were debated in great detail. But the apparent democracy was only skin-deep.

Hans had a masterful way of handling divergent opinions. After offering a long and exhausting summary of other people's viewpoints, he would enumerate their weaknesses and explain their implausibility. Then, having made his listeners feel they were at an impasse, he would unveil his own proposal, and cajole everyone into approving it. Of course, they were free to debate the particulars at length. But in the end, the game must always be played according to Hans's rules.

At other times, Hans made no attempt to play games at all and acted with open cruelty. When Norah, a young mother with emotional problems, went through one of her bad patches, he decided that she should be punished for her "unfaithfulness" by a period of exclusion from the community. Others felt that Norah could have used counseling and encouragement. Yet Hans would have none of it, and got his way, supported as so often by Georg.

Heiner, who knew Norah well, was horrified, remembering his own solitary confinement. "Norah's done nothing wrong. She's just not coping," he said to himself. "To put a woman in a hut in the jungle all by herself—it's simply heartless!" But it was the first time since coming back that he had consciously opposed Hans, and the memory of his own punishment kept him from approaching anyone who might feel the same—at most, he hinted at his thoughts to old friends like his former teacher Trudi. As for questioning Hans or Georg about the matter, he knew that would be futile. Whenever he so much as raised a question about something, they warned him that he was relapsing into his destructive tendency to criticize. And so, when the wagon came to take Norah's children away—they were to be cared for by a couple in the new village—she ran after it, sobbing and crying their names. With a feeling of helplessness, he went into the woods and wept.

Heiner found a measure of peace by devoting himself to his work. In the mornings he worked in the stables or ran errands as a wagon driver. In the afternoons, he supervised the schoolchildren after classes were over. There were a good two dozen of them, ranging from the first to the seventh grade, and occupying them would have been a challenge for most adults. School had been interrupted constantly for the last three years, what with emigration from England and repeated bouts of isolation for sickness. The ongoing lack of private living space in the quickly constructed buildings also took a toll on family life. Given Primavera's primitive conditions, it was not surprising that some teachers threw up their hands now and then and let the children run wild. But Heiner, who had worked off and on with children for years, had gained a reputation for keeping them happy. He knew how to draw the best out of the most difficult child.

Heiner demanded hard work from his charges – the community depended on their help in the vegetable garden, and they spent many afternoons setting out seedlings and weeding the rows. But where other adults might have exerted their will by means of discipline and control, Heiner sought to win the children's hearts through trust, not threats.

One day a group of boys disobeyed Heiner. It was orange season, and he had told them not to pick from the one tangerine tree. "That fruit," he said, "is reserved for the elderly." When he was out of sight, several boys picked from it anyway. When he found out, he called them together. He stood looking down at them, quiet and so sad that their eyes dropped to the ground to avoid meeting his. "How could you do this to me? I trusted you," he said – and walked away. The shame they felt was worse than any punishment.

Once Heiner took the children camping on the banks of a nearby river. It was six miles to the clearing where they would sleep, and a few of the boys rode ahead on horseback, while Heiner followed with the other children, and the supplies. As soon as his cart pulled into the campsite, Heiner saw that one of the riding horses was in trouble. Guilty-faced, the boys explained that they had galloped all the way and then let the horses straight into the water. Because of the shock, one of the mares had started to give birth prematurely.

Heiner beckoned the children to come near. Standing around the mare in a half-circle, they watched in silence until at last the foal lay on the grass. Then Heiner cut open the sac with a camp knife. The foal was dead. He turned toward the children. "Children, this is the result of your irresponsibility. Always treat animals with reverence. They are made by God."

Heiner did not tolerate disrespect to other people. Especially not mockery. Once one of the boys in his care mimicked an older man whose mannerisms and way of speaking had struck him as peculiar. Heiner's indignation burst out of him like a thunderclap: "How dare you mock him! How dare you mock anyone!" The offender apologized, and Heiner never mentioned it again. What made the incident memorable to the children was that Heiner so rarely raised his voice. Decades later, the times the children remembered most vividly were the afternoons they had each week for "free play." These took place in the School Wood, a grove of trees with two or three modest shelters where lessons were held and lunch served. On such afternoons, Heiner gave the children what to them seemed like total freedom. Some played at being knights or princesses or robbers. Others worked on crafts, using mud to make pottery and firing it in a kiln made by Karl's son, Ulrich. Hans's daughter, Heidi, and her best friend, Jennie Harries, worked for days with a fretsaw on a piece of wood latticework. In the meantime, Heiner stretched himself under a large tree with a storybook, watching the children as unobtrusively as possible and intervening only when necessary.

At the end of the afternoon, as they ate, Heiner retold the newest stories he had read. Often he improvised to fit a tale to the happenings of the day. If Heidi and Jennie had quarreled that afternoon, he might describe the fate of two princesses who refused to reconcile after a fight. If an older child had bossed around younger ones, he might tell how a bully received his comeuppance. Because the story was told with good humor, no child was ever made to feel stupid. Yet the point of each story was clear, and Heiner didn't need to spell out a moral.

He told them tales from real life as well: about the suffering of the Jews in Europe, underground resisters in Nazi Germany, early Christian martyrs, and people like Rachoff. That was their favorite story, and he told it many times.

Heiner's childhood was another topic that captured their imagination. They loved to hear about the Sun Troop, Hans-in-Luck, Sundar Singh, and Tata. And Heiner loved to talk about these things as much as they did. Here among children, he could speak freely about what mattered most to him, as he could not with his adult peers.

Once, inspired by all they had heard, Heidi and Jennie wrote a script for a little drama. The play portrayed an angel who visits earth dressed as a beggar in order to test the compassion of those he meets. The girls soon got the other children involved in the production. On their own, they memorized their lines and sewed their simple costumes. They even chose and rehearsed songs to go with the story. Heiner helped them construct a rough stage, and Annemarie found blankets for curtains. The whole community was to be invited to the performance.

Then, just when things were at their best, it was all shattered. One afternoon in August 1944, the children came to the School Wood to find that Heiner was gone. A new teacher, Jan, was there in his place.

Mystified at first, they were quick to find out what had happened. Heiner, along with Emmy and Hardy and several others, was in some sort of trouble. Even more worrying, they were forbidden to talk with him. Heidi vowed to Jennie that she would speak to Heiner anyway. "He has done nothing wrong as far as we are concerned. We must show that we stand by him." And they did.

At school, the children refused to accept their new teacher Jan—not because he was unkind, but simply because they did not know him.

"Who can help us with our play now that Heiner is gone?" Heidi wept at home.

"Your new teacher," her father Hans said.

"But he doesn't understand us! We can't do it with him."

In the end the girls pulled off the performance on their own.

A few days later, Jennie saw Heiner heading toward his house. He was carrying a small suitcase—a rare sight in Primavera, and one that almost always meant someone was about to leave on a trip. As Jennie watched, Annemarie came out, and Heiner said something inaudible to her. Then he said something that she clearly overheard. "Hans said to me, 'You have always wanted to go out on mission. Now you can go to Asunción and convert as many people as you want.'"

Heiner spoke with such pain that Jennie ached for him. But she felt as if she were eavesdropping, and quickly slipped away.

Heidi was shocked when Jennie broke the news—in fact, she couldn't quite believe that Heiner was really going away. They decided to hide in the bushes and watch the main road out of Primavera. Before long, they saw a wagon approaching. Behind the driver sat Heiner with his head in his hands. The girls jumped from the bushes to wave goodbye, but Heiner didn't see them. He never even looked up.

25

Banished

The storm had been brewing for months before Heiner's sudden departure. It had all started with a chance meeting one morning while Heiner was driving a wagon between the community's two villages. About halfway, as he was coming through a stretch of jungle, he heard the rumble of a wagon approaching from the opposite direction. Soon it appeared through the trees, and he saw it was Hardy. Both men stopped their horses.

Heiner longed to ask his brother how he was doing—to talk over everything that had happened in the last two years. At home it was so difficult; he felt they were being watched. Here in the privacy of the jungle, it should be safe to bare one's soul. But neither of them said anything. "Have we really become so practiced at hiding our true feelings?" Heiner wondered.

At last Hardy broke the silence. "You know . . . Hans and Georg— they don't come down on people with hammers. If they did, people would feel it and revolt. No, the way they squeeze people is like a hydraulic press—slowly, but in the end crushing every last bit of life."

Heiner sought an answer. It was only the truth. But he simply did not have it in him to reply. Slapping the reins, he drove on without a word.

In April 1943, Hardy's wife Edith had died at the age of thirty-two, leaving him to raise four young children—aged four, five, seven, and eight—on his own. The signs of appendicitis had not been recognized early enough, and her appendix had ruptured. The blow devastated the young father, as it would have anyone. But what made it far worse was that—alongside the heartfelt sympathy of many—others seemed embarrassed by Hardy's anguish. Emmy wrote to Hans asking to join Hardy's family to help care for her orphaned grandchildren, but her request was turned down.

Heiner knew a little what Hardy must be going through; the last few months had been hard for him and Annemarie as well. Annemarie, like most women in Primavera, worked a strenuous day for the community in addition to caring for her family—their fourth child, a daughter, had been born shortly after Edith died (they named the baby after her), and she and Heiner had been looking forward to another. But in March, Annemarie had lost the baby in the fifth month of pregnancy, possibly because of overwork.

Fourteen months after Edith's passing, Heiner gave Hardy a poem he had composed for him. Reflecting his boyhood love of mystics such as Meister Eckhart, it was a written prayer, titled "Dialogue between Christ and the Soul":

SOUL. My heart is sick and full of fear. O Jesus, give me the words to say everything to you. I see how serious our situation is. I have no clarity. My soul flares up and is cowardly. Only you know the way to go forward in humility yet with courage, in patience yet in truthfulness, without false martyrdom or flaring up in pride. Whatever I do, whether I speak or am silent, my soul feels guilty. Only you know the way.

JESUS. Hold on to me. Do you trust me completely? Do you have faith in me?

SOUL. Yes. Lord, I trust, I have faith! But my heart is so cold, so stubborn.

JESUS. I am here for you. I saw all your sins as you committed them; I saw you in dark despair. I am ready to open the door to you, so that streams of blessings may pour over you.

SOUL. Our prayers are so lame, our knocking so timid. I am an impure man. I am not single-hearted.

JESUS. I am full of mercy and will give without ceasing to those who ask.

SOUL. Oh how wonderful it is when you are near! We forgive our brothers and sisters. We love you. We wait for you. Amen.

These thoughts worked in Heiner, and he was not alone. During the next weeks, he and Annemarie talked about it, first alone and then with others. A group began to form. They never met together all at once. At most there would be three or four at a time talking quietly on someone's veranda. But eventually there were sixteen who knew they all felt the same: Primavera had lost its moorings and become a place of fear and division. It must be re-won for the cause—for love and unity.

The core consisted of several old-timers: Hardy, Fritz and Martha, Hans-Hermann and Gertrud, and of course, Emmy. Joining them were a diverse bunch that included three Swiss members—Peter and Anni Mathis, and Dorli Bolli, a disabled woman—and Bruce Sumner and his wife, Luise, Heiner's old classmate from Sannerz. Gradually all sixteen came to agree on a plan: they would stand up at a members' meeting and lay their concerns before the community. It was a gamble, but surely others would join them. Perhaps if they gave it just a little more time . . .

In the interim they voiced their feelings in other ways. That August Emmy wrote in her diary, "There is so much need among us. The Bible says we should bear one another's burdens. But do we? What about those who are struggling inwardly? Do we try to put ourselves in their position, to feel their needs, loneliness, and temptations? Do we concern ourselves with those who are grieving? I am writing this at night by the bedside of a sick child.

"I can't help going back to the last months of 1941. At that time God wanted to restore everything among us. Yes, the last dregs of bitterness were to disappear from among us. A great love broke through. But then the devil made game of us once more, and sowed mistrust again.

"It makes me especially sad that we have so little true understanding for each other. How quick people are to say, 'Oh, you are just revolving around yourself!' Might it not be sorrow for God's cause — and for the lack of love among us? The way people talk mockingly of 'compassion' is wounding in the deepest sense."

The crisis broke in September, before they were ready for it. Peter had tried to enlist one more person, and misjudged — the hoped-for supporter scurried to inform Hans. Late that night, Peter crept into Heiner and Annemarie's room and woke them, whispering, "The fight is on. Now we have to stand together."

Again, Hans and Georg moved fast. They called a meeting and announced that another conspiracy had been discovered. "The Gang of Korah," Hans dubbed the sixteen, after an Israelite clan in the Old Testament who were swallowed alive by the earth as divine punishment for plotting against Moses.

Secretly, many in the community admired the sixteen. Heiner's old teacher, Trudi, was one — she even wished she had joined them. And she could have: there was a brief moment when she and others like her could have stood up and turned the tide. But they stayed silent, and the moment passed. After that, all Hans and Georg had to do was mop up, which they did in a series of meetings in which they worked the rebels over.

Some of the sixteen bowed to the pressure right away. As the meetings went on, even Hardy started to waver. Without Edith, he did not have the confidence to face down what seemed to be Primavera's unanimous will. Finally he caved in, telling Heiner: "I will not be responsible for splitting the community."

Heiner at least had Annemarie to confer with, and she reassured him she would fight to the finish. "Stand firm," she urged him. "I'll stand with you." But in the end, every one of them – Fritz, Hans-Hermann, Heiner, and their wives, and all the rest – backed down during a single meeting, one after the other.

As the last one spoke, a piercing scream rose from the back of the room. It was Emmy, and those present said they would never forget the look of abandonment on her face as all those she had counted on deserted her. Falling unconscious, she was transported from the room. In the hospital the doctors diagnosed a stroke.

The rebellion had been crushed, but Hans and Georg were still not satisfied. Now they must stamp out every shred of support for the sixteen. In a new series of meetings they questioned each person whom they suspected of sympathizing with the "gang."

"Why did you talk to them?" Hans wanted to know. "And what did you talk about, and when, and where?" Annemarie's old friend Marianne was asked why she and her husband had invited Hardy to their house so often.

"Because we felt sorry for him and his motherless children," she answered. Now even basic kindness was suspect.

The meetings dragged on. Then Hans and Georg presented the community with a document. It summarized all that had come to light and determined punishments for those involved. Each member of Primavera was asked to approve it. Though many were shocked by the proposals, all did so, some doubtless out of fear.

The sixteen were summoned to a special session at which their fates were read out. Heiner was to be expelled from the community's lands, as were Hardy, Fritz, Peter, Bruce, and Dorli, the disabled woman. Annemarie, Anni, and Luise were to live in isolation at the edge of the village until their husbands were able to provide for them;

their children would be placed with foster parents. As for Emmy, the last of the "ringleaders," she was still recovering from her stroke, so it was not clear exactly how she would be punished. (She would later be formally excluded from membership for three months, living by herself much as Heiner had done two years earlier. According to the doctor's notes, she suffered a breakdown during this time.)

The rest of them received various disciplines but were allowed to stay. Hans-Hermann, for instance, was separated from his family but allowed to remain in Primavera. The document warned him "to finally separate himself from the influence of his brothers."

"We challenge those concerned to truly turn around," the document concluded. "There has to be a fundamental change in your whole attitude. You must come to feel disgust about yourselves and must completely give up all personal, wrong thoughts. Once more we warn you of the fallacy that humility and repentance might so cleanse you that you would be all the more able to represent your ideas. Only when you have come to the end of your opinions, your efforts, your hypocrisy and untruthfulness, is there hope for help – in no other way. Otherwise you are lost people."

Dazed, Heiner walked home with Annemarie and packed up his clothes. His heart cried out for Annemarie as he thought of their impending separation. Last time, she had only lost him; this time, she would also lose their children. Who knew if they would ever be a family again?

He had only a few minutes to pack. She helped him. Then he woke up Roswith, Christoph, and little Anneli to say goodbye. They were so sleepy they didn't realize what was happening. Heiner and Annemarie embraced, and took leave of one another.

(Days later, at three in the morning, Cyril and his wife Margot would arrive at the house, where Annemarie was already up and dressed. In an act of compassion, they had volunteered to care for the children so they would not be split up among foster families. Now it was time for Annemarie to go. The children were all asleep, and Annemarie wept as she kissed them one last time. She took with her a lock she had cut from each child's head. When the children woke, five-year-old Roswith kept asking, "Why did you take out Papa and Mama's beds? They are coming back, aren't they?")

Heiner turned and trudged toward the isolation hut, each step taking him farther from his family and closer to the terror of being alone. In the morning he was to leave for the river port and Asunción.

It was then that Heidi and Jennie caught sight of him on the wagon. After watching him pass by and disappear down the track, the girls agreed to meet again that evening after dark. When dinner was over, they slipped away from home to a secluded place where they prayed for Heiner. "Please let him—and all the others—return!" The two girls kept vigil like this for weeks.

One night the sky was particularly clear and full of stars, and as they looked up at it they saw a meteor speed toward the horizon. "It's a sign that our prayer has been heard!" the girls told each other. Surely someday, Heiner would come back.

Leper Colony

October 1944

The minute Heiner stepped off the riverboat in Asunción he started looking for work. But he soon discovered that employment was almost impossible to find. Since he couldn't speak Spanish or Guaraní, the country's official languages, no Paraguayan firm would hire him. Nor would British and American businessmen. Who wanted to hire a German when the war against Hitler was in full swing? As for the city's own German expatriates, most were Nazi sympathizers and saw Heiner as a traitor.

Heiner was hungry. All he had been given on leaving Primavera was twenty-five guaranís—barely enough for a day's meals. Now and then he found odd jobs like house painting, which paid enough to cover rent and basic groceries. But even when he had work, there was nothing to do in the evening. Often he would sit for hours on end in a café, ordering nothing and talking to no one. At least he could be among other human beings and hear happy voices and see friendly faces. Without that, he felt, he would go mad.

Heiner's landlady had similar fears. Contacting Gwynn, who now had become Hans's close collaborator, she told him that as a Catholic, she understood the need for discipline in a religious order. Still, she was of the opinion that Heiner's conditions were far too harsh. On a second occasion, she met with Hans while he was on business in the city to plead with him to help Heiner in his inner suffering. Hans reassured her, and told Emy-Margret about the conversation, but nothing was done.

Hardy and Fritz were in Asunción too, and were having as hard a time as Heiner. Eventually both found jobs (Hardy as an English teacher), but even with regular work their loneliness pressed down on them like a terrible weight. On leaving Primavera, they had been instructed not to contact each other. They could easily have broken their isolation in defiance of Primavera. The capital was not a large place, and they each knew where the other two lived. But by the same token, that would have been a gamble. There were always people from Primavera in the city, and what if the wrong one found out?

In the end, they did communicate – though without words – at a park where, in the evenings, they sat on separate benches – in silence, but together. In a sense, there was nothing to talk about anyway. They knew they were brothers, and that was enough. But Hardy found another way of expressing his feelings. One day he walked by Heiner's room and threw an envelope through the window. Heiner opened it and found a wad of cash. It was an unforgettable act of compassion.

Heiner (and Fritz and Hardy) could have easily abandoned the Bruderhof at this point. He would only have had to return, load Annemarie and the children onto a wagon, and take them elsewhere – anywhere – beyond Hans and Georg's reach. In their new home, they could have waited for Primavera to come back to its senses.

But tempting as such a plan might have seemed, Heiner never seriously considered it. Never, that is, except once, when a Primavera member came to check up on him – and the meeting went so badly that it made the idea seem tempting. But he soon rejected the thought. Long ago at the Sparhof, when he had decided to join the community, he had known that hard times would surely come. Already then, he had worried about what might happen after his father's death, especially when Georg and others had smirked at his involvement in the

Sun Troop. He remembered Tata's words to him when he had confided his fears to her: "Following Jesus just *will* demand struggle."

And so, in the years since, Heiner had never questioned his commitment. He had promised lifelong faithfulness to his vocation, which he believed came from Christ himself, to serve within this particular church community. He could not and would not undo that commitment now. Distorted as Primavera had become, the spark his parents had first kindled at Sannerz glowed even now, however dimly, in the hearts of many there. Trudi, Adolf, Karl and Irmgard, Alfred, and Moni—he knew they must long for it to blaze up again. There was still life beneath the embers.

Yet still he could not bring himself to ask to come back. It would mean saying yes to things he knew he could never say yes to. Some nights it felt as if he were being torn to pieces.

When Heiner had been in Asunción two months, he found a steady job, though he took it only out of desperation. He had sent an application to STICA, an American-funded development program, and when they saw his credentials as a farmer, they offered him a position: director of agriculture at the Santa Isabel leper colony.

The leper colony was located near the village of Sapucai, in the hinterland fifty miles southeast of Asunción, set among scenic wooded hills. It was reachable only by an outmoded wood-burning train, and the journey took more than four hours. Emerging from the train, Heiner found himself in a backwoods village whose one feature was a ramshackle mechanic shop for locomotive repair. When he asked the locals for directions to Colonia Santa Isabel, they backed away from him fearfully—outsiders here were usually new patients.

The leper colony lay a two-hour hike beyond the village, and when Heiner got to the main entrance he was taken aback. There was no barbed wire, and no guard towers, just a light perimeter fence, a farm gate, and an adobe administration house. Everything appeared to be relaxed and pleasant. (Later he found that appearances were deceiving. Patients who fled the colony were arrested and brought back, and some had even been lynched along the way. Soldiers were posted in the colony as well – four years earlier, a violent uprising by the patients against corrupt management had resulted in six deaths.)

Heiner checked in and entered the gate, and soon found himself among dozens of little homesteads where the healthier patients lived. Most had one room and a veranda, with a thatched roof and mud walls. Chickens, pigs, and cows went in and out of them freely.

Walking farther, Heiner came to the central village, with a church, a carpentry shed, a storehouse where rations were distributed, and a jail for the colony's thieves, fornicators, and drunks. Two long sheds served as men's and women's hospital wards, and in front of them spread a little plaza where the residents socialized.

On most afternoons, a dozen men could be found sitting in a circle, stark naked and drinking maté from a shared gourd. Some were missing eyes or noses, while others had lost fingers and toes.

Heiner tried not to stare, but it took him days to get used to such sights. How could it happen, he agonized, that a man is so completely stripped of his dignity? It wasn't so much the lack of clothing, or the way the lepers dragged themselves along the ground. Those things evoked his pity. Far worse was their hopelessness.

In the wards, men and women who could no longer walk or crawl lay packed side by side. In a sense, they were already dead, having nothing to live for. And that was true even of some who had been declared cured – so strong was the centuries-old stigma of this disease.

One young man, given a clean bill of health, had left the colony to return home, only to find out through a third party that the girl he loved wanted nothing more to do with him. His old friends crossed to the other side of the road when they saw him coming, and his own brothers and sisters refused to eat with him. His mother suggested that he move to a faraway place and take a new name. In the end, he returned to Santa Isabel. "Here I won't have to lie about my identity," he explained. There were several like him in the colony.

As for the law, it treated them all as *de facto* criminals. At Santa Isabel, convicted murderers lived on an equal footing with everyone else. Some had contracted leprosy while in prison for their crime; others had killed fellow patients. One young man had stabbed his fiancée to death the same day he was diagnosed – she had just told him she was leaving him because he was a leper. Paraguayan judges tended to deal with such cases pragmatically: since confinement in a leper colony already amounted to a life sentence, it would be an empty formality to imprison them elsewhere.

As director of agriculture at Santa Isabel, Heiner was responsible for running the food cooperative for the colony's four hundred patients. Whatever it produced was distributed to supplement the patients' government rations, which lacked vegetables and meat and were often inedible. (On occasion they also "failed to arrive," though Heiner suspected this had more to do with the commissary officer's greed than with poor service or delivery problems.)

Heiner did not realize it at first, but as director of agriculture he was an important figure in colony life. At the time, the best weapon in fighting leprosy was good nutrition, and the co-op may have done more to preserve health than the colony's doctors did. It also was one of the few places at Santa Isabel where a patient could earn a regular income, since there were funds to hire patients as field hands.

In time he got to know and love the men who worked under him. Despite their frequent fights over food and women, they could also be selfless, and would help each other. Heiner enjoyed their black humor as well. Speaking of poisonous snakes, one boasted that no one ever got bitten in the colony. "Do you think they want to become lepers too? Of course, it's not our disease they're scared of. It's the sulfa drugs we take. We stink so much they'd never bite us!"

That part was true: the patients did stink terribly. It made Heiner think of the story Tata had told him as a child – the story of Francis of Assisi and the leper. The son of a wealthy man, Francis had grown up despising the poor and diseased. Whenever he saw a leper, even from far off, he would hold his nose. But then one day, while riding outside Assisi, he had seen a sore-covered leper on the side of the road. Suddenly, as if gripped by a power stronger than himself, he had dismounted his horse and embraced and kissed the man. And this act of compassion had set off the change that made him a saint.

At Santa Isabel, Heiner thought a lot about Francis. But he never got off his horse and embraced a leper. Unlike the saint, he was too afraid of getting infected. If a man caught leprosy, he could be confined to the colony permanently. (Leprosy was then believed to be contagious — after all, that was why the lepers were quarantined in Santa Isabel — and the drug dapsone, which cures the disease, would only be introduced here two years after Heiner left.) And so he kept his distance from the men and women under him, assigning them work from the saddle of his horse and dropping their pay and supplies into an extended poncho. He always avoided their touch — for Annemarie and the children. Later he would accuse himself of having been unnecessarily cold.

At night, alone in his cabin, one of the administration huts some distance from the wards, he tormented himself with such thoughts for hours on end. He also despaired about Primavera: that he would never be allowed back; that he would never see his family again. Sometimes he fantasized that perhaps it could be worked out. "If only they would let me live a quiet life with my family! Then I would gladly promise not to cause any more trouble." But such thoughts usually lasted only a few moments. Deep down, he knew the only thing that Hans would ever accept from him was a statement of unconditional loyalty — and he would never, ever give that. To do that, he felt, would be to betray everything.

The one thread he clung to was Annemarie's faithfulness to him, which he never doubted, even though for the first months at Santa Isabel he heard from her infrequently. She was living at the edge of Primavera with Anni, Luise, and Dorli — all four women were under discipline – and working with them in the laundry. Though both she and Anni were pregnant, they were lifting heavy bundles of wet clothing for several hours each day – a job which would continue to within a month of the baby's birth.

To Annemarie, as for Heiner, their separation was excruciating. She often thought as she worked (she told him later) of the day she had first come to the Sparhof. Of Tata's death, and Eberhard's welcome – of the joy and unity she had sensed. Now the tension was almost unbearable. On the one side, she was of one heart with Heiner, especially in his opposition to the cold and loveless spirit that had taken over the community. On the other, she felt torn by her loyalty to her calling and to her brothers and sisters in the community. "I know for sure that I was called to live here," she thought. "And so I must believe that the truth, whatever it is, will come out in the end."

In February 1945, Hans and Georg deemed Annemarie sufficiently chastened, and allowed her to move back with her children. She had been separated from them for fifteen weeks. From then on, she wrote to Heiner more regularly. Her letters often concerned their children. "When I saw the children again for the first time after my months away," she wrote, "they all came running to me – except Christoph. He followed quietly and solemnly, with beaming eyes, expecting a big hug just like the others." A month later, she wrote from the hospital to announce the new baby. It was a girl, and she had named her Lisa, a form of "Else" – in memory of Tata.

But as time went on, her letters took on another tone. Some were even severe, as when she reproached him for being stubborn. In order to return to the community, she had agreed to remain loyal to it absolutely, and that is what she did. (Emmy, too, had resolved to leave behind all "dissention," and wrote to Hardy begging him to abandon his "scruples" so he could come home: "We really should be able to forget!") Even so, what mattered most to Heiner was the fact that she kept sharing her thoughts with him. It was his one link to life – to his wife, to his son and his daughters. He replied to every letter as soon as he could, and whenever he had saved up enough to buy something, he sent gifts to the children too.

Ten months passed. Auschwitz was liberated, Berlin conquered and divided, Hiroshima incinerated. Then peace was proclaimed. To Heiner in Santa Isabel, the noise of these events came faintly and belatedly, like far-off thunder. Christmas was approaching; it would mark more than a year since he had seen his family. Then, out of the blue, a telegram arrived. It was from Primavera, and it told him to come home.

Heiner was elated at the thought of spending Christmas with his family. During the next days, he bought something for each of the children. They had grown up without him for a whole year. Roswith was six now, and Christoph five. He had to make the most of his long-awaited homecoming, to spare nothing in showing them that he loved them more than ever.

On December 23 – it was his thirty-second birthday – he began the two-day trip home, taking the boat upriver from Asunción. At the dock, he found Albert, a man from Primavera, waiting for him. Heiner hurried to greet him, but Albert was strangely reserved. Heiner sensed immediately that something was wrong, and his Christmas joy vanished.

They drove in silence until they got to a field just outside Primavera, where Albert let the horses graze until nightfall. Then he led Heiner to a spot by the gatehouse. "Wait here. I'll be back." Heiner sat in the dark, waiting. Two hours passed. Then Peter, a man Heiner knew well from Ashton Fields days, was standing in front of him, and telling him to follow. They went to an outlying shack where equipment for beekeeping was stored. "You'll find everything you need there," Peter said, and then he was gone.

Christmas Eve had always been the high point of the holidays. A few days before it, the Arnold children would crowd together, leaving one bedroom empty for their mother to set up shop. This was the Christmas Room, and she kept it under lock and key—just as her mother had done when she was a girl.

On Christmas Eve, after sunset, she would tell Heiner to ring the Christmas bell. The children would come in, awestruck and hushed, staring at the lighted tree and the bulging tablecloth-covered mounds at its base. Those were the gifts, and each child got one, carefully selected and almost always handmade. Afterward, Heiner would read the Christmas story, and they would sing carols together until the children's bedtime.

But tonight, on this Christmas Eve, Heiner could only imagine them. He sat in the dark, defeated. They were only a few hundred yards away! Had he traveled two whole days to get here, for this—a lonely night in the beekeeper's shack? He slumped, so fatigued that he was unable to stir. His mind wandered. He recalled that it was the eleventh anniversary of their engagement. It all seemed so distant now—that moonlit walk, that celebration at Silum.

Finally he lit a candle from his bag and looked around. No bed had been prepared, though there was a sack of straw he could use as a mattress. Hours later, he fell asleep.

Heiner awoke on Christmas Day and went outside. He was still alone. All morning he waited, and then all afternoon. The hours dragged by. Evening came, and a sleepless night. What were they planning? Why had they called him home? Could it really be that they had forgotten he was here? Two more days passed—an eternity—and still no visitors came, or even a message.

On the third day, Hans and Georg appeared in the clearing. They did not explain why they had called Heiner home, nor did they so much as mention the way he had just spent Christmas. But Heiner had something else on his mind. "If I'm gone from Santa Isabel any longer without giving notice, I'll be putting my job in danger—and it wasn't easy to get."

Hans grew livid. "If that is all you have to say for yourself, there's no point in even talking with you!" he said as the two men turned away.

That evening, Heiner was instructed to go to the cabin behind the Primavera hospital. After a short wait, Annemarie came in — his Annemarie, whom he had not seen for over a year. She was carrying Lisa, who had been born in his absence. Lisa was nine months old, and he had never even laid eyes on her till now.

Annemarie laid the baby in his arms and looked at Heiner searchingly, desperate for a sign that their separation might soon be over. She noted his blank expression and his awkwardness. He was so unlike the husband she had known. "Are you a stone?" she chided him suddenly. "Can't you break down even now?"

But Heiner couldn't — he was simply unable to respond. His chest was heaving with pain and confusion, yet sometime during the last hellish months, he had lost the ability to shed tears. He could still weep inside — he was weeping this very moment. But how should Annemarie know that?

She told him she was only to show him the baby, and then go. After three minutes, she took the baby back from him and strode out, slamming the door behind her. Heiner was crushed. That evening, he was called in for questions by Primavera's leadership committee; still he could say nothing. He spent another endless night by himself — and then left the next morning for the riverboat, and the lepers in Sapucai.

◆ ◆ ◆

The year 1946 began, and from January to June, Heiner killed time at the leper colony. The nights alone in his hut were the worst. How many years would they keep him from his family? He longed to see Annemarie; to take her into his arms. It was true that she had seemed distant to him at Christmas. But he was sure it was frustration rather than coldness. After all, she was raising five children single-handedly. And no matter how much she understood his convictions — his stubbornness, as Primavera saw it — they were still keeping him from her, and from the community. He fought the anger as it rose in him.

But if Heiner often felt desperate, his coworkers would not have known it. They saw him as a competent and understanding overseer, and noticed how the cooperative thrived under his direction. They weren't the only ones to appreciate his management. Soon the American Mission to Lepers heard about his work, and its director, a Dr. Eugene Kellersberger, traveled to Sapucai to meet Heiner. Perhaps the cooperative's success could be transplanted to other colonies. The visit took place, and Dr. Kellersberger and his wife took to Heiner immediately. Afterward they corresponded, and soon counted Heiner as a friend.

Oddly, it was this friendship that convinced Hans to invite Heiner back home. Dr. Kellersberger had come to Primavera to look over the hospital, and he hinted that his organization might be able to fund the community's leprosy work. Hans—and Cyril, now head surgeon—knew such financial support could transform the clinic. Up till now they had barely been able to afford the most basic drugs and supplies. Hopes for a big donation soared. But Dr. Kellersberger's friendship with Heiner caused Primavera's leaders worry. What if he began to inquire why Heiner was away? Hans hastened to summon Heiner home.

This time as he traveled upriver, Heiner had no illusions. He was isolated in the same shack as before. He did odd jobs—clearing brush, repairing fences, and maintaining the hives. Francis Beels, the beekeeper, brought him his food. A gentle, kindly man, Francis ignored orders not to talk with him. But otherwise it was a lonely existence, and he saw no one else. No one, that is, except the children he saw through his binoculars. Though the yard they played in was about a quarter of a mile away, they were still visible enough to tantalize him as he tried to make out which were his. Roswith, Christoph, Anneli, Edith—what did they look like after all this time?

Two more months passed, and at long last the day came when Hans appeared at the shack and announced that Heiner could now join his family. He was still in disgrace as a member, Hans warned him, but that did not matter to Heiner. His happiness at the prospect of rejoining his family was too enormous.

It was a jubilant reunion, though not for one-year-old Lisa, who had never seen a man at the table before. When she saw Heiner sit down by her mother, she burst into tears and hid her face. Five-year-old Christoph, on the other hand, sat brimming with happiness and pride. For twenty months, he had stayed devoted to his father—so much so that when he refused to obey, Annemarie could bring him round just by showing him Heiner's picture. "Your Papa wouldn't like it," she'd tell him, and he'd give in.

Now, on the first morning his father was back, Christoph insisted on taking him right through the middle of Primavera to pick up their allotment of breakfast at the communal kitchen. Ignoring the disapproving stares, the boy waved his arms to everyone they met. "Papa is back! My Papa is back!"

Fatherhood

When Heiner returned home in August 1946, no fatted calves were killed. To most in Primavera, his long absence had made him a stranger, even to the young English members who had once looked to him for guidance. Now they were farm bosses, accountants, and hospital administrators – part of the establishment. And immersed in their work, they were too busy to concern themselves with what had happened to him. The vast majority knew next to nothing about his year and a half at Sapucai, or about his disastrous Christmas visit. Newer members did not even know why he had been away. Since both he and Annemarie were determined to forgive fully and to avoid sowing mistrust toward their fellow members, they never talked about what happened to anyone. This silence extended to their own children, who would be adults before they dared to ask their father why he had been gone. Of those who had been banished in October 1944, Heiner was the last to be allowed back. (Dorli never returned.) Fritz, Hardy, Bruce, and Peter were all back with their families, and Emmy was back too, after a three-month isolation.

But Mama was not her old self, Heiner noticed. Ever since the very first years in Sannerz, she had been the community's housemother, looking out for guests, caring for whoever was sick, and attending to the needs of the women, children, and babies. On her return, deemed unfit for this kind of service, she had at first been assigned by Hans to work as an orderly in the hospital—even on Sundays, and even though she was over sixty.

Hans took something else away from Emmy too: her treasured collection of Eberhard's papers, several volumes of correspondence from the time of their courtship, and her diary of the last days before his death in Darmstadt. Telling her, "they're not good for you," he locked them away in what he dubbed "the poison cupboard."

In a similar vein, Hans saw to it that the Arnolds were not housed near each other, but divided between Primavera's two villages. "We must see to it that they never live in the same place again," he told Georg. He also warned Heiner and Fritz not to resume their earlier friendship, saying, "It's clear that you are a bad influence on each other." Heiner talked to Fritz anyway, but only when no one was watching. The two never entered each other's houses.

What hurt Heiner most was not the prohibition on their friendship, but that Fritz (like others of the sixteen) was in obvious inner need and had no one to look out for him. There was little he could do about it, though. Stripped of his membership, he had no voice in decision-making.

In one way, Heiner was satisfied with this arrangement. As long as Primavera stayed as it was now, he had no desire to be a member again. He remembered too well his mother's scream in the meeting and Norah's tears as she ran after the wagon that was taking her children away. "I can never be party to such things," Heiner thought.

And so he threw himself into making up for lost time with his children. He taught them how to ride and how to care for a horse. How to cut and stack wood. How to lay a fire. In the evenings, he played to them (he had taught himself the violin) or held them on his lap as Annemarie read them stories or sang them lullabies.

Aside from playing, Heiner took up another hobby: making violins. He sent Christoph and Roswith in search of the best seasoned planks and then, as they watched, showed them how to bend the side strips and carve the belly. His tools were crude, and he had to experiment with the tropical woods. Paraguay had no beech or spruce. But the violins he turned out, while not concert-class, were playable. And that was all that mattered to Primavera's musicians.

Heiner's children took it for granted that their father could do or repair anything. They had the same confidence in his skills as a gardener, and here they may not have been far off. In a climate where European roses withered, he had soon planted the gardens around the house with thriving bushes, one displaying ten different colors of bloom. Visitors to Primavera were brought to admire the blossoms, and one – Mrs. Kellersberger – demanded Heiner reveal the secret of his success. (The trick was grafting, using a hardy native rose as the stock.)

Heiner threw himself into his daily work. He had his old job of wagoning again, which also meant maintaining the stables and training the horses. Most of the time, his errands took him back and forth on the wooded track between Primavera's two villages. But once in a while there were longer trips, such as pick-ups to make from the river port at Rosario.

One of these trips became a favorite family story. Heiner had gone to Rosario to pick up a woman from Montevideo – and not just any woman, but a wealthy European. She had expressed interest in supporting Primavera's hospital, and it was Heiner's task to make a positive first impression.

Trouble began the moment the woman stepped off the riverboat. She was dressed as if she were driving to a fashionable luncheon rather than into the jungle, and as soon as she got into the wagon she started complaining about the mud and the mosquitoes. The wagon, which had no springs, lurched through ruts, puddles and washouts. Ducking was a constant necessity because of low-hanging lianas, and detours around fallen trees made an already long journey even longer. As the sun climbed and the day went on – it was thirty-seven miles from Rosario to Primavera – the temperature rose, and so did the woman's ire.

Suddenly the wagon slid into a mud hole, sinking right down to its axles. One of the horses panicked and got stuck too, and now Heiner was forced to ask his passenger to get out. She flew into a tantrum—the mud would ruin her shoes—but Heiner persuaded her that she had no choice. Then he set to prying out the horse, using a long pole as a lever. While he worked, she perspired, ranted, and wept. Finally, both horse and wagon were free, and they could continue their journey.

Heiner drove on for several miles, until—as luck would have it—they had to stop again. This time the problem was more serious than a mud hole: one of the horses collapsed and died. Finally, late in the evening, they pulled up to the Primavera gatehouse. Heiner gave a sigh—they were finally there. But his passenger was beside herself and demanded a shower and a refrigerator at once. Informed that neither was to be had, she announced her intention to leave again the very next day.

Needless to say, no one dared ask about the hoped-for loan, which—no surprise—never materialized. To Heiner's relief, someone else had the pleasure of driving her back.

On shorter trips, Heiner often brought one of the children along—never before had he been able to spend so much time with them, and he reveled in the opportunity. When it was Christoph, Heiner spent the journey teaching him how to drive. Though the boy was only six, he soon had learned the basics, and Heiner would hand him the reins for long stretches.

Once as they were passing through the jungle, a mane wolf trotted out onto the trail in front of them. The horses shied, then bolted. Heiner grabbed the reins from Christoph and threw him into the back of the wagon, where he would be safest. "Hold on!" he yelled. He himself stood crouched in the box like a charioteer, feet pressed against the cleat and elbows locked, pulling against the reins with all his weight. He kept his head just high enough to see over the horses but no higher because of the low branches hurtling over him.

The horses ran on and on. Heiner kept speaking to them calmly and soothingly while trying to slow them by pulling the reins with every ounce of his strength. Finally, he managed to slow them to a controlled trot—and to wipe the sweat streaming from his forehead. It was then that Christoph bounced from the back of the wagon, elated over the wildest ride he had ever had and bursting with pride at his father's skill in driving.

A less dramatic and far unhappier trip took place the time they took the monkey back to the jungle. A gift to Heiner from a Paraguayan friend, the animal was tame and clean and had made a good pet. But unfortunately it was fond of the neighbor's tomatoes, and eventually the man lost his patience. "The monkey must go," he told Heiner one day. "If it doesn't, I'll kill it."

Heiner told the children that they would have to release the monkey into the wild, and after a tearful farewell from the girls, he set out into the jungle with Christoph. Several miles in, they left the monkey under a tree, said goodbye, and headed home. A surprise awaited them when they arrived. On the doorstep stood the monkey, its tiny body trembling with laughter. Further attempts were equally unsuccessful, until they finally took the monkey to a river several miles away and rowed it to the opposite bank. It never came back.

Heiner's trip (all that trouble just to avoid killing a monkey!) raised eyebrows in Primavera. In this place where every foot of farmland had to be wrested from the forest, a place of snakes and locusts and insect-borne diseases, many saw nature solely as a hostile force. By necessity, killing had become part of daily life, but from here it was a short leap to killing for the thrill of it. At least among the community's boys and young men, brutality to animals had become a mark of machismo.

A lifelong farmer, Heiner was no sentimentalist, but he could not tolerate such an attitude. Once he caught several boys playfully shooting at an owl with their slingshots until it died. "Who do you think made that bird?" he demanded. "Was it any of you? Can any of you bring it back to life?" He glared at them. "If you can't, then who gives you the right to kill it?"

A few boys looked up, embarrassed and remorseful. But most stared right past him, their faces stony and sullen. To Heiner, that was the worst of it: not the dead owl, but their hardness. Who had they learned it from, and how could it be dissolved?

Incidents like these strengthened Heiner's resolve to raise his own family differently. Without preaching, he instilled in them a reverence for nature and for the Creator behind nature. Often he told them stories about his boyhood in Sannerz.

Once one of the houseguests had cornered Hans-Hermann and asked him where Heiner kept his dog. Hans-Hermann, then ten, worried that the man had malicious intentions, but told himself it was none of his business and agreed to show him. The next day the dog died of poisoning. When Hans-Hermann confessed his role in what had happened, Eberhard was stern. "You are guilty of taking innocent life. Today you have lost your childhood." (Afterward, Hans-Hermann had confided to Heiner that although he was a little sorry to have lost his childhood, he was glad to be a grownup now.)

Heiner also told tales of adventure, often from the German novelist Karl May. The heroes of these tales were a varied lot—desert sheiks, Afghan tribesmen, noble Sioux warriors. But all of them modeled chivalric values: honesty, bravery, and generosity.

Above all, he tried to teach by example, as during a rash of armed burglaries at Primavera. The thieves, Paraguayan natives, would come at night and steal tools, clothes, or household utensils, or—in the case of Hans-Hermann and Gertrud's house—everything they could find. Once they fired their guns right into a house, just missing a sleeper by inches and wounding a young man who had rushed to the door.

So when Heiner's retriever began barking furiously one night, waking the whole family, he suspected the worst. Lighting a storm lantern, he went outside to investigate. Sure enough, he saw a figure running. He loosed the dog and followed its barks, and found it snarling at the base of a tree.

Heiner held up the lantern and saw the fugitive, an unarmed man, who—to Heiner's amusement—was trembling with fear. Calling off the dog, Heiner coaxed the man to come down and invited him to the house, where he offered him a meal. Over food, the man relaxed and told his story piece by piece. He was from a nearby village, the sole breadwinner of a large family, and he was not making ends meet. As he spoke, the children, who had all crowded into the living room, watched him with a mixture of fascination and fear. After the man left Heiner said to them, "God loves everybody. But especially people like him."

Heiner and Annemarie had an open door. One who came often was Günther Homann, a tall, bookish bachelor who worked as Primavera's librarian. In a community that idolized the gregarious and capable, Günther was not popular; even the children made fun of him. But he knew he was welcome at the Arnolds. So did Niklaus, a shy stutterer, and Friedel, the disabled man who had been at Heiner's side the day the Nazis raided the Sparhof. Little was said as the men sat in the arbor with their maté, but the solidarity they felt spoke louder than any words.

The Arnold home was not conventionally religious: there was no regular family prayer, and no Bible reading. No grace was said at meals. Still, there was never any doubt about the center of the family's life. If Heiner overheard a nasty or degrading comment from one of his children, a row was sure to follow—and he could thunder. Later he would ask them, "How could you? Have you forgotten about Jesus?" They knew what he meant without any further explanation, and were ashamed.

Heiner was their security, especially at night, which terrified them. When Primavera's electric power was turned off at ten o'clock, everything went black. Then the night howls of the mane wolf and the wavering tremolo of the *Totenvogel*, or "death bird," could be heard—and what they didn't hear, they imagined. Heiner taught them a song to comfort them:

> When shadows hide the sun,
> and lions roaring come,
> I know that still in darkness deep
> my Jesus watch will keep.

Heiner was now a full member of the community again, thanks to Adolf Braun, a comrade since Sannerz days. Recently named as a leader of Primavera, he visited Heiner and Annemarie evening after evening and tried to argue him into becoming a member again. Hans and Georg didn't stop these efforts. Perhaps they felt Heiner no longer posed a threat, or perhaps it was simply that their attention had shifted. (Now that the war was over, the two made back-to-back year-long journeys to Europe. Apart from visiting Wheathill, the five-year-old Bruderhof in England, they also sought to arrange with the German government to send sixty war orphans to Primavera; in the end the Germans sent 114 refugees instead.) Whatever the case, after several weeks Adolf's persistence eventually paid off, and Heiner asked the community to reaccept him, which they did. With that, his long exile officially came to an end.

He would never be able to understand everything that had happened—especially why, when he was at Sapucai, Hans and Georg had treated him as they did. But that didn't matter now; all he wanted was to forgive them and to be forgiven. After all these years during which the cause had been held back, wasn't it high time they trusted each other and got on with life? Besides, Heiner was convinced that he was to blame too. "If I had stayed completely faithful to the call I received as a boy, things could never have gone so far wrong," he told himself. "That's what I repented for while working in the leper colony—not for opposing Hans and Georg, even if that's why they sent me away."

28

Marianne

ONE EVENING AT THE END OF July 1947, Heiner took the children outside their house for a talk. He led them to the picnic table, saying it was a good night for stargazing. Sitting side by side, they stared up at the Southern Cross and the Milky Way sweeping vast and speckled from horizon to horizon.

Heiner said nothing. He just pointed at the stars. Then, as they watched, they saw a shooting star. "God might send us a baby soon," he told the children. "Maybe that was the little soul coming down." They were silent, staring, transfixed with awe. Up there among the stars was their Opa, Eberhard. So was Tata, and Emmy Maria, whose birthday they celebrated every year. Would the baby come down to them from up there?

Heiner's thoughts were in the hospital, where he had taken Annemarie that morning. "Hospital" was perhaps too grandiose a name for it. A two-story structure built of air-dried bricks, it had room for a dozen beds, a few exam rooms, a surgery, a pharmacy, and a lab. Nearby stood a shed with a fireplace where instruments were sterilized in boiling water.

It was a primitive setup, but well-staffed and well-run, and Heiner knew that Annemarie was in good hands. Phyllis, the midwife, had delivered their last three babies, and today she had welcomed

Annemarie with such warmth and cheer. And Annemarie herself had left the house confident and happy. "I can't wait," Heiner thought.

Annemarie, in the meantime, was trying to sleep. All day the labor pangs had come and gone—as they would all the night, and all the next day as well. "I began to feel discouraged," she wrote in her diary. "When would this little being within me come into the world?"

On the evening of the second day, a new series of contractions began, more painful than the first and lasting without any real break for the next twenty hours.

"I had strong labor pangs throughout—so strong that we were sure from hour to hour that the baby would be born. Heiner was up all night; I could not be without him. In the morning I felt exhausted. Phyllis had given me something to hasten matters, but it had been of no use. Ruth came, and I begged her to bring the child to birth by artificial means. On examination, she found that the child was not in the right position—that was why I had not given birth."

For Heiner, it was becoming a waking nightmare. During her first six births, Annemarie had always been brave. But now, as her labor stretched on, she became desperate. Never had he seen her in such a state. She begged; she pleaded; she wept for help. When he had gone to the doctors to ask them to do something—anything—they had told him it was best to let nature take its course. He trusted their judgment but could not bear to see Annemarie suffer. Love for her, and a sense of responsibility—as the baby's father, he had caused all this—swept over him, wave after wave.

Annemarie wrote in her diary: "After that came the most agonizing hours, for while the pangs grew increasingly stronger and more frequent, I now knew that they would do nothing. All that pain, as if wasted. Finally, the doctors decided to deliver the baby under general anesthesia, with the help of forceps. But first they had to sterilize the instruments by boiling them for twenty minutes. The wait seemed like an eternity.

"When at last everything was ready, they put the ether mask on me and told me to breathe deeply and quietly. I could still feel the beginning of the next labor pang as I sank deeper and deeper into unconsciousness. My one thought was that now I could escape the pains. Then I knew no more."

Now Heiner was standing at her head, gripping her hand. The doctors—Cyril and Ruth—were working to get the baby out with forceps. The baby lay wrong, with a face presentation. They tried for what seemed like hours, then suddenly grew alarmed. Annemarie was turning bluish. She had stopped breathing.

They broke off the operation at once and yanked the ether-soaked wad from her nose so that she would wake up. Cyril examined her. "Her heart has given way!"

Seconds ticked by. Then Annemarie started breathing again, and coming out of the ether. Relief ran around the room. But Cyril was still anxious. "I can't help her with the birth anymore. It's too late."

As soon as Annemarie woke up, sharp pains wracked her, and she pleaded for help. Heiner turned to Cyril. "Can't you do a Caesarean?"

Cyril shook his head. "Her heart won't stand the anesthetic. There's too big a risk of losing her."

Then came the moment Heiner would never forget: Cyril asked him to step outside. "The only way to save Annemarie is to abort the baby," he said bluntly. "If we don't, both will surely die."

Heiner looked at him dumbfounded, and fled outside into the banana plantation behind the hospital. It was pitch dark and drizzling. He had hardly ever felt so lonely, not even in the leper colony, although the delivery room was full of people eager to help. An abortion? It was out of the question, especially now. How could he ever let their baby be dismembered? The very idea was evil; it sickened him. "But Cyril says Annemarie is dying," he thought.

Heiner lifted his face into the blackness and the rain. He wept and prayed as he had never wept or prayed before. "God, show me your will. May your will alone be done." He went back into the hospital, and ran into Cyril. "The baby can be aborted painlessly," Cyril repeated. "It's the only way to save Annemarie's life." Heiner said nothing, but walked past him into the delivery room.

"I awoke from the ether with a jolt," Annemarie wrote later. "High above me, heads and bodies were moving here and there — Moni, Cyril, Phyllis, Ruth — and the craziest pangs seemed to tear me to pieces, allowing me only the shortest intervals of relief. I didn't know what it meant, or if the baby had been born. Then I heard a voice say, 'It won't be long now,' and realized that they were all standing around me, helpless. I was in so much pain, and every minute seemed endless.

"Suddenly the child was born, and voices were exclaiming, 'A girl, a girl!'

"'She is alive,' Cyril added. I wondered what he meant. Then, straining every nerve, I kept on until the birth had finished its course, and at long last the agony ceased — for the first time in sixty hours.

"I was not in any state to see the baby, but fell asleep again right away. When I awoke, I finally saw her. There was a blue-black mark on her head from the instruments, and her little face had suffered too — it was swollen, the lips especially. She had swallowed a lot of fluid and breathed with a snoring sound, as though something was still lodged in her windpipe. The hospital had no bottled oxygen, and no way to suction out the fluid. They told me she had to be kept quiet. They did not want to wash her, but let her lie undisturbed.

"In spite of all this, there she was — our baby, lying in the crib. She looked big and strong, at least nine pounds, and healthy, or so I thought. I was happy that she was a girl.

"I kept falling asleep — I could hardly move my body from exhaustion. Once as I woke up, Phyllis was lifting her, and saying with satisfaction, 'She has soiled everything — her blanket, booties, everything.' And then I saw how round her legs were, with little folds, and

I saw her feet. Her little chest too—it was broad and round. That was the only time I saw her. Then they tucked her under the blanket again.

"At times her cry was like that of a strong baby. But other times it was high, like the cry of a little kitten. Her breathing often sounded plaintive and whimpering. I could not see her face.

"Heiner was there. He was so happy to see me. He told me what had happened, and we decided to name the baby Marianne. Then I slept—a deep, refreshing sleep.

"When I woke again, I couldn't see the baby, but her breathing sounded very fast to me. Was she in danger? I was terrified. The doctors reassured me. They even said that the swelling of her face was going down. Ruth pushed the crib closer so I could see her face. She lay on her side, with chubby cheeks, a wide nose, a triangular mouth, a determined chin, and two well-formed little ears.

"How I longed to have her in my arms, to feel her little body and breathe in the delicate fragrance that belongs only to a newborn child!

"I fell asleep again, and woke in the middle of the night. Heiner and Emmy and Ruth were in the room with me. The generator had gone off for the night, so there was only an oil lamp. Heiner pushed the crib next to my bed. Marianne's face looked all wrong. Or was it just the lamplight? They lit a second lamp to see better. It was true— her color was terribly dark.

"There was not much we could do. Ruth tried to clean Marianne's throat by sucking through a thin rubber tube. The baby opened her eyes. Ruth said, 'Look—she's trying to nurse on the tube.' We told each other that it was a good sign.

"Minutes passed, and Ruth felt the baby's color had improved. I could not see much difference, but I was only too glad to believe her. Then the sound of her breathing grew softer and softer.

"Filled with fear, I said, 'Her breath is so shallow.' Ruth asked Heiner to fetch Cyril. Then, as I watched, Marianne closed her eyes. Her breathing became quieter and quieter, and then died away. Her little chest did not rise again. 'She's stopped breathing!' I cried out. 'She's stopped breathing!'

"Ruth hastened to give her an injection of adrenaline, hoping to start her heart again. Cyril rushed in, and listened for a long time with a stethoscope. I knew already—yet I was still hoping they would say they had found some sign of life.

"But they didn't. There she lay, as if asleep. I kept looking at her, watching, waiting to see if she might take another breath after all.

"Mama picked her up and put her into my arms. I felt her weight. Her hands were already cool, but her neck and cheeks were warm. I can still feel her. Her legs, too, were quite warm. It was the first and the last time I had her in my arms. I could not get my fill of looking at my beloved child. And it was so hard to grasp that this little girl, so greatly longed-for, born under such pain, had now left us before we had even gotten to know her, before we knew what kind of person she would be.

"I held her as long as I could. I looked at her again and again. Then came the final parting. Heiner's mother carried her out of the room to prepare her body for burial. My heart felt as if something were tearing it.

"How glad I was that in those hard, hard hours my dear Heiner was with me, and that our souls were now so close together! He looked so disconsolate. How he had looked forward to holding a little baby again, for the first time in four years! He had been far away in Sapucai when Lisa was born.

"Visitors came. They said how happy they were that I was still alive. It was only then that I gradually understood how dangerous it all had been.

"When I awoke the next morning, our room was quiet and empty. There was no baby. In a burst it all rushed back into my mind. I looked out the window. It was raining. It rained and rained. I looked out at the somber autumn landscape—the bare linden trees, the brown meadows, a few last roses. Now and then I heard the cry of birds. And in my room, the oppressive silence, the bare white walls."

◆ ◆ ◆

Now that the baby was gone, Heiner felt a sudden spasm of guilt. At the time of the birth, Annemarie had taken all his attention. As her labor had continued hour after hour, the danger mounting, he had despaired of her survival. And then the baby had come so quickly and naturally—a miracle. Of course he had been glad about the baby, but all his thoughts were with Annemarie. A feeling of gratitude had surged through him, so intense that it hurt. "She is alive!" he thought. "And the baby also . . ." But as long as Annemarie had been in danger, he had thought only of her, and hardly at all of Marianne. He had not even held the baby. He had neglected her. Now she was gone.

He planned to tell the children at breakfast. He knew it would be hard—for the last two days, they had been waiting for him, full of anticipation, every time he came back from the hospital. Each time they had met him with such eager questions. Little Anneli had been telling everyone, "Mama has gone to heaven, to Mary in order to get the baby." On the second day, she had become impatient, demanding. "Why isn't it here yet? Is God still finishing it?" When at last Heiner had announced that they had a little sister, the children had gone wild with excitement.

His step slowed as he approached the house. How should he break the news? Then they were rushing out to meet him, clamoring and clinging all over him. "How did she sleep last night?" Roswith wanted to know.

"Come. Let's go inside and sit down for breakfast," he told her.

"But Papa, you only have to say yes or no. Did she sleep well or not?" Roswith insisted.

Heiner took the chair at the head of the table, while Anna, the baby-sitter, took the chair at the other end. As she sat down, the children saw that tears were streaming down her face. They looked to Heiner for an explanation.

"Children," he said, "I have to tell you that your little sister went back to heaven."

Christoph's eyes grew big. "Does that mean she's not our sister anymore?" Roswith started sobbing, and Anneli cried over and over, "Get her back! Get her back!" They all wept.

Later, Heiner found Roswith in the woods picking wildflowers for a bouquet. He asked her if she wanted to visit the baby. "Marianne's soul has gone up to heaven," he explained. "But her body is still here on earth, and we can see her now, if you would like to."

Marianne was lying on a table in a tiny casket, wearing a garland and holding roses in her hand. Someone had decorated the room with palm branches, and the fronds seemed to bend protectively over the baby. Roswith's face beamed as she took in the sight—it struck her, she said later, as a picture of heaven. "She's only sleeping!" she exclaimed. "When will she wake back up?"

Heiner answered that someday everyone who had died *would* wake again. "Also Opa and Emmy Maria?" Roswith wanted to know. His answer reassured her. After they got home, Roswith told Christoph and her sisters about what she had seen, and in the following days, Heiner often overheard them talking about heaven. They seemed to believe it was a place they all might visit any time.

The funeral was on a Sunday morning, and since the cemetery was a few miles from the hospital, the community went out in wagons. Heiner got up early and visited Annemarie. He told her that Marianne's body was still the same, "sweet and unchanged." Then he went with a heavy heart to close the casket and carry it to the wagon. Like Marianne's room, it had been decorated with palms.

Annemarie, who was in no condition to attend the funeral, watched from the window as the wagons filled with people. Just at that moment, a harsh wailing broke out from the other end of the hospital. As she later found out, it was the family of a Paraguayan woman who had just died after bearing her twentieth child, a still-born. To Annemarie, that wailing – so hopeless of anything beyond its pain – seemed to contain all the misery of an unredeemed earth.

It was raining as the first wagon left – Heiner with the casket, Hardy driving. The procession passed below Annemarie's window in silence. She strained but could see nothing of the little casket as it went by. A few hours later Heiner returned. It was still pouring outside.

"These are incomprehensible days and hours," Annemarie wrote that night in her diary. "Sometimes it all seems so unreal to me, as if it had never happened. And now it is not easy to find the way back to reality, to pick up the broken thread again. It would all seem like a passing dream if I did not remember again and again that our little one had lain in the crib right beside me, so warm and so alive. Marianne! Our so dearly beloved, yet so little-known child."

29

On the Road

FOUR MONTHS AFTER MARIANNE'S DEATH, Fritz was struck in the forehead by a block of wood thrown from a turning lathe. The blow left a gaping wound just above the right eye. Moni rushed to the workshop to bandage him, and soon Cyril was there, too, with a wagon to transport him to the hospital. Despite the severity of his injury, Fritz tried to calm everyone, even joking with his wife. But forty-eight hours later infection set in, and his condition worsened quickly. He was dying.

The community was called, and soon they were standing outside his window singing carols (it was December) and praying for him. Heiner stood at the back and craned his neck. How he longed to see his old friend up close! He decided to ask if he might say goodbye. But when he did, Georg turned him down. Three days later Fritz took his last breath. He was forty-two years old.

The following months were black. But they passed, and a year later Annemarie gave birth to another baby girl. They called her Monika Renate—"Renate" meaning "reborn," in memory of Marianne. Another year passed, and another baby arrived: Else.

Heiner treated both girls with special tenderness—the loss of their sister was still fresh for him and Annemarie. At low moments, they clung to their memories of the time around Marianne's death, when so many in the community had responded from the heart, from Phyllis and Ruth in the hospital to the schoolchildren who had brought bouquets of flowers. That unfeigned warmth gave Heiner hope that somehow, despite all, Primavera would find its way back to its first love. In the meantime, he vowed to re-dedicate himself to supporting others in their joy and grief.

Else was seven weeks old when, in September 1950, Heiner left home on a journey. Christoph accompanied him as far as the river port.

Night had already fallen when the boat pulled away from the bank, and as Heiner waved from the rail, he thought that his son, who was standing alone on the dock embankment, looked terribly sad. The ten-year-old was going to find another long separation from his father hard. Heiner kept calling out "Goodbye! Goodbye!" and at first Christoph answered him confidently. Then his voice grew more uncertain and broke off.

Heiner turned from the rail and reviewed the itinerary before him. In Asunción he would board a plane for Bolivia, fly to Panama, and then on to Havana. Once there, it would only be a short hop to North America.

The purpose for the trip was fundraising. Primavera continued to be desperate for cash. Births and new arrivals from Europe were swelling its population, and the farm, while productive, was not bringing in any income. Meanwhile, the hospital needed money to treat a growing stream of indigent patients. The previous year, the community had sent four men to the United States on a similar mission, and they had raised tens of thousands of dollars and sent back tons of donated goods and farm machinery.

Yet the situation at home was still basically unchanged. Many men wore clothes with more patches than original cloth, the women lacked enough thread to sew on buttons, and the hospital and nursery were continually short of diapers and bed linen. A second attempt must be made, everyone agreed. And who better to send than Heiner, known since childhood for his knack of touching people's hearts?

His traveling companion was to be Will Marchant, a fifty-year-old Englishman whom Heiner had known for a decade, ever since he and his wife Kathleen had joined the community in Ashton Fields in 1940.

Emerging from the plane in Miami, Heiner and Will met the first contacts on their list, a young American couple from Georgia who had come to pick them up. They drove six hundred miles northwest, and arrived at a small peanut farm near Americus, Georgia. This was Koinonia, a faith-based cooperative and one of the first outposts of the great movement against segregation that was just beginning to stir. Koinonia's founder, Clarence Jordan, was a radical Southern Baptist who aimed at putting the Sermon on the Mount into practice in daily life — much like Heiner's parents had in Sannerz. Clarence called his community "a seminary in a cotton patch," and as if that wasn't enough of an affront to his hidebound neighbors, he welcomed blacks as well as whites. (A few years later, segregationists would bomb Koinonia's store and initiate a boycott of its produce. On occasion, shots were even fired into the homes of the cooperative's families.)

It was Heiner's first taste of America, and it excited him. On the surface, the country he was encountering was the land of the Tupperware party, the wood-paneled station wagon, the Burma-Shave billboard. This America had had enough of sacrifice. During the war, it had bled for a righteous cause in Europe and the Pacific. Now the age of thrift and of ration cards was over. Thousands of G.I.s and their brides and babies were settling down, eager to start living the good life.

But underneath the nation's optimism ran a current of disillusionment. Trying as the war years had been, they had seemed to unite the country behind a noble, and ennobling, cause — to defeat the forces of evil, as personified by Adolf Hitler. Now Hitler was gone. But had evil really been defeated? The war had not even succeeded in making the world safe. Russia had the bomb, and Communists were taking over everywhere, from Eastern Europe to Korea.

On the home front, things were not much better. After so much heroism, everyday life seemed petty and drab—and shadowed by uncertainty. Even President Eisenhower was worrying over the "military-industrial complex" and its threat to American freedom. Meanwhile, in the big cities, racism and poverty were slowly pressing out at the seams that would, twenty years later, burst violently apart.

Now, in 1950, the vast majority of young America shrugged off its discontent and hurried to join suburbia. But not all. A few made pilgrimages to San Francisco and Greenwich Village to join the Beat Generation. Hundreds of others turned their backs on middle-class expectations, and set to building up the kind of world *they* wanted: a society based not on money and credentials, but on cooperation and creativity. Communes sprang up everywhere from California to New Jersey. It was a tiny advance wave of the Sixties, and as Heiner and Will went from place to place, meeting new people and answering their questions about Primavera, they found themselves caught up in it.

Clarence proved to be a warm friend, and so did the other people at Koinonia. In fact, their hospitality went further than Heiner would have preferred. He and Will had arrived early in the morning, and when Clarence had brought them to the home where they were to stay, their hosts, a couple, were still in bed. Seeing Heiner and Will, they climbed out and invited them to make themselves at home. "Unappetizing," Heiner remarked to Will as soon as they were alone. Covering the pillow with his handkerchief, and putting his jacket back on, he lay down gingerly on *top* of the bedspread.

They spent half a week there, working at the farm and talking with Clarence about his battle to create an island of integration in the midst of the Deep South. On the last day of their visit, Koinonia gave them their first donation: a hundred dollars. Heiner and Will were amazed, since anyone could see that the cooperative was struggling. And that wasn't all. Clarence offered to drive them up to Washington, DC, so they could begin raising funds in earnest.

They arrived in the capital in the late afternoon. Clarence dropped them off, and now they were on their own with nothing except for a list of names, the money from Koinonia, and their own ingenuity. And there was no time to lose. They knew what high expectations people at home had for their journey—and what a dressing-down the team before them had received when at first they failed to bring in as much as had been hoped for. Heiner could understand such impatience. Still, you couldn't just land in a new city and buttonhole strangers for cash. Heiner and Will decided to set what they felt was a reasonable goal: one thousand dollars in donations every month.

They would have to sweat for it. For starters, their appearance worked against them. In the United States of the fifties, where everyone was clean-shaven except for old men and bums, their beards gave them an outlandish look. Both were unfamiliar with American social conventions, and Heiner, whose English was rusty, had to get used to the language again. Though Heiner knew his way around tractors, neither he nor Will could drive a car.

But Heiner had a plan. Leaving Will in their hostel, he set out to locate a well-placed cousin of his, a certain Thurman Arnold from an American branch of the family. Heiner was nervous—he had never met this relative. But he knew that if Thurman Arnold wished, he could launch him in Washington. A former Yale law professor and federal judge, Thurman had been Assistant Attorney General under Franklin Roosevelt, in whose administration he gained fame by busting war profiteers and monopolies. Now he was founding partner of Arnold & Porter, a powerful Washington law firm.

Heiner knew that Thurman admired Eberhard and his family for their attitude toward Hitler, but he wondered just what his cousin thought of their communal way of life. With Senator Joseph McCarthy's anticommunist crusade in full swing, Thurman might balk at risking his reputation for the sake of the Bruderhof. Having taken on, pro bono, the defense of several alleged Communist sympathizers, he had plenty of trouble on his hands already.

The offices of Arnold & Porter gave Heiner a glimpse of an America far different from the one he had seen in Koinonia. Secretaries looked him over with surprise when he told them whom he had come to see. One of them ushered him into Thurman's office, where personally inscribed portraits of Roosevelt and Truman hung over the desk. Heiner introduced himself.

Thurman shook his hand, a little amused by his strange cousin but also curious about him. "Bourbon or whiskey?" he asked, gesturing for Heiner to help himself from the cart a secretary had pushed in. Heiner hesitated. How big was a standard drink in America? In Paraguay men were expected to drink *caña* by the pint. Taking a wild guess, he dumped several shots of Scotch into his glass and topped it with a little soda. Then he threw down most of the glass, as Thurman watched him with mounting respect.

"Four drinks in one go, and you act like it's nothing!" said Thurman. He had grown up in Wyoming when it was still the Old West, and liked a man who could hold his liquor. By the time they got up from their drinks, he had invited Heiner and Will to stay at his house. He would pay all their expenses, he said, and they could eat for free in the firm's cafeteria.

"I'll bring you home right now, if you like," Thurman said. Leaving the office building, he strode into the middle of the street, right through the rush hour traffic, and commandeered the first taxi — in order to ride one-and-a-half blocks to his car. (This was, Heiner would learn, his usual routine.) Then, after collecting Will from the hostel, they drove out of town into the Virginia suburbs, pulling up to a big house on top of a hill. Thurman ushered his two guests in and introduced them to his wife, Frances.

"A hundred-percent society lady," Heiner thought, as Frances looked over the odd-looking pair with obvious lack of enthusiasm. Heiner, tall and thin, his windblown hair sticking straight up, towered over Will, who was short and wore a pointy beard. Heiner was uncomfortable under her gaze. In the stiff new black suit he had been given for the journey, he was sure he looked like a sailor, or worse, a parson.

At dinner Frances was courteous but cool, and that is how she remained during the next few days. Heiner did his best to put her at ease, but he was nervous that Will would unintentionally undo his efforts—having grown up in a working-class family, Will thought nothing of cleaning his nails at breakfast or taking up the topic of his false teeth during dinner. At such moments Heiner winced inwardly. Frances, fortunately, found it all terrifically amusing, and gradually warmed to her guests.

Soon even Will was popular with her—"he's so unaffected!" But it was Heiner whom she especially befriended. There was something about her husband's cousin—was it his sensitivity?—that she could not but respond to, and before long she was confiding in him as if he were an old friend. Not only did he seem like someone you could trust your fears and troubles with. He always seemed able to cheer you up, even though he'd usually do little more than listen.

Over the next few weeks, Frances's reserve melted. She started pestering Thurman to give Heiner more help. She even took to serving him breakfast in bed.

"Frances, you shouldn't do this," he protested. "You're spoiling me."

"I'll be repaid a thousand times if only you sometimes pray for me."

On her prompting, Thurman not only offered to cover Heiner's travel expenses but also loaned him two hundred dollars to buy a used car, and outfitted him with shirts, a watch, a never-ending supply of Chesterfields, and a bottle of single malt. (Heiner accepted the bottle, but picturing the poverty he had left behind him in Primavera, he could not bring himself to drink it. Eventually he traded it to an acquaintance in return for a cash donation.)

By day, once they got into the city, Heiner and Will separated and went from door to door on foot. It was winter, and bitter cold. In the beginning Heiner used a card file of addresses made by the previous fundraising team, but he was soon wondering if he wouldn't do better picking names at random from the phone book. "Sympathizes with our cause," the card might say under one name. Heiner would knock on the door full of hope—only to find himself coldly dismissed. One man covered his ears before Heiner had even finished his plea, then threw him out.

Even when welcomed in, he made little headway. Rich old ladies would sit him down and tell him how much they admired the Bruderhof. "How wonderful it is that there are people who sacrifice everything out of love to humanity!" they would exclaim, as servants in tails brought in the silver tea service. What donations he did get were small: twenty dollars here, fifty there, and occasionally, a hundred. Heiner's visit with a certain Mrs. Roberts was typical. He had to call three times and mail a letter of introduction before she finally agreed to meet him. At the long-awaited appointment, she listened intently to all he said; in fact, she was visibly moved by what he told her about Primavera. Yet when Heiner finally made his pitch, she said, "It's only sad you've come so late in the year. The money I set aside for donating in 1950 is already gone. Would you come back and see me next year?"

After visits like this it was a relief to come home to the Arnolds, who by now treated Heiner like a son. Thurman might be a prominent Washington lawyer, but at home he was easy-going and absent-minded, his shirt covered with coffee stains and burn holes from his cigars. After dinner he produced whiskey and Cuban cigars, and the four of them talked, Thurman growing expansive as he contemplated the charitable foundations they ought to approach, and how they should manage the nonprofit corporation he was administering for them.

Sometimes the conversation meandered to his firm, and then he would grow fiery, especially when he told Heiner and Will about his pro bono work. It enraged him that "decent people" were losing their jobs and reputations because of a witch hunt fed by anonymous informers. "Washington today is in a state of hysteria!" he ranted. "The cloak and dagger intrigue is unthinkable. It's getting so that attorneys are afraid to touch these cases for fear of losing respectable clients!" At other times, both he and Frances were in tears.

Now and then they took Heiner along to social events, such as the birthday party of Francis Biddle, formerly the primary American judge at Nuremberg. (Heiner was astonished that such a kind-faced old man could have hanged all those generals.) But while many showed interest in Heiner's story, few reached for their pocketbooks – an unexpected blow, since he had hoped that at least here, donations would be easy to come by. These people all seemed so unbelievably rich; even Thurman's cook came to work in a brand-new car. By the end of November, Heiner was falling far short of the thousand-dollar-a-month target.

Will met even less success. He could rarely bring himself to ask for money outright, and tactfulness was not his strong suit – without intending any harm, he once reduced their hostess to tears by teasing her about her bad driving. Tensions between him and Heiner grew. One morning Heiner woke to see someone at the foot of his bed going through his trouser pockets. It was Will. Opening Heiner's wallet, he emptied out what Heiner had collected the day before, and slipped from the room. He did not reappear till late that night. "I guess he also wants to send some money back to Primavera," Heiner joked in a letter home to Annemarie. Still, he worried at the lack of teamwork.

Then came the day when Will up and left. Taking the two hundred dollars that Thurman had loaned, he bought a car with it and told Heiner he wanted to drive to Cleveland. "Why Cleveland?" Heiner wondered. They had a few leads there, but none of them were definite or even promising. Still, Will was determined, so Heiner agreed, consoling himself that Will's absence might be a blessing when it came to his own begging.

Soon afterward, having run out of new addresses in Washington, Heiner concluded it was time to move on. He chose Philadelphia, where he had several likely leads. The Arnolds sent him off with a special farewell breakfast, and he caught a Greyhound north.

On arriving in Philadelphia, Heiner checked in his luggage and went to a nearby post office to send a telegram to Will. At the counter, he reached for his wallet. It was gone.

It was about five o'clock on a frigid December evening. Except for a few coins, he was without money in a strange city. His card file of prospective donors was with his bags in the bus terminal, but his ticket stubs were in the lost wallet, and you couldn't retrieve luggage without them.

More than just a stolen wallet was at stake. How could he explain the loss of its contents—some three hundred dollars—to Primavera? "When they hear about this at home," he thought, "they are bound to summon me back in disgrace." How hard that would be for Annemarie! Had all his efforts been for nothing?

Dejected and aimless, he walked down Arch Street to the Quaker bookstore that served as Primavera's mailing address for North American travelers. Perhaps Samuel Cooper, the manager, would be able to help him. Just then the name Pendle Hill crossed his mind. What kind of place was it? He had no idea except that someone had recommended it to him. Now it beckoned as his only hope. He crossed his fingers that Mr. Cooper would have the address. He did. It was in Wallingford, about half an hour away.

"How much does it cost to get there?" Heiner wanted to know.

"Two dollars."

It might as well have been two hundred dollars, as far as Heiner was concerned. But the manager was bustling forward with an envelope, saying. "I have some mail for you." Inside the letter was cash: exactly two dollars.

Pendle Hill turned out to be a Quaker retreat and study center. Anna Brinton, the director's wife, offered Heiner a bed as soon as she heard he was from Primavera. Then she sailed away, forgetting to tell Heiner that he'd have to work for it. He discovered this soon afterward, when he walked past a notice on the center's main bulletin board: "Heiner Arnold, of the Bruderhof in South America, will be this evening's featured speaker."

The audience numbered several dozen. In his halting English, Heiner told them the story of the community in Paraguay, describing Primavera's need for machinery and equipment, and the hospital's need for drugs. At the end of his presentation, he told the story of his stolen wallet—and found his listeners taking up a collection for him. When he counted it afterward, it came to nine hundred dollars: triple what he had lost. Without the theft of his wallet he would have taken weeks to accomplish so much. What's more, tonight's event had launched him in a whole new circle.

After the meeting ended, an energetic woman of about fifty came up and introduced herself to Heiner as Grace Rhoads. A member of the board at Pendle Hill, Grace was widely known and respected among Friends because of her work for peace and social change. Deeply imbued in Quaker spirituality, she was an admirer of George Fox, the seventeenth-century radical preacher who started the movement. She invited Heiner to spend the weekend at her family farm, and he accepted.

Hereshome, near Moorestown, New Jersey, was not a working farm, though it had over a hundred acres and a hired farming staff. The Rhoads family, who had made their money in manufacturing, had bought it long ago as a kind of countryseat. All five children had come of age years ago, but two—Grace and Betty—still lived here with their mother.

The house was austere but elegant, and smelled of money and tradition: Grace's aunts had been among the last Philadelphia Quakers to wear bonnets and long black dresses. Even now, worldly amusements like alcohol and smoking were forbidden here—though Heiner discovered Betty with a cigarette, furtively blowing smoke up the fireplace chimney. Eighty-year-old Mother Rhoads was treated with a respect bordering on reverence.

They spent most of the weekend by the fireplace in the living room, with Mother Rhoads enthroned in her armchair. As they talked, Heiner gradually learned more about Grace. As a young woman, she had vowed to dedicate her life to peace, and now she had given away most of her inheritance to post-war relief programs and Gandhian ashrams. Along the way she had picked up a Ph.D. in international relations, worked with Jane Addams of Hull House and Pierre Cérésole of the Fellowship of Reconciliation, chaired committees for conscientious objectors, and traveled the world on goodwill missions.

But Grace wanted more than to merely add Primavera to her list of good causes. She peppered Heiner with questions. Was it really possible for people to live in community? Wasn't it an escape from the problems of the world? Would someone like her be welcome in Primavera? "I'm standing at a crossroads in my life," she told Heiner.

One thing that especially bothered her was the way her taxes went to subsidize war. "I cannot go on paying them; my conscience will not allow it. Either I must refuse and risk being jailed, or I must choose voluntary poverty and join your brothers and sisters in Paraguay."

Looking at Grace's earnest face, Heiner was sure that she meant every word. Yet he could not help smiling inside as he tried to imagine her in a thatched hut in Primavera. From childhood on, she had been accustomed to luxury – and yet in her mind, her lifestyle was simple. He also suspected she was more attached to her social life than she realized. And so, in his answers to her questions, Heiner played up the hardships she would meet in Primavera, and stressed that he was here to find donors, not to recruit members.

All the same, he was bursting with an excitement that he could barely conceal. Finally, without planning it, he had begun to do what he had always dreamed of. And though it was unexpected, it made sense. In order to get people to donate, you had to touch their hearts. And once their hearts were touched, they would not stop with giving money. By the end of the weekend, Betty also wanted to know everything about Primavera.

Mother Rhoads listened as her daughters plied Heiner with questions, and as their enthusiasm grew, so did her nervousness. It wasn't him personally; he was a model guest. But surely they wouldn't leave Hereshome for this strange German community. She dismissed the thought. It was too much to bear.

When the weekend was over, Grace arranged for Heiner to stay with other friends of hers. During the day, she drove with him to visit people she thought likely to donate. Moorestown was a good place to start, she said—it was supposed to be a town of seventy-two millionaires. Owing to her longstanding work for humanitarian causes, Grace had an extensive network to which she could introduce him. And Heiner had a long list of things Primavera needed, from laboratory equipment to bedding and shoes. As they drove, they talked and talked. One day Grace invited him to celebrate Christmas at Hereshome.

It was a delicate situation. Will arrived just before dinner on December 23, Heiner's thirty-seventh birthday. Cleveland had been a bust—in a month, Will had garnered just $250. Heiner could not wait to pull him aside to clear the air, but a private talk proved to be impossible. As soon as the meal was over, Grace brought in a huge birthday cake. After that, there was the Christmas tree to decorate, and the next day was taken up with holiday preparations.

After dinner on Christmas Eve they sang carols, and Mother Rhoads read the Christmas story. Then they opened gifts, including several packages marked "For Annemarie," which the Rhoadses had filled with household supplies for Primavera. Afterward they sat in silence around the tree, on which hung cards with the names of loved ones.

Heiner looked at them and thought of his family. Annemarie had written that Edith, who was seven, had lost part of a finger in an accident with a hatchet, and that Monika was learning to talk. He thought of his farewell from Christoph at Rosario, and wondered how Else looked now. Last he had seen her, she was just a baby. He imagined them all opening the gifts he had sent, mostly Christmas cards and balloons—cheap here, but rarities at home.

He thought of Annemarie, too, and—as he always did on Christmas Eve—the night of their engagement. Now they were thousands of miles apart.

Two days after Christmas, Heiner finally found an opportunity to pull Will aside for a man-to-man talk. At first Will tried to laugh off Heiner's concerns. But not for long. Waiting till the peace-loving Rhoadses were out of earshot, Heiner blew up at him. By the end of the conversation, the two had come to an understanding. They each promised that from now on they would work as a team.

As for Grace and Betty, they had more questions than ever. Could the peace work to which they had given their energies—action committees, lobbying, and international aid projects—actually solve anything? What did it mean to follow Jesus all the way, without compromise? Was it possible to live in comfort and still claim to love one's neighbor as oneself?

In a family like the Rhoadses, such questions were explosive. For days on end, there were heated discussions and emotional scenes, moments of decision followed by hours of gloom and sleepless nights. Heiner tried to stay out of it all, but listened and answered questions as he could.

At the end of January, Grace decided to go see Primavera for herself, and a few weeks later she left for Paraguay. After a few months, Betty did the same. In the furor that followed, word about "the brothers from Paraguay" spread like wildfire. Hereshome, once such a bastion of respectability, would never be the same again. But Heiner and Will got many more invitations to dinner.

30

Changes

Philadelphia, January 1951

Florrie Potts was kindhearted to strays, and could afford to be. Educated at Holyoke and married to the vice president of a thriving steel wholesaling company, she kept up a busy social life. For the first few years of her marriage, she'd filled her days by serving on committees for progressive causes such as sharecropping and racial justice. Now, with a son and two daughters, she concentrated on hosting "interesting people" in her spacious three-story home in Germantown, a section of Philadelphia.

One day in January she got a phone call from Grace Rhoads, her husband's cousin and a fellow Quaker. "There are two men in town from South America who are fundraising for a church and hospital they run down there," Grace said. "They've just moved into your area. If you run across them anywhere, do invite them for a meal. They're very hungry and so poor they don't have two beans to rub together."

Florrie promised to keep an eye out. Germantown was a small world, so she wasn't surprised to run into them a few days later in a friend's home. After introductions Florrie said, "Please come to dinner."

During the meal, Heiner and Will made a mixed impression on Florrie and her husband, Tom. At first glance, their odd collarless suits made them look foreign and even a little disreputable. But as Heiner began to talk, the Potts's skepticism started to crumble. He spoke about the hospital, which was short of basic medicines and supplies. He also described his community and how they tried to live out the teaching of Jesus in the Sermon on the Mount. They could not afford things like toys for children, nor even basic dry goods and material for clothes.

Tom and Florrie listened, intrigued. "He's sincere," Florrie felt. "He really cares about that hospital in Paraguay—he's giving his all for it." The hospital itself was nothing to her, but she wanted to help this man. She asked Heiner and his comrade where they were staying. When he said, "At the YMCA," she offered her guestroom. "It's empty, and I can quickly make up the beds."

After that, it was easier to persuade the two to accept hospitality for another night, and then another. Soon Florrie's house was serving as their headquarters. She became Heiner's strategist (and Will's, when he wasn't fundraising elsewhere). The two usually stayed out late in the evenings at speaking engagements, then slept in the next day. By the time they got up, Tom was already on his way to work. Florrie would cook a second breakfast, sit with them in the kitchen as they ate, and get a report on the previous night's work. She coached them on whom to approach next—and what and what *not* to say.

This routine was ideal for everyone except Tom, who hardly ever saw his two guests. One day Florrie spoke up on his behalf. "It's not fair! You tell me everything, but Tom has to go to work, and by the time he comes home, you've gone off someplace for the evening."

"Then tonight we'll stay home and talk with you and Tom," Heiner said immediately, and went to the phone to cancel his evening appointment. Florrie gasped, remembering what it was: a dinner invitation from a wealthy couple who were on the verge of making a donation. "And yet he responded to me without a moment's hesitation," she thought.

After that, Florrie found herself wanting to do more and more to help him. She invited acquaintances – sometimes thirty at a time – for informal evening get-togethers and had Heiner speak to them. (They were all, she told him, "people with extra money.") After small talk was over, and the guests had been shepherded into the dining room, Heiner would describe the hospital and life at Primavera. And not only Heiner. Often Florrie's enthusiasm was such that she could not refrain from interrupting him to add points he forgot.

Tom and Florrie had meant to help Heiner "just as friends." But as the weeks passed, they asked themselves what it was that drew them to him. "It wasn't anything to do with him as a person," Florrie later said, "but rather that he represented a whole new way of being." There was, for instance, his way with a friend of theirs who, though a college man from a good family, just couldn't manage to hold down a job. Currently he was working part-time, delivering milk. Heiner noticed his defeated look and set about befriending him. On several evenings, the time of day most valuable for fundraising, he even passed up chances to meet prospective donors in favor of visiting him and his wife.

Another of Florrie's friends, a doctor, was putting his son through medical school, against the son's wishes. The young man was miserable. Heiner would get up early to go bird watching with him, even after a late night speaking engagement.

Tom made his own observations. He noticed how perfect strangers would walk up to Heiner on the trolley and share their troubles. Heiner claimed this was because of his unusual clothes, but Tom believed it was because of his face and the man he was. "He's so child-like, he'll make friends right away with anyone," Tom told Florrie. "He'll look you in the eye so that you feel, 'Here is somebody who is interested in me.'" (With regard to Heiner's clothes, Florrie later learned that various friends had tried to spruce up his wardrobe. In every case, he gratefully accepted the money they pressed on him but then sent it on to the hospital—and continued to wear the same shabby suit.)

Soon the Pottses realized that through meeting Heiner, the ground had begun shifting under their feet. Till now, they had assumed that the life they were living was good enough. Their family was close and loving; Tom was scrupulously fair in his business dealings; Florrie was social-minded and gave generously to charity. God couldn't demand more than that.

Or could he? "We're still not really living the kind of brotherly life Jesus demanded," Florrie said to Tom. "And perhaps this man and his community in South America *are.*"

Such thoughts were threatening—and so their criticisms began in earnest. Florrie launched into it one morning when she and Heiner were washing dishes. "People who choose to live in a place like Primavera," she said, "cut themselves off from the broader world. They aren't pulling their weight for others. It strikes me as a selfish way to live."

Even while speaking, Florrie was surprised at herself for getting so heated. But Heiner just kept washing dishes and listening. Then he said gently, "You and Tom have a nice house, don't you? You have rooms for your children to play in, and money to send them to private schools. Your family takes beautiful vacations together.

"I am grateful, very grateful, for all the help you have given us for Primavera. But aren't you actually a self-contained cell? Don't you always care for your family first, and worry about the needs of the world only when you have a surplus? Do you ever share your inmost thoughts and feelings with anybody else? How often do you have discussions with others about things that really matter?"

Florrie had to admit that Heiner had a point, and in the weeks that followed, she could not forget what he had said. She asked more questions. Heiner tried to answer, but always ended up by saying, "You have to experience our life. Come down and visit the community for a while. Then you'll see the answers to your questions yourself."

One day Florrie demanded, "How can you stand living so close together with other people? There's no privacy. You must all live on top of each other."

"Come down to Primavera and see," he repeated.

Around this time, she and Tom decided to take him at his word. Grace was there now, and they had been devouring her reports. Not everything about her new life had been easy. But as far as they could tell, she was as convinced as ever that this was how she was meant to live. "We'll come—next summer," they told Heiner.

In the meantime, they gave him and Will the run of their house. They kept a guest room free for them, and always left the front door unlocked. When Florrie woke up in the mornings she would look out of her bedroom window to see if the battered black Ford they drove was under the tree—her way of knowing they had come in during the night. Whenever she saw it, she felt her heart lift.

In May 1951, Heiner and Will received word from Primavera that they should make plans to return home. After making a round of farewell visits, including a stop at Thurman and Frances's Virginia home, they boarded a ship for South America. They arrived home in July to a warm welcome, having netted over $12,000 in donations.

The Pottses visited Paraguay for six weeks in the summer of 1952, and their apartment in Primavera was next door to the Arnolds'. Every few days, Heiner would walk by their living room window, which—like all windows in Primavera—was simply an opening with no glass. Leaning into the room where Florrie was busy with housework, he would wait for her to notice him and then ask, with a twinkle in his eye, "Are you getting enough privacy?"

On the last day of their visit, at a communal farewell meal, Heiner asked Tom if he had any parting words. Tom said, "Well, I guess I feel like the New York debutante who went out to Arizona to a dude ranch for the summer and fell in love with a cowboy. She thought, 'If I marry that cowboy, he won't know anything about New York. He doesn't know how to act in high society. He knows nothing. What shall I do?' She decided to go back to New York and see if she still liked him.

"That's what I'm going to do. I'm going to go back and see if I still like the cowboy."

It didn't take long for the Pottses to find out. When they had been back in Philadelphia for about a month, Tom came home one day and said to Florrie, "I don't know about you, but I want to go back and join the Brothers." Florrie felt the same. Within days Tom told his surprised colleagues that he wanted to resign, and the family began preparing for the move to South America.

It wasn't without a flap that people like the Pottses were able to extricate themselves from their world. In circles like theirs – circles which prized not only financial security and social connections, but also propriety and clearheadedness – the rashness of the move demanded an explanation. Tom was glad to provide one.

In an open letter addressed to the members of his Friends' meeting, he wrote: "For all my adult life, I have been frustrated by the contradiction between 'ordinary' American life and the 'impossible' teaching of Jesus' commandment: 'Love thy neighbor as thyself.'

"During the week, I make out all right. I have a good job and am part owner of a steel warehouse. We like working together and enjoy the game of competing for the available business. We advertise honestly; we charge fair prices; we are concerned about good employee relations; we have a Christmas party; we give generously to the community chest; we have a profit-sharing scheme.

"But do I love my neighbor as myself? Am I concerned for the clerk who has to come to work by streetcar while I drive a recent-model car? Do I help a competitor's salesman get the big order? Do I give to the chest just what I don't need anyway? Jesus did not say, 'Love your neighbor after taking care of yourself.'

"Then on Sunday I worship with the Society of Friends. Like other Friends, I believe that all men are children of God, and brothers to each other. But what do I do about it? Periodically we ask ourselves searching queries such as, 'Do you keep to simplicity and moderation in your manner of living and your pursuit of business?' In the case of my wife and me, we have two cars; we send our children to private schools, and buy them everything they need to keep up with the Joneses; we ourselves can buy pretty much whatever we want. Is that simplicity?

"And how about my 'pursuit of business'? Today it's impossible, in my opinion, to run a competitive business without trying constantly to make it bigger. But to what purpose would I spend the next twenty years in building our business to two, three, or ten times its present size? I would double my income, triple my worries, and perhaps donate more to good causes. But would these donations, however large, serve to bring the kingdom here on earth as much as the devoting of my waning energies to a really Christian way of life?"

It was around this time that a new chapter began for Heiner in Primavera. Perhaps it was the fresh air he brought back with him from his travels. Whatever the reason, people began to turn to him as they hadn't for at least a decade, coming to him with their problems and seeking his advice on everything from child rearing to difficulties at work. Heiner was humbled by the trust they showed him, but his mind mostly ranged further afield.

Hardy and others were now in the United States, continuing where he and Will had left off. Like them, Hardy was finding seekers as well as a startling variety of supporters, from Clarence Jordan of Koinonia, to Henry Regnery, the conservative publisher, to the Doris Duke Foundation; he was working on Marlene Dietrich. Heiner read his brother's reports eagerly and lived in the excitement of every new development.

Then, toward the end of 1952, Heiner was chosen to replace Hardy and – to his great surprise – was told to take Annemarie with him. They traveled in December, leaving their children in the care of Gwynn and his wife.

Heiner and Annemarie headed first to Philadelphia, where the Pottses put them up and introduced Annemarie to all their friends. "She was so direct and down-to-earth," remembered Jane Tyson Clement, a poet whom Florrie had invited to hear the Arnolds. To Jane and others, "community" called up the otherworldly image of a medieval cloister. Yet here was this motherly woman in a blue jumper and peasant blouse, her hair braided around her head, her eyes shining. When she spoke, she was matter-of-fact. She described Primavera's nursery, its school, and its other work departments. She summarized their reasons for living together. There was no persuasiveness, and certainly no oratory. And yet she conveyed something that her listeners wanted more of.

In between staying at the Pottses, their home base, Heiner and Annemarie canvassed new addresses for donations. After collecting a large pile of rags with which to clean the windshield (the wipers weren't electric yet, and stopped whenever the car was going uphill) they would set off. Heiner drove, and Annemarie tried to keep the panes clear. She also wheedled money from Heiner for gifts — things for adults and children that you couldn't get in Primavera. Every few weeks she'd send down a care package: yarn for a girls' knitting class; pen knives for schoolboys; paints, books, and puzzles and other things for the school.

As they travelled from house to house, Heiner and Annemarie felt freer and freer. The weight of the past and its unsolved riddles slipped off them. Annemarie bubbled over with the excitement of new faces and new friends. To those they met, they talked about Primavera with unqualified enthusiasm. The community at home had weaknesses, they admitted. As Heiner said, laughing, "We know them only too well." And if someone seemed especially serious about visiting or joining Primavera, they made no bones about the sacrifice it would demand. But they never, ever mentioned what they themselves had been made to suffer. Despite its flaws, they insisted, the community had been built on a solid foundation.

In the summer of 1953 they had to return home. The Bruderhof had been branching out steadily of late, and Primavera's leaders wished to take stock of its growth. A conference was announced, and Heiner and Annemarie were summoned to participate.

They flew down with Dorie Greaves, a young woman from Minnesota whom they had grown close to. Dorie had long wanted to visit Primavera, and she jumped at the chance of traveling with them.

In Montevideo, they stopped at El Arado, an outpost of Primavera that had opened the previous year. The reception was warm, and a welcome dinner was held. But during it, Dorie stood up and fled. Heiner and Annemarie followed her to her room, and found her crying inconsolably.

"What's the matter?" Annemarie asked. Dorie said she couldn't put it into words. It wasn't the people—they were friendly enough. But something was amiss and it had dashed her expectations. "Maybe it's just the atmosphere," she finally blurted out. "It's so self-satisfied and small."

Heiner stood tongue-tied. He felt just the same as Dorie did.

The Bruderhof World Conference, as it was nicknamed by the Pottses, went on day after day for three weeks, with representatives from each community getting a slot to report. The event was a triumph of careful bureaucratic planning. There were committees, agendas, and long meetings to discuss detailed questions: "What types of people can be expected to respond best to our message?" "Where and how can the most money be raised?" "How can our movement help to establish worldwide brotherhood?"

To be sure, Heiner was thrilled at Primavera's enthusiasm to carry forward the mission in the United States. American attendees were invited to tell their stories, including Tom and Florrie, who had returned to Primavera bringing forty-five hatching eggs for the poultry operation. And in a sign of new openness, one session commemorated Eberhard Arnold's seventieth birthday; Emmy Arnold was invited to tell about the community's founding in Sannerz, and Hans Zumpe read selections of Eberhard's writings.

All the same, the longer the conference went on, the more uncomfortable Heiner and Annemarie became about its self-congratulatory tone. "What's going on here?" they asked each other privately. "For months we have been telling people about following Jesus – and here we are with writing pads making schemes for expansion." To Heiner, the discussions seemed arrogant and academic; he wondered what they had to do with real people and problems. "Has Primavera really changed so much in our absence? Or is it we who have changed?" he asked Annemarie one night.

Before the conference ended, a new fundraising team was announced: Hans-Hermann and Gertrud were to go to the United States. Heiner and Annemarie were relieved to be staying home. Much as they had loved traveling, they had seven growing children to raise. But they were still excited about the trip: Hans-Hermann and his wife were going not only to raise funds, but also to find a house and build up a North American outpost.

As it turned out, a house would not be enough. Within months of their arrival, Hans-Hermann and Gertrud had met dozens of people who had heard of "the Brothers" and were begging to join them. Clearly, a larger place was needed to accommodate them all.

In the end, Woodcrest, a rural property in upstate New York, was found, and in June 1954 the first residents moved in. By the end of the year, they numbered eighty. Hans-Hermann and Gertrud served as house parents, but they could not stay in America indefinitely – their family of nine was still in Paraguay, and they had traveled on temporary visas.

Hans thought Heiner and Annemarie were the most obvious replacements. Like Hardy, Heiner had proved to have a knack for raising cash, and if anything made sense, it was putting him where there was money. As Hans once put it, "One doesn't kill the goose that lays the golden eggs."

The Arnolds were to travel as soon as they got their immigration papers; Clarence Jordan gave the required affidavit of support. The paperwork took a whole year, and the children grew impatient. So did Heiner and Annemarie. But they found leaving Primavera harder than they had expected. For six years, Mama had been part of their family. She lived quietly next door, occupying herself with her knitting, her grandchildren, and her parrot, which could sing snatches of Handel's *Messiah*. She was mentally astute, but almost seventy, and growing frail . . .

Emmy was not the only one Heiner and Annemarie would miss. Despite everything, the last fourteen years in Paraguay had brought them close to many of their comrades. Together they had struggled to build a home in the jungle, to feed their growing families, to bring up their children. And they had shared losses: Edith, Fritz, the many children, and their own baby, Marianne.

Of course, the dark times—isolation and banishment—had left their mark too. There was much that had never been resolved. But both Heiner and Annemarie were determined to leave behind the past when they moved to their new home. And so, not wishing to be reminded of it, they burned all the letters they had written to each other while separated. They would forgive.

31

Woodcrest

Rifton, New York, February 1955

It was a snowy February morning when Heiner and his family stepped out of the car, the girls in sandals and carrying coconuts picked up during their stopover in Miami. They shivered in the unfamiliar cold of a New York winter.

"So this is Woodcrest," Heiner thought. It sat on top of a hill rising from the Wallkill River valley, overlooking the glistening white Catskills. The view was exquisite. Woodcrest itself was not. The main building was a hulking, rundown mansion built fifty years earlier by a textile baron. In his day, the grounds had imitated an English manor park, with lawns, terraces, hedges, and fountains. Now they were overrun with knee-high poison ivy and untidy brush that pushed through the snow. Laundry hung out of windows at rakish angles, frozen stiff.

The Arnolds followed Doug and Ruby Moody, the young Americans who had picked them up from the airport, to their new home. It was a chicken house that had just been fixed up for people, and in the yard you could still smell the chickens. The apartment had no plumbing (bathrooms were in the next house) and was heated by a pot-bellied coal stove that squatted in the living room. The bedroom in which four of the girls were to live could barely accommodate their bunks. Ruby was curious how the newcomers would react. To her amazement, Annemarie went from room to room, clapping her hands and exclaiming, *"Wie schön!"* – "How wonderful!"

Doug and Ruby lived in similar quarters just across the hall. Doug had grown up in a straitlaced missionary home. "I'm thirty-four, and I've never had a beer," he confided when Heiner offered him a drink one evening. In fact, his scruples had kept him from drinking even coffee. But Heiner's easygoing manner relaxed him, and soon it was as if the two had been friends all their lives. As the weather grew warmer they could be seen sitting in the low, open windowsills at the end of the day, Pall Malls and beers in hand. Heiner would tell Doug about his childhood, his father, and Tata. The stories poured out of him, Doug later said, as if he had been waiting to tell them for years.

Annemarie took to Woodcrest immediately: "It's impossible to be bored here," she wrote home to Emmy. "Each day when I wake up, I don't know what's going to happen."

As summer came, new people arrived every week, and living spaces had to be juggled continuously. Whole families crowded into one-room apartments. A handful of single women pitched a tent on a lawn, and moved in until frost drove them back indoors.

Good weather inspired impromptu picnics, and sometimes a planned meeting would be scotched in favor of an informal singing evening on the front porch. Then, as the mismatched dishes were cleared away, someone would run for the newly mimeographed collection of folksongs while another fetched his guitar.

Woodcrest was a different world from prim and proper Primavera. Here, work assignments were fluid (greenhorns easily outnumbered old hands) and the daily schedule so flexible that a visitor might not have noticed there was one. Here, people had lax ideas of cleanliness – some didn't make their beds or wash their dishes for days. Here, women wore jeans and were as likely to exercise as to knit. Some mornings a white-clad student of yoga could be seen hanging upside down from the lowest branch of a tree.

Other, older community members might have raised their eyebrows at this, but Heiner and Annemarie approached it all with humor and pragmatism or—where something rubbed them wrong—a frank question or admonition. If there were issues to hash out, let them be hashed out. How late should children be allowed to stay up? Should the common pantry be locked, or should they depend on an honor system? Should they call the cops on the junk man when he drove off with more than he had paid for? Such discussions often took place at meals. Everyone chimed in, whether a casual guest or a veteran of community living. When a thornier question came up and agreement seemed impossible, Heiner would not press for a resolution. "Let's leave this one for another time. Love will find a way."

Heiner was not blind to the dangers of spontaneity. He knew from experience how quickly it can turn to chaos, and how friendly disagreements can balloon into serious tensions. He had seen youthful idealism spring up only to die a few days later. But he loved Woodcrest for what it was. Here at long last he had been given a chance to experience his father's dream come true: a community that was not just an organization but a living organism. And so he fought all attempts to tame it with rules. A degree of structure was necessary—he knew that—but he was wary of anything that stifled enthusiasm.

It wasn't always easy to strike the right balance. Zealous members sometimes tried to impose order on the mayhem—often when Heiner was away—and he would return from a trip to be told of a new ban on cats or go-carts or bubble gum. "Every time I come home, you've made a new rule," he would joke. Luckily, it usually took no more than a few days for the new regulation to die a natural death.

In Woodcrest it was common to laugh about "when things get back to normal," the point being that things never did. The stream of guests was endless, and included everyone from would-be members to the merely curious. One weekend a group of young Zionists dropped in for discussions on community and an evening of dancing. Russian Communists visited from a collective farm. Dorothy Day took a bus up from Manhattan, stayed a weekend, and described Woodcrest in the next issue of *The Catholic Worker*. Peace Pilgrim, a woman who crisscrossed the country wearing her name in big letters, came through regularly and was a favorite with the children. K. K. Chandy, the head of the Fellowship of Reconciliation in India, visited and became a lifelong friend.

Eleanor Roosevelt came for a day, and followed up her visit with two pieces for her nationally syndicated column praising both Woodcrest's cooperative lifestyle and the lamb stew served at lunch. Little did she know that the cooks had gone out of their way to spare her the community's usual fare: low-budget menus heavy on cottage cheese and boiled chard. Grocery money was usually short, and as often as not it was lavished on the wheat germ, stone-ground flour, and molasses-based "tiger's milk" craved by Woodcrest's many health-conscious eaters. Heiner remarked drily, "It's wonderful to eat only carrots, and live a few extra days. But the important question is: How are you going to use those days?"

Hundreds came to Woodcrest and left after a short visit; dozens of others stayed for good. Those who did were a ragtag bunch. Claud Nelson was a sports reporter from Atlanta; Carroll King, the first socialist elected to the Minnesota state legislature; Bertha Mills, an Episcopalian missionary to Alaska. Don and Marilyn Noble were supporters of Cesar Chavez's farm workers movement and hailed from the orchards of central California. John Houssman, a former manager for Dow Chemical, had financed the entire down payment on Woodcrest the year before. Dwight and Norann Blough, twenty-one-year-olds from Kansas, came after reading descriptions of the Bruderhof by Pitirim Sorokin, a Harvard sociologist. Paul Willis, a black carpenter whose previous home was a shelter, was a magnet for any youngster who needed help with a model ship. Bob Clement was a successful Philadelphia lawyer.

Whole groups joined. One was Macedonia, a cooperative community that ran a dairy and manufacturing business in the hills of

Georgia. Dick Mommsen was a typical member. He had come there ten years before, shortly after his release from the Civilian Public Service camp where, as a conscientious objector, he had spent World War II. He and his wife, Dot, lived in the log cabin they had built. Heiner and Annemarie had visited them in 1953, and hearing about Primavera had impressed them and other Macedonians. But it also left them apprehensive. Admirers of Gandhi and Albert Schweitzer, they tended toward a humanist idealism. To them, Christianity was narrow and dogmatic. They had no use for it.

In the summer of 1957 that began to change. Outwardly Macedonia was finally flourishing after more than a decade of dogged efforts. But Dick and Dot felt that something was not working. Among those coming to Macedonia were people dogged by alcoholism, adultery, involvement in the occult – and how did one address such issues in a humanist community? After deciding that a common spiritual basis would help, Macedonia planned out a course of group study. First they would read together from the New Testament, and then from the Koran, and then from the Bhagavad-Gita.

They didn't get far. Only a few chapters into the Gospel of Luke, they found that the text was taking hold of them in a way they had never expected. Reading about Jesus stirred them deeply. Many were in tears. They called Woodcrest for guidance, and Heiner and Annemarie traveled down. After a few days, to Heiner's astonishment, the members called him into a meeting and presented him with the keys to the place. "We feel that Macedonia belongs to Woodcrest," they explained.

Shortly after this, everyone at Macedonia moved to Woodcrest, including Dick and Dot, who, despite earlier misgivings, now wanted to stay. They were still homesick for Georgia, especially Dot. But something powerful had drawn them to Woodcrest, and they couldn't evade it: "This is where we want to spend the rest of our lives."

With additions like the Mommsens, Woodcrest urgently needed more housing, and began work on a new two-story dwelling. The lumber bought for the frame was green—so green that when you hammered in a nail, sap squirted in your eye. It was also far heavier than it looked. Doug, who worked with Heiner, marveled that someone so thin was able to carry the two-by-ten planks all the way up to the second floor.

Buying better lumber was out of the question. Woodcrest's income hardly covered operating costs, let alone maintenance for its 150 inhabitants. Not that they were going to allow money worries to dampen their spirits. On the contrary, they thought nothing of embarking on new projects without any idea of how to finance them. Almost always, a donation or a loan would arrive in time to keep everything afloat. And when one did, people didn't merely sigh with relief. "It's time to celebrate," Heiner would announce, and even if the cash box contained only a few dollars, they'd all take off in cars and pickups for the neighborhood Dairy Queen.

But no one can keep borrowing forever. Fortunately, the Macedonians had brought with them a toy-making business, Community Playthings, and over the next years Woodcrest poured every available resource into it. Tom and Florrie Potts were called back to the United States from Paraguay so that Tom, an experienced manager, could take the helm. A barn was converted into a factory, and machines sent up from Macedonia were installed. Some were quite functional, others mainly ingenious. One had a saw blade mounted directly on the drive shaft of a dismembered car that dangled overhead. Next to it was the ripsaw, an angle-iron monster whose operator sometimes needed a sledgehammer to bludgeon the lumber past the blade. Meanwhile, upstairs, attic rooms became sales offices—never mind the absence of windows, heaters, or other niceties.

Aside from establishing a livelihood for Woodcrest, a myriad of other activities kept Heiner and Annemarie up till twelve or one most nights. Heiner spent hours in his study – the cramped turret of an old carriage house – just trying to keep up with the correspondence that came his way. Primavera's leaders expected detailed reports every week. He had to write replies to those asking to visit or join. On top of that, the accountant, the factory foreman, and the school principal – all new to communal living – stopped by often to consult with him. Now he appreciated his father's foresight in sending him to the Strickhof. The subjects he had detested most while there – bookkeeping, construction, and business management – stood him in good stead here.

But practical oversight was the half of his job that Heiner cared least about. Far more important, he believed, were his responsibilities as a counselor – in particular, *Seelsorge*, or "care of souls." Often he could be seen walking the circle around the mansion deep in talk, his arm resting firmly on a companion's shoulders. His study was usually open for guests or anyone else. And many came daily for counseling or encouragement.

When people told Heiner their problems, he rarely did more than listen – even if it meant sitting with them for hours. As Ellen, a young woman from Brooklyn, put it, "Heiner takes your problems seriously." His advice, when he gave any, was brief – usually only a sentence or two. Yet visitors almost always left feeling strengthened and refreshed.

Heiner didn't stroke feathers, however. Once Janice, a new member, came to him to lament her lack of gifts. "I want so much to bring the community something that would be an asset."

"All the others bring nothing but their sins," Heiner told her. "But you insist on coming like Father Christmas!"

Janice looked stung. But by the next day, she saw what Heiner was trying to do – free her of self-concern. It worked. So did humor. One day George Burleson, a novice member, visited Heiner to admit to backbiting. Heiner sat quietly while he went through all the things that were troubling him. When done, George looked up, expecting a sharp rebuke. But Heiner, who saw that he was remorseful, looked him in the eye. "Boring, isn't it," he said gently, and offered his hand. George returned home jubilant.

As a pastoral counselor, Heiner was often presented with situations that had no easy solution, and he soon developed a circle of trusted individuals that he could turn to for advice. This was true not only for cases of emotional illness – for these he worked closely with a respected local psychiatrist – but also for matters of spiritual direction. He especially valued the advice of Dietrich von Hildebrand, a prominent Catholic philosopher at Fordham University who had opposed the Nazis. (Pope John Paul II would later call Hildebrand "one of the great ethicists of the twentieth century.") Heiner, who studied Hildebrand's writings on marriage and sexuality, would visit him to consult on how to help those struggling with problems in this area.

Annemarie assisted him closely in his tasks, her cheerfulness and bluntness keeping every challenge in the right perspective. On the face of it, the two had opposite characters. As Heiner's mother Emmy had noted decades before, he had a "leaning toward mysticism, and an outstanding sensitivity and devotion to others." Meanwhile, Annemarie didn't seem to have a contemplative bone in her body.

Both had strong personalities and could disagree heartily in public, even in the members' meetings held three or four evenings a week. On occasion the exchange got heated, and they seemed to forget themselves. They acted as unguarded as if they were in their living room. But their love was so obvious that it hardly ever put others on edge – two such determined wills, yet such harmony about fundamentals. Eventually they always came to an agreement.

Annemarie mostly came late. Often, after conversations had fallen to a hush, and people sat waiting for the meeting to begin, she would slip in and make a hurried beeline for the empty chair next to Heiner. "And where have you been?" he would ask her loudly.

Like Dick and Dot, almost everyone at Woodcrest recoiled from religion. But that didn't mean they weren't searching for God. Heiner understood this, and perhaps that is why they trusted him. One evening at supper, a guest asked, "What does the Bruderhof teach about the devil and hell?" In Primavera, such a question might have prompted a lengthy explanation. But not here.

Heiner put down his cigarette and sized up his questioner. "God is God," he answered, "and anything else is of no importance whatsoever." Seeing the guest was bewildered, he went on: "At the final judgment we can only stand trembling before God. What the Bruderhof or anyone else teaches will not change God's will one bit; we have no right to interpret him. Jesus says, 'Sell what you have and give it to the poor; sin no more; love your neighbor as yourself.' But we are not to interpret this. We are to do it."

One day Sibyl Sender, another guest, found herself in Heiner's study. By age twenty-two, she had gone to Harvard and dropped out (too phony), married and split (too stifling), and had a child. Now an editor at a glossy magazine, she had come up from New York City solely to pacify her ex-husband, who kept pestering her to visit and saying, "You'll love the place."

Sibyl arrived determined to hate it and to shock the uptight believers she expected to find. It shouldn't have been hard. Her motto was summed up by a line from a movie – "Live fast, die young, and leave a good-looking corpse" – and what with her atheism and studied sensuality, she was sure this religious community would be no match.

Yet she had been disarmed at once by the atmosphere that met her – by genuineness and warmth and the complete absence of anything pious or phony. And now she was sitting in this shabby little study with this stranger called Heiner, and he had made her coffee. She had unraveled the whole messy tangle of her life to him. At the end, when she ran out of things to say, he said, "Thank you for trusting me enough to share all this."

Sibyl warned him that she wasn't about to change her lifestyle. "I need to get back home to New York."

"That is death," Heiner said.

"I know. But I can't stay here."

Three months later, she was back, having tried – and failed – to shake off whatever it was that drew her. "This time I'm staying for good," she told Heiner.

◆ ◆ ◆

One thing that struck Heiner and Annemarie almost daily was how straightforward people were at Woodcrest. Not always and not everyone, to be sure; but still, there were none of the intrigues and decades-long grudges that had come to poison Primavera. Instead, there was an insistence on open, honest relationships, and people took literally the "First Law in Sannerz," a brief house rule Heiner's father had composed in 1925:

> There is no law but love. Love is joy in others. What then is anger at them? Words of love convey the joy we have in the presence of our brothers and sisters. It is out of the question to speak about another person in a spirit of irritation or vexation. There must never be talk, either in open remarks or by insinuation, against any brother or sister, or against their individual characteristics – and under no circumstances behind their back. Gossiping in one's family is no exception. Without this rule of silence there can be no loyalty and thus no community.
>
> Direct address is the only way possible; it is the brotherly or sisterly service we owe anyone whose weaknesses cause a negative reaction in us. An open word spoken directly to another person deepens friendship and will not be resented. Only when two people do not come to an agreement quickly is it necessary to draw in a third person whom both of them trust. In this way they can be led to a solution that unites them on the highest and deepest levels.

At Woodcrest, people went at it hammer and tongs. Even short-term guests felt compelled to be candid, though anywhere else they would have taken pains to conceal their true feelings. Once Heiner saw Dick chewing out a guest over a snide comment he had made. Afterward, Heiner tapped Dick on the shoulder. "I wonder if it was really wise to speak in such strong terms."

Dick looked surprised. "But if it's the truth, why not say it? I wouldn't know what to say to guests if I couldn't say the truth."

Heiner laughed, admitting Dick had a point. It was just how Sannerz had been. And he could be brusque himself, especially toward those closest to him. Once he saw Doug lighting into a young man whom Doug suspected of lying. Nothing wrong so far: Heiner appreciated Doug's gift of seeing through slick characters, and this young man was one. But what bothered Heiner was Doug's judgmental tone. "Doug," he told his friend, "until now I thought your peering through the defenses of others was a gift. But when it's without love, it's from the devil."

Not everyone enjoyed Woodcrest's brashness. When Gwynn came to visit, he was invited to hold the Sunday morning service. He chose a long inspirational reading as his text—standard fare in Primavera. Sibyl, who was sitting near him, was visibly bored. As soon as he was done, she leaned over to Heiner and whispered to him, too loudly, "What do I do if I got *absolutely nothing* out of what he just read?" Gwynn looked startled. But Heiner, who saw that Sibyl was completely sincere, tried to hide his amusement while thinking up a diplomatic answer.

Normally, meetings were as lively as mealtimes—a spontaneous back-and-forth, a favorite song, a question followed by further discussion. There were tough things to address, from money troubles to rocky marriages. Still, the general tone was that of a family gathering, and many of the women brought their knitting. And when things got too heavy, Heiner tried to inject some humor. "Five minutes' laughter is worth a dozen eggs," he loved to repeat. He could tease people too, especially Annemarie, who would respond with a friendly jab of her knitting needle.

There was one bone of contention between them that everyone seemed to know about: Heiner's beard. It was not a new issue. Their first quarrel, just days after getting engaged, had been over the same topic, and in the twenty-five years since, neither had backed down. The conversation might start with a discussion of when he should get a haircut.

"Heiner, your hair is too long."

"Ach, Annemarie, what's wrong with it? Think of Beethoven."

"You aren't Beethoven."

"Then think of Einstein."

"And your beard. It makes you look like an Amish man."

"Annemarie! What do you have against the Amish?"

Annemarie had a strong will, and never gave up without a fight. One night several women gathered on an impromptu stage at dinner. Sibyl gave a speech, and they banged on pans and waved signs plagiarized from BurmaShave ads:

Men Who Don't Shave

Belong in a Cave

Children Find It Scary

To See a Man That's Hairy

Beards: A Fire Hazard

Apparently it worked. Photographs prove that for the next several years, Heiner restricted himself to a mustache.

After the building team finished work on the new dwelling house, the Arnolds were among the first to move in. Their new apartment was bigger but just as rugged. True, it had plumbing, but that was a mixed blessing. A bathroom had been installed just inside the front door, in order to serve the nearby houses. There was never any mistaking when a chamber pot had been emptied. Annemarie would murmur her disgust, and Heiner would hurry her into the living room. "Don't worry, Annemarie, I'll smoke a cigarette." The walls were thin, and each night they could hear the neighbors brushing their teeth. *"Eine kleine Nachtmusik,"* said fifteen-year-old Christoph. "But not by Mozart."

Christoph and his two oldest sisters had started public school by now and came home nightly with tales of their newest discoveries: the Pledge of Allegiance, the Brooklyn Dodgers, nuclear bomb drills, and a practice called "dating." The younger children had their own adjustments to make. Monika, who pined for Paraguay, was judged "a little stupid" by her first-grade teacher and moved back to kindergarten. Edith discovered the woods and filled the house with wild animals that she caught and kept as pets: a flying squirrel, a fawn, a fox cub, and a raccoon.

To the children's joy, Emmy moved to Woodcrest to join them. In good weather, she would sit in front of the Arnolds' house, knitting, and talking to everybody who went by. Guests, awed at meeting the community's co-founder, came to sit by her chair and hear her tell about Sannerz and Berlin.

As a boy, Heiner had sometimes grumbled that he rarely had his father and mother to himself. Now the pattern was repeating itself. Often breakfast was the only time the family spent together, so every morning when Heiner came in to the living room, he would go around the table from child to child, look into their eyes, and ask them how they were. He could tell if something was troubling one of them and would make a point of finding out what it was.

College-age men made up a big part of the community, and inevitably several of them started noticing Roswith and Anneli. And vice versa. The girls found that their father usually seemed to know when they had a crush on someone. "You're so quiet," Heiner would say to Anneli. "What is it? Is there somebody you like? Tell me about him." And then he would take her out for a drive.

Anneli didn't feel uncomfortable talking about such things with her father. He assured her that falling in love was the most natural thing in the world. But he was also very direct. When she had finished telling him about this or that new friend, he'd say, "I understand, but he's not for you. Put it out of your mind." And because Anneli trusted her father, that took care of the matter as far as she was concerned.

The children always hoped Heiner would be free at the end of the day – to sit together around the coffee table and talk or sing until late. Much to their dismay, it was just this time that other people often took, demanding long conversations alone with their father. And because he could rarely bring himself to refuse a person who needed an ear, Heiner would disappear with them and be gone the rest of the evening.

Woodcrest seemed to attract people with broken minds and spirits. Heiner welcomed each one into his home and made sure his children spoke English whenever a guest was there. As a result, the family almost always included one or two troubled young people. Some stayed for months, rooming with Christoph or with the girls. A few were just emotionally fragile; others were mentally ill. Heiner was matter-of-fact about this: "We live in a neurotic age. Just by growing up in modern society, all of us are touched by mental illness to one degree or another."

There were two sisters who were both suicidal, and Heiner was ready to respond to them day and night. Even when battling a fever or the flu, he could be seen shuffling down the snow-covered walk in slippers, hurrying to their apartment because he'd been called to help them through a rough patch.

Another troubled young woman, Leila (not her real name), grew to be like a daughter to Heiner and Annemarie. She was twenty-two, exactly the same age Emmy Maria would have been, and soon she started calling them "Papa" and "Mama." Leila had seemed balanced enough on her arrival at Woodcrest, but after several months, she began going into hysterics, weeping uncontrollably, shuddering at the mere mention of God, and exhibiting other symptoms of possession.

Heiner and Annemarie were guarded in speaking about Leila's ailments. To them it was enough to know that she had been exposed to the occult as a child, and that she was now struggling with forces larger than herself.

Sometimes Leila tried to kill herself. She climbed out on balconies, ran toward a busy highway, and once punched out a window, slicing open her arm. Heiner and Annemarie moved her in with Roswith so that she could be watched in case she had attacks. When she did, she grew violent, striking anyone who tried to calm her or scratching at them with her nails. For weeks, they watched her day and night. Even so, she sometimes succeeded in slipping out at night. Finally Annemarie moved a mattress in front of her door and slept there to prevent an escape.

In between these bouts Leila was carefree and considerate and impressed casual visitors with her childlike happiness. Monika and Else loved to play with her or have her read them stories—it never crossed their minds that they should be scared of her. Sadly, Leila's dark impulses continued to torment her. About half a year later she signed herself into a hospital.

Meanwhile Heiner was kept busy with the constant pastoral round of births and weddings—and illnesses and deaths. After Doug and Ruby lost a stillborn child, their third, they turned to Heiner for help. Ruby was beside herself with grief, and Doug said he'd had to fight the urge to jump out an upper story window at the hospital.

Heiner felt their pain as deeply as they did—hadn't he and Annemarie lost children themselves? But he did not offer the Moodys cheap consolation. Instead, he told them about losing Emmy Maria despite praying for her, and about the choice he had been presented with at Marianne's birth. Finally he said, "Doug and Ruby, no life—or even a hope in the direction of life—is in vain." These words made all the difference to them.

Later Doug tried to express his gratefulness to Heiner. "I want you to know how much I appreciate the way you relate to people." Heiner was quiet. How frustrating it was – this assumption that he had a way with people; that he had answers! How could Doug or anyone else at Woodcrest know how often the past plagued him, how conflicting emotions filled him every time he thought of Primavera? Worse was that feeling that had gnawed at him since 1941 – his sense of guilt for having reinstated Hans and Georg as leaders. Even now, the community had not come out from under their tight grip. But what was the point of stirring up the past? Hadn't he and Annemarie decided to forgive? And so he simply replied, "Doug, none of it comes from me personally. Whatever I have comes from God. If only you knew how many mistakes I've made!"

Not long after this, Hans visited Woodcrest, and Heiner made Doug feel that this was someone to be respected – as if he were one of Heiner's oldest, truest friends.

Ruby found that Annemarie was the same in the way she constantly thought of the people in Primavera. When donations came to Woodcrest, she would sort through the boxes and select the best things to send down to Paraguay. Everything she sent could have easily been used in Woodcrest. But such was her generosity and eagerness to share. While stowing clothes, books, and sewing machines into fifty-five gallon metal drums, Annemarie would describe the brothers and sisters who would be receiving them in such glowing terms that Ruby longed to go to Primavera herself.

There was something in the air at Woodcrest, Doug and Ruby felt. It was as if they had discovered an inheritance or uncovered long-lost roots. "Coming up the hill to Woodcrest for the first time, our hearts beat faster," Doug recalled. "Only later did we take in the weeds, the run-down buildings, and the unheated factory. A charged atmosphere pervaded the place. At mealtimes the singing and the exuberance was a living presence. We felt that something far beyond us wanted to happen."

He added, "It was like finding an oasis after wandering in the desert, seeking vainly for decades for a meaningful life. We were suddenly transported into peace and lightness of heart."

One visitor at Woodcrest met friends there whom he had known earlier in life, and remarked, "I've never experienced such a change in people. It radiated from them!"

Donna Ford, a young teacher from Kansas, said that when she came up the drive she "was gripped by a mounting sense of expectation. When I got out of the van, tears came to my eyes. I felt that I'd come home."

Dwight Blough, another Midwesterner fresh out of college, had the same experience. "When I came up the drive, I felt: this is it! – though I had never been at Woodcrest before. I told my wife, 'If this is what we've heard and read about, we will stay for good.'" (They did, and Dwight became one of Heiner's closest friends and coworkers.)

Heiner and Annemarie rejoiced over every such arrival, but they were careful not to recruit. Guests had to decide to stay (or leave) on their own accord. In any case, building a big movement had never been a goal. Heiner wrote at the time, "Let us consider the community of believers we Christians are always talking about – this one organism alive through all the centuries. What is the Bruderhof, then, with its culture? What are all the other denominations, Quakers, Mennonites, and Brethren? Whatever good is in them has come about only because they are surrendered to, and gripped by, this stream of life. We must not lay too much stress on the Bruderhof or any other movement. Our community will pass away just as many others have passed away. But the stream of life to which we are surrendered can never pass away. That is what matters."

It was surely this stream, Heiner felt, that drew Woodcrest's guests. How else could one explain the diversity of their backgrounds? And how else to explain their reasons for staying?

"It was disturbingly religious," said Don Peters, an activist filmmaker from Canada, "but the new community was so real. Its clear-eyed directness saw right into my phoniness. My wife and I looked at each other in a new way. Our lives had been brought to a standstill by what we had found—there was no possibility of continuing with our old half-life!"

As for Sibyl, she recalled, "I was shaking like a leaf when I came back that second time. I wondered what kind of religious nut I was turning into. But there on the door of our room was a sign scrawled by a child: 'Welcome Home.' That was it; I had come home at last. Sure, there were struggles. But even they were punctuated by laughter, of all things. I had been expecting gloomy introspection, but what I found was prayer, forgiveness, God. The people I met were just normal human beings like myself, but sharing life with them was like participating in an ongoing adventure. By coming to Woodcrest, it was as if I had found a pearl. I was as one in love, utterly consumed by my joy."

Here was the Youth Movement in a new form, but with all the same freshness, innocence, and enthusiasm. It transported Heiner to the happiness of his boyhood. Here, the vision of his parents and Tata was finally coming back to life.

It was March 1955, Woodcrest's first Easter. Heiner hoped to mark the occasion with a celebration of the Lord's Supper. Annemarie arranged the tables so that all two-dozen members could face each other. She decorated them with white linen, candles, and wildflowers. In the evening, after all of them were gathered, Heiner broke the bread. The loaf went from hand to hand around the table, and then a jug of wine was passed around.

Many years before, when Heiner was twelve, Luise had visited relatives and come back to Sannerz with a bottle of wine. She and Sophie and Heiner had wondered what to do with it, and decided that the Sun Troop should celebrate the Lord's Supper. They didn't know how to go about it—Heiner had only a sketchy idea—but they knew that it had to do with loving Jesus and each other. When they were done, they got rid of the leftover wine by smashing the bottle.

Heiner later worried that they had desecrated something holy. He rushed to Tata and told her everything. Touched by his earnestness, she reassured him, "There was nothing wrong in what you did." But she had one reproach: "Why on earth did you smash the bottle afterward? Your father would have enjoyed the rest of the wine so much! We can hardly ever afford to buy him any."

Papa, Tata, Adolf, and Fritz—here in Woodcrest, they were all alive, all present. "This is the greatest grace of my life," Heiner wrote to Georg back in Primavera. "I have been allowed to start over—to be a child again." Here in a decrepit mansion in upstate New York, the spirit of Sannerz was reawakening. Heiner looked around the room with a radiant face. As they all shook hands and embraced, he exclaimed, "The spirit has come again!"

For days afterward, the music of Handel's Hallelujah Chorus boomed through the windows of his office, out over the laundry lines and the uncut lawns.

The Crucible

THE SAME YEAR THAT HEINER AND ANNEMARIE moved to Woodcrest, Hans began a branch community in Germany. It was high time to return to the old country, he believed. Europe was opening up again after the war, and financing would come mostly from the German government, which was compensating expatriates who had fled Hitler. Hans hoped that donations raised by Woodcrest would cover the rest. In his mind, rich Americans were in great supply. Those in charge of Primavera thought similarly.

Primavera was at this time still living hand-to-mouth, with an income that covered far less than expenses. But it was also the oldest and biggest community, and the Bruderhof's undisputed hub. It was where the movement's finances were coordinated, where the archives were located, where conferences were held. It was Primavera's leaders — in consultation with Hans — who called the shots, and everyone knew it. And so its financial managers gradually came to expect that other communities would cover its shortfalls. The biggest burden fell on Woodcrest, which was supposed to send tens of thousands of dollars a year. Still deeply indebted itself, Woodcrest had to raise every dollar of that money by begging for loans and donations.

Heiner knew the poverty of Primavera all too well, and knew how hard it was to keep the farm and other businesses running. All the more, he was baffled by its plans to pour money and labor into loss-making projects: a wood gas plant, a new hospital complex, and a plan to turn a hundred acres of swamp into a rice plantation. How could the financial team reconcile these costly schemes with the hard fact that Primavera was already spending beyond its means? Did they take the generosity of North American donors for granted? Apparently they did, for in late 1958 they sent one letter after another asking why the flow of cash from Woodcrest had slowed. Heiner was nonplussed: "Do they have any idea how hard it is to beg $10,000, let alone $100,000?" He wrote back reminding Primavera that such complaints were perhaps unrealistic, and that he worried that a lack of thankfulness and humility would threaten an open relationship.

This was risky, as Heiner was aware. He would surely be accused of promoting Woodcrest at the expense of the mother community. Knowing that sooner or later Hans would become involved, he first phoned him in Germany and then sent a series of letters to explain what he was doing.

Hans's response seemed to assure Heiner of his support. It was somewhat vague, which was a little puzzling, but there was no question that it was warm. "As long as Hans is happy," Heiner felt, "we can work out our differences with Primavera like brothers."

But Hans wasn't really happy. Two weeks after his letter arrived at Woodcrest, Gwynn, who had recently been in Europe, stopped in at Woodcrest for a few days. During his visit, he mentioned to Heiner that Hans was fuming about "the anti-Primavera mood" at Woodcrest—and that he held Heiner responsible for it. Hans had even told Gwynn before his departure, "It's a good thing you're going to America instead of me. If I came to Woodcrest, I'd smash it to pieces."

Heiner was floored. That Hans had taken Primavera's side in the dispute was not surprising. But such calculated double-dealing—this was a low blow. And it wasn't the first time—there had been other disturbing incidents recently. "Gwynn," Heiner asked him, "If you heard Hans say *that*, don't you owe it to the community to find out what he means?" Gwynn admitted he ought to, but begged Heiner to come with him. He seemed terribly nervous about confronting Hans alone.

Heiner was scared too. He had faced down his brother-in-law before, and each time it had taken years to recover from the consequences. The first time, in Silum, after his father's death, he had almost lost Annemarie when Hans had turned her against him. The second time, in Paraguay, when he had challenged Hans and Georg's ruthlessness, he had landed up starving in an isolation hut. The third face-off had earned him a year in a leper colony. Heiner could not risk a fourth confrontation. Or could he? To yield to Hans now would be to betray all those who had believed what he told them about a way of brotherly and sisterly community, and had left everything to follow the call. In any case, this dispute wasn't a personal one. The soul of the whole movement was at stake.

Heiner told no one except Annemarie about the looming conflict. To the others in Woodcrest, he said only, "I need to go to Europe to resolve a disagreement with a brother."

In Germany, they met at a hotel, and Hans tried to explain away his two-facedness. It was all a huge misunderstanding, he said. "If you only knew how much stress I've been under! Then you'd understand how I meant it."

"But how did you mean it, Hans?" Heiner asked him.

There were days of strenuous wrangling. After four days, they flew to England and continued. Every time they met to talk, Hans tried to play Heiner and Gwynn against each other, until both grew disgusted. Finally Hans realized that his game was up. Suddenly conciliatory, he asked Heiner and Gwynn what they would advise him to do.

The two withdrew to discuss their answer. Heiner pointed out that the way Hans had been acting, he could hardly be trusted as a leader of the community. "Wouldn't it be better if he stepped down, at least until this mess is clear?" Gwynn agreed but added—suddenly defensive of Hans—"Let's only be sure to do it without embarrassing him.

Hans has done more for the Bruderhof than any man I know, and out of gratefulness to him we have to be lenient."

Hans was sullen at the prospect of stepping down, but he did consent to it, and to another request: to clarify the matter by apologizing to the community.

Hans's apology was to take place at Bulstrode, a sprawling manor house near London, and the Bruderhof's newest European base. When everyone had assembled, Hans rose to speak. Heiner expected him to make a simple statement: apologize and announce his intent to lay down his responsibilities. But here, surrounded by supporters, Hans's contrition evaporated. It was as if he forgot that Heiner and Gwynn were there. After a few introductory comments, he veered wildly to a new subject—his wife's poor health: "Emy-Margret is about to undergo thyroid surgery next week," he said. "It will be a very difficult time for her. This morning I ask that we consider how we can support her."

Bulstrode's members responded as if on cue. One after the next, they sprang to their feet to declare their sympathy and support. By the end of the meeting, a celebration of the Lord's Supper had been suggested—as an affirmation of unity, and to give Emy-Margret inner strength. Heiner sat helpless and unbelieving. Afterward he walked out in a daze. If people here supported Hans so firmly, what could he and Gwynn do?

Later, Heiner cornered Hans. "You are a liar and a deceiver," he told him.

That night, Heiner found that no one wanted to talk with him. It was not as if he were a stranger here: many of the people at Bulstrode had lived with him in Primavera and knew him well. But now they wanted nothing to do with him. At first, Heiner was mystified, but he soon discovered why. Apparently, anyone who had a position here owed it to staying in Hans's good graces, and everyone else was terrified of provoking him.

Not long before, Hans had expelled Heiner's old teacher Trudi and her husband, largely because she had crossed him. After they were gone he had ransacked their apartment, gathered what they had left behind, and hauled it into a members' meeting. Then he had picked through clothes, letters, toiletries, and pictures, mocking Trudi's "materialism" as he held up item after item. No one had dared to say a word.

Nor did they dare to oppose Hans now. True, there had been no showdown, but the tension could be cut with a knife.

Heiner felt like a pariah. In the evening, as he walked down the mansion's long, vaulted corridors, looking for someone who might invite him in, doors swung shut as he approached. Finally, lonely and sick at heart, he slipped out of the big house and went across the open fields to the nearest village pub. At least there he might find a friendly face.

Over the next days, the three men met with four mediators — Bulstrode's suggestion for solving the stalemate. As before, Hans argued and evaded and played for sympathy. But this time Gwynn and Heiner were resolute. When at last the mediators made their report to a full members' meeting, everyone was in agreement: Hans was clearly in the wrong.

Heiner was relieved, but even more so by what happened next. People began to voice their true feelings about Hans. Each had his own story: his imperious manner, his use of flattery, and — when that didn't work — his biting sarcasm and veiled threats.

Many mentioned his tendency to categorize people, and to snub them by means of casually dropped comments. One outspoken member was a "thorn in his flesh," another was put down because he was "much too quiet," still another was suspect because she was Jewish. (Hans warned her fiancé against marrying her.) Almost everyone knew of Hans's penchant for such gossip, and many were co-guilty themselves. But on the whole, they had shrugged it off. Now, as one incident after another came to light, a disturbing picture emerged. Soon everyone had heard enough. Bulstrode asked Hans not only to step down, but to move to a community in the United States for a time of self-examination.

Late that night, Heiner was alone in his room. He stood for a while looking out of the window. It opened onto the flagstone court-yard that separated the two main wings of the mansion. At this late hour, all the rooms opposite him were dark, except for one – Hans's. Heiner was sure Hans was awake, though he could not see anyone through the lighted pane. Then, as he stood, he felt a dark ray of hatred beaming from that window toward his own. The conviction seized him: "Hans wants me dead." Shuddering, he locked the door to his room, lay down on the bed, and prayed. Then on an impulse he got up again, went to the heavy wardrobe in the corner, and shoved it against the door.

Heiner lay awake for hours. Sometime after midnight, he heard footsteps coming down the corridor. They stopped outside the door, and the knob turned slightly until stopped by the lock. First the would-be intruder rattled it, then he beat furiously on the door. Neither of them said a word; the only sound was a hollow pounding. Then the noise stopped abruptly, and the footsteps retreated.

Emy-Margret underwent her thyroid operation, recovered, and moved with Hans to a Bruderhof in Connecticut. (After a few months, Heiner, hoping for reconciliation, invited the Zumpes to move to Woodcrest.) Meanwhile, in South America, England, Germany, and the United States, everyone in the movement breathed a sigh of relief.

For the first few months after Hans's departure, it seemed that community life had taken a turn for the better. New members were joining every week, business was up, and public interest was at an all-time high. With almost 1300 members of two dozen different nationalities spread over eleven communities in five countries, the movement seemed to be flowering as never before. Certainly, there were problems; there would always be. But now that Hans was gone, many thought, they should be solvable. "This will be the year without crises," it was said. "A year of jubilee," others called it.

Emboldened by a new sense of freedom, members who had held back from expressing themselves made their voices heard for the first time in years. People expounded on every possible topic; many meetings were a hubbub of half-baked opinions. Emmy was one of the few who did not share in the general euphoria. "Everybody is happy that so-and-so is speaking up. But a lot of it is utter nonsense," she blurted out one day to Ben, her grandson and Hans's son. "Nobody listens to what is actually being said."

Or to what wasn't being said. One subject no one broached was why Hans had got his way for so long. Actually, the answer to this question was simple: without a large following, he never could have held onto his power for so many years. But until such a recognition could be honestly faced, it was more convenient – and far less painful – to let the blame fall to one scapegoat.

◆ ◆ ◆

Midsummer Day 1960 marked the fortieth anniversary of the Bruderhof's beginning in Sannerz. Heiner was in Sinntal, the community's German branch, but Hans-Hermann was in Woodcrest on a visit, and he and Annemarie had planned a festival. In the evening a special dinner was held, with flowers and music and readings from Emmy's memoirs.

But despite the happy atmosphere, trouble was brewing. Hans had disappeared, and though it was getting dark, he had still not returned. It wasn't the first time it had happened – all through the spring he had been morose, sometimes leaving his work for hours to wander along a nearby interstate. But before, he had always been home by sundown. Now it was ten o'clock, and Emy-Margret was worried. Several small parties had been sent out to look for him, but to no avail.

When Hans finally returned, he was in a black mood. Doug, Hans-Hermann, and a handful of others confronted him. Where on earth had he been all day? Hans said he had been depressed again—so depressed that he wanted to kill himself. He had set off for the interstate, intending to jump off an overpass. Then he had returned to Woodcrest and hidden in a bush. He had spent the entire evening watching the men search for him.

"Perhaps you don't realize how serious your situation is," one of them told him. "This is not a private matter, but a matter for the whole church."

Hans sat pale, expressionless. When he finally began to speak, none of them was prepared for what came out. "I know," he said. "It was a heavy sin . . . with Helene."

There was a long silence. They knew that Helene, a trusted member of the community, had been Hans's secretary for years. But such a thing had never crossed their minds. Why was he volunteering it now? They soon found out. Hans, who knew that Heiner was visiting the German Bruderhof where Helene lived, had worried that she would reveal his adultery. Now that he was not there to keep her quiet, he had guiltily assumed that she had spilled out everything to Heiner.

She hadn't, as Doug discovered when he called Heiner the same night. But she did the next morning. Relieved when told why Heiner wanted to talk, she said the affair had been tormenting her since it began almost a decade ago. But Hans had threatened her to keep her mouth shut. Now she freely poured out the whole sordid tale.

Two days later, Hans flew alone to Germany, where he had made arrangements to live with friends. (Emy-Margret, staggered by the revelation of her husband's infidelity, remained at Woodcrest with the children.) Heiner met his brother-in-law at the airport in Frankfurt and pled with him to turn his life around. It would be the last time they met.

Meanwhile, a wave of disbelief swept the entire movement, leaving everyone unsettled and braced for what might happen next. Not a household was unaffected. For years, Hans had married their children and buried their parents. He had counseled them and heard their confessions (and had earned a reputation for special severity when it came to sexual sin). What is more, Hans was also among those whom Eberhard had named to guide the community after his death. As much as he had been feared, he had also been revered. How should one respond to a betrayal of this magnitude?

For many, it was too much to stomach. One by one, like the first rolling balls that set off an avalanche, several long-time members announced that they had had enough. Soon a half dozen families had packed up and left.

Newer members were equally devastated, but they tended to see the situation as a call to arms. Here was the community they had given up everything to join, on the brink of a crisis that was deepening every day. To run away from it now was out of the question. If anything, it was a time for firmness and resolve. Besides, many sensed a shakeup was due. As Hans-Hermann put it, "Our movement has undergone an operation for cancer. The main growth has been removed. But the body still needs to become healthy again, and it is not yet at all certain that everything has been removed that needs removing."

Hans-Hermann proved right. With Hans's dictatorship toppling, the power structures that had supported it began to crash down too. As had happened at Bulstrode after Hans's unmasking there, people throughout the movement began speaking up for the first time in years. Bit by bit, Hans's goals came into focus.

According to his closest coworkers, he had cherished grand dreams for the future of the community in Germany. He had hoped to outshine anything Eberhard had accomplished. But to his chagrin, it had not worked out that way. Instead, the movement had flourished at *Bekehrungsanstalt Woodcrest*—Woodcrest Conversion Institute, as Hans called it derisively. And so, smoldering with concealed jealousy, he had determined to outdo Heiner and his band of upstart Americans at all costs. Woodcrest could attract all the new members it wanted, but he would see to it that "his" Bruderhofs were flooded with the same. Soon an aggressive drive for European members was underway.

Now it was all over, and those whom Hans had buttonholed – some of them idealists unprepared for the demands of communal life – were left wondering what they had come to.

In January 1961, Heiner planned a trip to Primavera, whose leadership had requested a visit after the events of the previous months had left the community anxious and discouraged. He hoped that this sign of solidarity from Woodcrest would cheer up the members there. He traveled at the end of the month, accompanied by Doug Moody and Art Wiser, who had come from Macedonia a few years before. On the flight down, the two young Americans were in high spirits. This would be their first chance to see Primavera. They quizzed Heiner about his years there. "If Hans was living a double life so long, how was it possible that no one stopped him earlier? What was going on all those years?"

Heiner dodged the questions, saying only, "I don't want to influence you against anyone." Then, beaming, he began to tell them about each person they would meet. "Johnny Robinson will be there when we land in Asunción. If you want to know what he's like, draw a big heart and add arms and legs."

The Primavera they arrived at was far different from the Primavera of the 1940s. Back then it had been a hardscrabble pioneer outpost. Now it looked like an established missionary colony, with some of the well-known missionary problems: whites ran the machinery and supervised a hundred or more brown hired hands. Everyone and everything had a place, a position, and a role. If at times it felt stifling, at least it all ran smoothly.

Will, Heiner's old traveling companion, welcomed the visitors at their first meal, and soon Doug and Art noticed that he seemed to have a finger in every pie. He seemed to be running every meeting, ticking off each point on the agenda he had written down in a little book. In contrast to Woodcrest, the tone was curt and businesslike. When Will snapped his book shut, the meeting adjourned, and everyone scattered to his or her appointed place. By the end of the week, Doug and Art's enthusiasm for the mother community had worn off. Was this really what they had joined?

Four days into the visit, Will asked for a private talk. His personal life was in shambles, he told Heiner, Doug, and Art, and he was suffering from depression and ulcers. "My whole emphasis has been wrong," he went on. "I've become an expert at community – a communiteer. My focus was organization and protocol. But I just can't go on living like this." He looked defeated.

Will came to talk again two days later, and during the conversation, Doug mentioned Eberhard. Will trembled visibly. "I've always believed it was good that Eberhard Arnold died when he did," he said darkly. "Otherwise we could never have developed independent of his influence." Then, breaking down, he asked to be relieved of his responsibilities.

That night Primavera's members met to discuss Will's situation. As they gathered, a tropical storm exploded over them. Rain lashed the building, and those who spoke had to shout above the thunder. Will was invited to speak, and stood up. "The greatest fight of my life," he cried, "has been against the influence of Eberhard Arnold."

Lightning lit Will's face as he spoke, and as he sat down, the meeting erupted with expressions of indignation and astonishment. His statement seemed to demand immediate explanation. How long had he felt this way? Why would anyone have such a strong reaction to a man who had been dead for a quarter century – a man Will had never even met? What did it say about Primavera that a long-time leader felt this way about the community's founder?

Much as Will's bald confession shocked many in Primavera, it could not have completely surprised them. Even if it seemed to come from out of the blue, it brought into sudden focus a conflict that had been going on for decades. On the one side stood the vision of the community's original members: to live out Jesus' teachings as the first Christians did, in love and mutual service. On the other stood the vision that had guided Primavera for the last twenty years: a well-run, outwardly successful community led by the ablest man. It was a matter of two opposing goals.

The next days brought a spate of truth-telling about the past. It was as if Will had burst a dam, and old memories came surging out through the breach. Especially memories of the first years in Primavera. Ruth Land, the doctor, was one of those who shared recollections that troubled them, mentioning Emmy's stroke on the night the rebellion of the sixteen was crushed.

Art and Doug, to whom Heiner had told nothing about Primavera's past, reeled at hearing all this. It struck them that in the early 1940s the community had made a deliberate turn away from the spirit of Sannerz, choosing "objectivity" and "organization" instead. Will, through his harsh honesty, had forced the community to recognize that it would have to choose one or the other.

Art and Doug called a meeting of those who had been at Primavera since the beginning. "Don't we have to face – and repent for – the way Emmy Arnold was treated in 1944? If we don't, can there ever be a blessing on our community?" A chorus burst from all sides. "Yes, but that was only one incident! Do you know how they treated Emmy, Fritz, Hardy, and Heiner in 1942 and 1944?" As new details were remembered, the story came out in pieces: the enforced separation of Heiner and Annemarie's family (and many others), the poems in the outhouses, the widely shared distaste for talk about Sannerz and the Sparhof.

Many were struck with remorse; Alfred wept for most of the meeting. Others tried to wash their hands, saying they hadn't really known what was going on. But most looked relieved that they could finally talk about something that had been shrouded in silence far too long. As Ruth said later, "This was what we had wanted all the time. We'd all got caught up in our work—there had always been plenty of it. We were swamped with activities. At the same time, there was always this helpless feeling: Who can I talk to about what troubles me? Partly this was because of the very strong belief in the community that one should never bring up the past."

For many now looking back, one moment glowed out like a beacon: October 1941, when Heiner, at death's door, had appealed to them to seek repentance. Older members kept mentioning that time, and said it had been the decisive turning point. It had been Primavera's great chance to become a community of love. But it had been rejected, and they had allowed Hans to trample the movement of heart that Heiner's call had inspired.

By now almost everyone admitted that Primavera was inwardly rotten. "We've been experts at community, but mistreated each other. Communitarianism replaced Christ." As Gwynn Evans would later write, "To say that all this had nothing to do with the teaching of Jesus of Nazareth is far too mild. My attitude, at least, spurned the compassion and forgiving love of which the Gospels speak, and yet, most dreadful of all, it was all done in the name of brotherly love." The community's very soul was at stake.

Evening after evening, and sometimes even during the day, the entire Primavera brotherhood, or decision-making body, met to search for common ground and a way forward. Each meeting was more confused than the last. Everyone was eager to talk about what had gone wrong. They told of children who had been subjected to corporal punishment; of disabled or eccentric members who had been ostracized and ridiculed. They told how people caught in some small act of delinquency had sometimes been expelled with no second chance; how alienated teenagers were running wild in gangs.

Public confessions were followed by outcries. Long-winded explanations were interrupted, only to be resumed. Accusations were traded; defenses went up; apologies were made. At times, Art would acknowledge later, mob psychology took hold, and several members were told to pack their bags, sometimes over simple misunderstandings. "We cannot go on like this," Heiner would plead. "We have to listen to one another." But then, after a heavy silence, the pattern would be repeated yet again. At night, people came to Heiner full of fears for the future. What was going on? What would happen to them all? People began to announce their intention to leave the community.

One evening, after yet another meeting had turned to finger-pointing and shouting, Heiner said, "I wonder if it is Jesus of Nazareth who is being served here." Everyone was quiet, and the meeting closed.

Not all was bleak. Heiner saw cause for hope in Primavera's younger members, who were ready for radical change. These were the sons and daughters of his old comrades, the children of the Sparhof and Ashton Fields, who were now in their twenties. They sensed a new wind blowing from Woodcrest and asked Heiner over and over, "How can we find the same spirit here?" "Hold on," many older members said, "Things aren't as bad as you're making them out to be." For his part, Heiner sympathized with the younger ones but feared that undue zeal might only deepen the divisions. And so he cautioned them, "Don't push too hard. Go slow."

Knowing that Primavera was now entering uncharted waters, Heiner reported on the developments to the communities in Europe and the United States and asked if they were in agreement. He was particularly concerned about how Georg, who was now in England, would react. To his great relief, the three European communities sent a telegram confirming their support.

In Primavera, though, things kept getting worse. One evening the meeting turned to utter chaos. It began with long speeches from older members. Before long, several younger members snapped. One stood up shouting, "I can't stand it anymore. It will kill me if I have to listen to any more of this stuff." They were at an impasse.

Afterward, Heiner went into the woods alone. The jungle pressed in around him, wet and black. He was in such anguish that he did not know what to do with himself. "How will we get through this? Every meeting gets worse. I wish I had never come down here."

It was around this time that a small group approached Heiner. They said it was pointless to continue meeting with everyone—too many were confused or carrying baggage from the past. Why not dissolve the old brotherhood, and start over with only those who really wanted to be part of a new one? As Andreas Meier, a proponent of this idea, later explained, "There was no real brotherhood anyway, and we thought it was high time to recognize that."

Remarkably, though unable to agree on any other suggestion so far, the members at Primavera supported this move. They would disband the entire brotherhood, replace it with a new core, and then build it up again, member by member.

Many wanted a committee of five, including the visitors from Woodcrest, to decide who should form the new quorum, but Heiner flatly refused to act unilaterally: "That is something that has to be agreed to by your own circle." In the end, the Paraguayan members unanimously agreed to a list of twenty-three people and entrusted them with making decisions for the community while the rest tried to find their feet. Additional members were to be reinstated on an individual basis.

By early March, after more than a month of intensive meetings, Heiner was exhausted—and ready to fly home to Woodcrest. For one thing, he urgently needed to consult with Georg, who had come over from England to discuss the situation at hand. For another, he was anxious about Annemarie. Earlier, she had planned to fly down to support him, but in the meantime, heart trouble had prevented her from traveling. "Perhaps it was just as well she couldn't come," Heiner thought—there had been too many painful revelations.

Cyril, who was an enthusiastic member of the new core group, felt the same. After one of the meetings for truth-telling about the past, he had pulled Art aside to say he was glad Annemarie didn't have to hear it all. "Art, what she suffered over the years you just would not believe."

Heiner's return trip took him via Buenos Aires. Long layovers were common at the time, and it was three days before he could get a flight to New York. In other circumstances, it might have been a welcome break. But Heiner could neither rest nor relax. He was simply too taxed by the previous weeks.

Before he had left Primavera, the new core group had asked several "unclear" members to leave, among them his old friend Johnny. On one level, this was understandable as an emergency measure, painful as it was. With so much dissension in the ranks, it had become nearly impossible for the community to function. Furthermore, no one had been permanently expelled but rather simply asked to take a temporary leave for a time of consideration. The hope was that with time and space, tensions could be eased and attitudes reexamined. But Heiner had still pled with the new leadership to be cautious, fearing that some might despair.

Now, alone in Buenos Aires, he worried he had not done enough. Whenever he thought about Johnny, for instance, he agonized that an injustice had been done. Had he been able to, Heiner would have traveled back to Primavera then and there. But he did not have enough cash to change his ticket.

Days after Heiner arrived back in Woodcrest, a telegram came from Primavera announcing that over a hundred more people were leaving the community. Heiner was shocked, and made plans to return to Paraguay.

He begged Georg to come with him, but Georg said he couldn't. Several months before, his wife had suffered a debilitating stroke, and she had still not recovered. Heiner rushed back down without him, hoping to spend time with those who had been asked to leave. But he never got the chance. Primavera's business managers, asked to prepare for the eventual closing of the community, had prematurely sold the land it sat on, thus placing the whole community in danger of homelessness. For the next three weeks Heiner was consumed with trying to straighten out the affair, and then had to return to the United States – earlier than he wanted to – for negotiations with the Mennonite Central Committee, which was helping to finance the purchase.

By the time he got to Woodcrest again, he was so run down, and had such trouble breathing, that he could hardly walk. Milton Zimmerman, a young physician who had recently come to the community, took a cardiogram and told him, "You're on the verge of a heart attack. You need absolute rest."

Now Heiner could do little more than watch the storm from his bed. In fact, no one could have directed the flow of events – the rush of decisions, counter-decisions, and moves all followed each other too quickly. At one point Heiner told Georg, "If we can hold the communities in Primavera till fall, then we have won. Otherwise I do not see any way out."

In early May, Hardy came over to Woodcrest from Bulstrode, and one day while out driving and chatting with Heiner, Hardy made a passing reference to something he had recently found out about: an agreement Georg and Hans had made to silence Heiner in 1941.

"What agreement?" Heiner asked him. "What on earth are you talking about?"

"You know, the agreement he made with Hans when you were sick. They felt your talk about repentance was unhealthy, and decided to work against you as a team."

Hardy faltered, seeing Heiner's expression of horror. "According to Georg, you knew about this. He told you everything – or that's what he claimed, in Bulstrode."

"I know nothing. Georg never talked to me about this."

"But I assumed . . ."

Heiner cut off his brother. "Georg knelt down for me to bless him in 1941, while he and Hans were conspiring to get rid of me?"

For days Heiner could hardly eat. He was so agitated that he could not concentrate on anything, and had to withdraw even from his family. It was a week before he could gather his thoughts sufficiently to write to Georg. After asking him whether Hardy's report was true, he poured out his heart as he had never done before: "Now I come to the most difficult thing in my life, something I've had to struggle over right into this year. As a child I had an experience of Jesus that I valued like a pearl. You smiled at this experience and attacked it—yes, I could use even stronger expressions. But perhaps you yourself will remember what you said to me about it in Primavera, in private and in public. You told me, sharply, 'Christ is experienced only through the church!' . . . And yet the personal experience that led me to join this life was ridiculed and rejected, while the brotherhood that claimed to be this church tolerated hatred, lying, divisiveness, and impurity. Until now I have told no one into what pain and need this brought me. But I believe now that it is the heaviest sin of my life: that I listened to you. My life could have taken a different turn. It is the greatest grace of my life that here in America I have been allowed to start living again like a child."

Heiner was near a breakdown. Hans's deceit and the confusion he had left in his wake, the collapse of Primavera and the ongoing chaos there, the revelation of Georg's betrayal—who knew what might come next?

What hurt most was to see so many people turning their backs on the dreams of their youth. They had come to the Sparhof, to Silum, and to Ashton Fields so full of joy and so ready for sacrifice. They had left careers and families for the promise of a new life. Heiner had helped many of them fight through to find faith; he had heard their confessions, baptized, and married them. They had vowed faithfulness not only to God but to each other, and he felt a shepherd's responsibility for them. Now, middle-aged and bitter, they were leaving it all. To see so many disown the vision that had once awakened and transformed them broke Heiner's heart.

He felt it was his fault as well as theirs, especially when he thought about the early years in Primavera. He and the others had confronted Hans twice, and both times they had backed down for fear of splitting the community. Now, two decades later, the community had split anyway. "If only I had stayed true to what God called me to as a boy!" he told himself. "If only I had not backed down and compromised and twisted my conscience! Maybe then this disaster could have been avoided."

For most of May Heiner stayed indoors to rest, not even joining Annemarie and the older children when they went to the community's evening meetings. Monika and Else, who were too young to go, stayed home too, and heard him through the wall as they lay silently in bed. Often he wept, begging God for forgiveness. Some nights he didn't just weep, but cried out with grief, beating his head against the wall. Once he appeared in their room, his face streaked with tears, and said, "Children, forgive me for being such a bad father."

By June, Heiner was in such poor health that Doug arranged for him and Annemarie to take time off at a rental cottage near Woodcrest. They moved in on June 1, a Thursday. On Sunday would be Christoph's graduation from business school—an event Heiner was looking forward to celebrating with his son. But it didn't work out that way. On Saturday afternoon Heiner's nose started to bleed. It went on at intervals throughout the evening, for longer and longer spells and with increasing loss of blood. Around midnight Annemarie called Milton. For five hours he tried to stop the bleeding with cotton gauze. Finally he took Heiner to the emergency room.

Heiner underwent surgery, then stayed in the hospital for three weeks—aside from his nosebleed, he had developed a life-threatening heart condition from all the stress. Mail poured in from all corners of the movement, with many cries for help—far more than he could respond to. Heiner's own conscience convicted him for where he had been hard or judgmental in the past, and he wrote letters to a number of people asking forgiveness.

Meanwhile Primavera continued to melt down. By now the tremors had reached so far that they were toppling the Bruderhof's European branches as well; if anything, the situation in England and Germany was even more chaotic, as Heiner would learn only years later. (Gwynn, whom Heiner's children remembered so warmly as their foster father during their parents' trip to America, was among those who left at this time.) Annemarie spared Heiner the details, but it made little difference—as it was, he was plagued by the crisis even in his dreams.

It was nearly August by the time Heiner could begin regular work again, and by then, the tumult in Primavera had mostly passed. By year's end, out of a population of almost 1300, 246 members with 294 minor children—540 people in all—had left or been asked to leave. (Of these, 146 would eventually return.) Sibyl, who typed the reports Heiner dictated for the eleven other communities, found her job had become easier. A year ago, trying to make eleven carbon copies of each page, she had needed to bang down each key of her manual typewriter as hard as she could. Now she needed only four carbon copies—for Woodcrest, Bulstrode, and two other American branches. The other seven had all shut down.

The collapse left the remaining communities reeling—and deeply in debt. Heiner had urged that each adult and child leaving Primavera be given a ticket to their country of origin and $100 per person as landing money. It was a pittance, he knew, but still a great deal more than the community could afford. (As things turned out, there wasn't enough cash to go around, and some left with even less than the $100. In an effort to cover the costs, the Bruderhof took out heavy loans, which Woodcrest was still paying off years later.)

Even though Heiner could do nothing to produce money that simply wasn't there, the matter gave him no peace. Daily he ran through the names of those who had left over and over again, picturing each of them. How were they making out? Had he or anyone else who remained in the community wronged them in any way? He remembered all too well what it had been like to be sent penniless into a strange, unfriendly world.

Money was the least of it. How could anyone begin to grasp the full meaning of what had happened? It had burst upon them like a violent storm. No one had precipitated it; it just poured down on them all. The bill for twenty-five years of unresolved problems had been suddenly presented for payment – the mortgage called in all at once. And no one was without blame in letting things get to such a pass. It was not as if the guilty had all left and the innocent had all stayed behind. On the contrary, all were guilty, most simply by letting complacency and self-righteousness slowly extinguish what was once a radiant joy.

Clearly, the renewal they needed could only come through the agony of birth pains. Each community member, both those who stayed and those who left, had to face the question: Are you willing to take responsibility for your part in the mess? Are you personally willing to repent and to change?

Many found the change too excruciating. Their whole world had shattered, and they could not muster up the courage to start again. Some turned increasingly angry and bitter.

Others welcomed the upheaval. Ilse von Köller, a German member who left in 1961 (and returned in the 1970s) called it "a storm wind sent by Christ that had to come to sweep out what did not belong in the community." And Emmy, though she grieved deeply over those leaving, still compared it to a long-awaited change of season: "How I wish for us all that the coldness of the long winter passes soon! How I wish that we might soon experience the springtime that we already see the first signs of." Many others also saw it in this light – as an eleventh-hour chance for renewal – and embraced it.

Among these was Georg. After getting Heiner's letter in May, he had spent weeks wrestling to come to terms with his longstanding duplicity. Then he wrote back, acknowledging his guilt and asking not only forgiveness of Emmy, Heiner, and the others he had hurt (they gladly granted it to him) but also the entire brotherhood. Within months, he was serving again as a trusted pastor in the community.

And yet so many other much-loved brothers and sisters had left: Johnny, Will, Gwynn, and Cyril. Sophie and Luise. Hans. Two of Heiner's own siblings, Monika and Hans-Hermann. Heiner would spend the rest of his life working for reconciliation with each of them.

33

Liberation

FOR TWENTY YEARS, THE BRUDERHOF HAD lacked a helmsman. Ever since Heiner's sickness in 1941, Hans had acted as head of the movement, but he had waved off suggestions to officially name him to this position. He preferred to work as a puppet-master, keeping up the trappings of egalitarianism while pulling strings from behind the scenes to make others move as he wanted them to.

Now that he was gone, many were eager to name someone to provide unifying leadership—someone who would lead not as a manager or an executive, but as a shepherd. The trauma of the past three years had convinced them of the wisdom of the early Christian tradition of having a bishop—though they did not use the term—charged with ensuring that no one was neglected. It wasn't long before Heiner's name began to surface.

Heiner wasn't keen on the idea. "We all should be servants and slaves of Christ," he would say. "I only want to be a brother among brothers." Annemarie felt the same, saying she was reluctant to have anyone named to such a role after Hans had so badly misused his position as a leader for so many years.

But it was precisely his approach to leadership which gave people confidence that Heiner was the right one. As he would later express it: "True leadership means service, so it is a terrible thing to use it to control others. When such abuse takes place in our community, it is especially devilish, because brothers and sisters dedicate themselves voluntarily, trustingly, and openheartedly to the community. In a dictatorial state, people might yield to tyranny even though inwardly they reject it as evil. But in a brotherhood of believers, where members trust each other, the misuse of leadership for personal gain is nothing but soul-murder. If any of you ever feel that I am wielding power over anyone in the slightest way, I beg you to point it out to me. I would rather die than do that."

By the summer of 1962, there was widespread agreement that Heiner had the inner authority for this task. He and Annemarie finally gave in. On July 13, at Woodcrest, the community confirmed Heiner as senior pastor of the movement. Annemarie wept over the decision. Unlike newer members, she had an inkling of what burdens and hurts would come. When the meeting ended, however, she dried her tears and set to work helping him.

Annemarie never walked, she ran. She rose early and worked late, writing letters, knitting, tending her garden, cleaning her apartment (and then helping a neighbor clean hers), and babysitting. When a communal project was announced to tackle extra work before breakfast – hoeing corn or picking beans – she was often the first to arrive, even though as one of the older women she had every right to stay in bed. In the rare moments when she wasn't working, she went out walking, berry picking, or swimming.

Throughout Heiner's life, he drew intense reactions from people who met him. Some responded to him with deep respect, others with outsize animosity. Perhaps the latter were envious of the love and trust people gave him. Even in Primavera, when he was out of the community's good graces, many had turned to him to confide their personal struggles or problems with their children. Those jealous of such trust did not realize that he had earned it at a great cost.

After the near-collapse of the movement in 1961, some who had left turned on him – some angry that they had "given the best years of their lives" to the community, others understandably hurt by the circumstances of their parting from it. Even though Heiner might not respond to every communication, he thought constantly of those who had left the movement. In the years that followed, he visited dozens of them—in the United States, England, and Germany—and wrote them hundreds of letters. And he urged the rest of the community to help. Dwight, Doug, Art, Dick, and others traveled to Europe and South America year after year to seek reconciliation. Over the next years, a slow but steady trickle came back to the community, among them Sophie and dozens more.

Of the others Heiner visited, some were friendly but uninterested, while a few slammed doors in his face. Predictably if unfairly, many blamed him for Primavera's collapse. For his part, Heiner usually did not defend himself, but simply kept asking for forgiveness "wherever I or the community might have hurt you"—and gently kept reminding those who would listen that they had actually been part of that same community themselves.

Heiner's ceaseless efforts to reach out upset some people in Woodcrest. Why was he squandering his precious time on ghosts from the past? But Heiner persisted. He had no peace whenever he thought of his former comrades and pictured their faces. At one point he even asked to be stripped of his membership in the community, so that he and Annemarie could visit them as equals. Perhaps in this way, he hoped, he could reach the most antagonistic of them. When this request was denied him—other members could not agree with it in good conscience—he only redoubled his efforts. On a single trip to Europe in the spring of 1964, he made forty visits to former members. He found pockets of hostility, but open hearts too.

With such pressing demands on Heiner's attention, it would have been understandable if he had focused only on the internal problems of the community. But he had never forgotten his father's words to him that night as they looked down into the Rhine Valley from Silum.

Papa had warned him never to become so caught up in the problems at hand that he forgot the world beyond.

On August 4, 1964, the US destroyer *Maddox*, cruising off the coast of North Vietnam in the Gulf of Tonkin, reported being fired on. Hours later, President Lyndon Johnson ordered air strikes on North Vietnam. The Americanization of the Vietnam War had begun. That same day, in backwoods Mississippi, an FBI team investigating the disappearance of three civil rights workers got their big break. They were excavating an earthen dam, and halfway through the sweltering afternoon they uncovered a human hand. "We've struck oil," they radioed back in the code arranged with headquarters to foil snooping by the KKK-affiliated local police.

Under packed clay, they found the body of Michael Schwerner. A twenty-four-year-old from New York City, Schwerner and his wife Rita had come to Mississippi with the Congress for Racial Equality to register black voters. He had last been seen a month ago. Beneath his corpse were found the bodies of two coworkers, Andrew Goodman and James Chaney.

Michael Schwerner's remains were flown to New York a few days later for burial. On its front page, the *Times* carried a searing photograph of his mother as she waited in the airport to receive his casket. She was sobbing, her face twisted with raw grief. As soon as Heiner saw the picture, he felt he had to do something. Woodcrest was in contact with Martin Luther King, Jr. and had longstanding ties to the Civil Rights movement, thanks in part to relationships going back to Clarence Jordan and Koinonia. Here was a chance to show support for the family of a young man who had sacrificed everything for justice. Taking the newspaper to Dick Domer, a friend, Heiner showed him the photo and told him, "We have to reach out somehow. We have to do something."

Not long afterward, Heiner and Dick obtained an address and drove to Pelham, New York, the Schwerner family home. They had tried phoning earlier, but with no luck. "Let's pass by the house anyway," Heiner said.

It was around four o'clock when they parked in front of a modest two-story suburban home. Heiner rang the bell, and a short, motherly woman of around fifty opened the door. Heiner took off his hat. "Mrs. Schwerner?" he said. She nodded, and he introduced himself. "We are here because we have read about your son Michael."

Anne Schwerner paused, as if sizing him up. Logically, everything about this unannounced bearded visitor in secondhand clothes should have set her against him. He was obviously German, and he had said he was from a Christian community. That was two counts against him. The daughter of Orthodox Jews, Anne had grown up in the shadow of the Holocaust, and as a mother, she had just lost a son to the Christian Knights of the Ku Klux Klan. Just in the last weeks, anonymous racists had been phoning the house with death threats. Her husband Nat had warned her not to let in strangers.

Still, there was something about this man that had set her at ease as soon as she had peered through the crack in the door. She had seen his face and knew, *This is an honest man.* And so she opened the door and beckoned them inside: "Come in. I like to talk about Mickey."

They sat in the living room, and Anne wanted to know where they came from. Heiner briefly explained, and added, "It's like a kibbutz, but Christian, where we try to live in brotherhood."

Anne responded with enthusiasm. "Brotherhood—that's what Mickey wanted. He always said, 'I don't want social work, that's paternalistic.'" She got up and brought them drinks. Heiner noticed that she came alive as she talked, so that she seemed to be continually in motion, continuously shedding sparks of energy. "You know, I'm not religious. Mickey was not religious. But he believed that if man is an extension of God, he should be treated like a brother. He wanted to treat everyone he met as a brother. So he always wore jeans—overalls, actually—and a beard. Out of protest, you understand. That's how they recognized him in Mississippi, that he was the one to kill." She brought out photos of Mickey as a little boy.

Heiner and Dick stayed an hour and a half. When it was time to go, Heiner urged her, "We'd love to have you and your husband come visit us." She promised she would.

Anne and her husband, Nat, made their first visit to Woodcrest a few months later, and kept coming. Each visit was an occasion for passionate discussions of faith and politics. "Those racists are a bunch of bastards," she said. "Did you know that if a Negro woman has an appendicitis operation in Mississippi, they sterilize her? The government knows it, and they don't do a thing. It is like Hitler's Germany!"

As time went on, the Arnolds and Schwerners became close friends. It was an unlikely bond. Like her husband, Anne was a staunch atheist, having left the Judaism of her childhood. She was determined to understand how rational people who cared about social justice could base their lives on faith. As they sat together in the evening, she went around to everyone in the room asking incredulously: "Do you pray to God? Do you pray? Do you know that the Klan begin their ceremonies with a prayer to God? What is the difference between your belief in God and theirs?"

Despite their strong differences, they saw right into each other's hearts. Anne, in particular, always showed special love and respect for Heiner, and every time they met he had to stoop down so that she, stretching up on tiptoe, could embrace him.

Having come of age in a nation of Nazis, Heiner loved America for its freedoms. All the more, he was alarmed to see the same demons that had ruined Germany rearing their heads in his new homeland: militarism, economic oppression, and racism. But it heartened him to see so many people speaking out, and he felt drawn to add his voice to theirs.

In the fall of 1964, when the American public was only dimly aware that US forces had entered Vietnam, Heiner helped organize a crowd from Woodcrest to march against the war. He also concerned himself—for the next nine years—with the many young men then seeking recognition as conscientious objectors to war. He guided them as they applied for CO status, encouraged them before draft board hearings, and helped arrange their terms of alternative service when they received exemption.

Heiner's respect for Martin Luther King, Jr. was profound. "He is a prophetic voice," he often said. In February 1965, after the death of the Civil Rights martyr Jimmy Lee Jackson, he sent his son, Christoph, to the funeral along with Art. The following month, together with Dwight and Milton and others from Woodcrest, he joined King's second march from Selma to Montgomery. Tensions were high: on the first day they were there, a fellow Northerner, Viola Liuzzo, was shot and killed. But despite the risks, and despite his heart condition, Heiner walked a full day in the Alabama heat.

While Heiner sympathized with the movement's political goals—voting rights, school desegregation, equal-employment opportunities—he felt they were limited. What really struck a deep chord in him was that people were standing up for the oppressed. Remembering Christel and the other proletarian rebels who had been the heroes of his boyhood, he spoke often of his belief that at the root of any fight for justice lies an inspiration from God. As he wrote to Georg in Bulstrode, "They say that the murderers of Michael Schwerner marked him out as their victim because he was a Jew and wore a beard. Now one hears that nonbelievers are asking Christians: 'And what was Jesus? Wasn't he a Jew with a beard?' Many of them feel the pain of injustice more deeply than the Christians and point out that Jesus was also an outcast. For example, Nat and Anne told us that their son, who was not a Christian, had deep reverence for Jesus' teaching and called him 'the greatest man.' What is happening here is the opposite of the so-called revival movements that preach only personal salvation. For the people in this movement, it is the question of justice that is the starting point—and this leads them to look to Jesus."

◆ ◆ ◆

In May 1966 Nat and Anne attended Christoph's wedding. The bride was Verena Meier, a young woman whose parents had joined the Sparhof from Switzerland around the same time as Annemarie. Heiner held the wedding himself. Mindful of the Schwerners' discomfort with religion, he tailored the service to them, speaking about the couple's desire to dedicate their marriage to working for brotherhood and justice.

Christoph was the second of Heiner's children to marry. Anneli, now called Maria, had married the year before, and in September she had her first child, making Heiner and Annemarie grandparents.

Ever since his son was a teen, Heiner had felt a special bond with him. Earlier, he had been careful not to put him under any religious pressure. Yet he hoped that through his and Annemarie's example, Christoph might find a personal, living faith—just as he had, through Tata and his own parents. And this happened.

Christoph had always been sure, in a vague way, that he wanted to follow in his parents' footsteps. But one night when he was fourteen, as he sat on the hill overlooking Woodcrest watching the stars, he heard someone calling him—not a human voice, but one deep within him. It was a turning point. From that moment on he felt he must give his life to Jesus. He wanted to witness to the gospel as Rachoff, his grandparents, and his parents had done. Back at home, he went straight to his father and mother in their bedroom and told them of his decision. Tears came to their eyes. Christoph realized how much his parents had been praying for him. From that evening on, his relationship to his father changed. The two had always been close, but now father and son shared a deeper bond as well.

Heiner's daughters also made the same decision, each at her own time and in her own way. The turning point for Monika, the second-to-youngest, came in the summer after her ninth grade year. At a worship meeting one Sunday, Dwight spoke on the theme, "You are never too young to give your life to God." Overwhelmed by this thought, Monika felt she had received a direct call from God to follow him. She could hardly wait for the meeting to end, so she could talk to her father. "Yes, you are never too young," he said. And with that, she knew how she would spend the rest of her life.

By the spring of 1968, Monika, now nineteen and a pre-med student, was asking to become a full member of the community, and joining other would-be members in her parents' house for informal weekly discussions. In this relaxed atmosphere, the young men and women started plying Heiner with questions about the community's history. What had happened in 1961, when so many of their childhood friends left? And why were older members so tight-lipped about the early years in Paraguay?

Heiner had kept the silence like everyone else. He hadn't even spoken to Annemarie about all that had happened in the early 1940s. Nor had he told her everything he had heard at Primavera in 1961, when so many mysteries had finally become clear. Up till now he had felt that to talk would only tear open old scars. Besides, he and Annemarie had decided long ago to forgive those who had hurt them, "as we ourselves have been forgiven for our failings."

On the other hand, Heiner realized that his own children and others their age were growing up ignorant of their community's history. "The young people have a right to know about the past," he told himself. And so, for the first time, he decided to tell the whole story, starting with his father's death. Because others at Woodcrest were interested too, Heiner was asked to talk to the whole community – not just Monika and her peers.

As Heiner started telling, he took care to stress his own failings: "What I'm going to tell you tonight was perhaps the biggest mistake

I made in my life. In the months just before I went down to Paraguay, I was taken in by the notion that Hans Zumpe should be 'completely forgiven'—that he should be reinstalled and that the people Papa named in his last letter should work together as he had hoped. I really believed that if only Hans, Georg, Hardy, and I could work together, the destructive course that had been set after Papa's death could be reversed. I left England for South America with the firm intention, 'I will fight for this!'

"Then I got sick. The doctor told me I had only a few hours to live. As my last wish, I asked the brotherhood to appoint Hans, Hardy, and Georg—which is how I got it through. It's doubtful everyone would have agreed otherwise, from what I have heard since. Many of those who remembered Hans as a dictator were apprehensive, but agreed because I asked.

"Then it all went completely wrong. The close working together I had hoped for never happened, not even for twenty-four hours."

As he told the story of what had followed—his hallucinations when he was ill, Hans and Georg's plot to sideline and silence him, his separation from his family, and his banishment to the leper colony—the young people listened, horrified. So did his doctor, Milton, who was shocked to learn how close to death Heiner had been, and how his medical condition had been used against him.

Milton was also curious about the medical particulars. Later, in his office, he pulled out Heiner's files and started reading through the yellowing sheets covered with Cyril's neat handwriting. Soon he was jotting down notes, because an unexpected picture was emerging: it seemed that while Heiner was sick in 1941, he had been suffering from massive overdoses of bromide. Milton checked and re-checked his pharmacological manual to confirm that the symptoms Cyril recorded fit this diagnosis. It all matched up. When Milton was certain, he arranged a meeting with Heiner and Annemarie and explained to them that Heiner's abnormal mental symptoms in October and November of 1941, including his hallucinations, had been drug-induced.

As Milton spoke, he saw relief flood over their faces. The memory of Heiner's hallucinations had been a source of self-doubt to both of them for decades. Hans and Georg had insisted that these nightmares were a sign of instability or even spiritual darkness, and for twenty-six years, Heiner had been left to worry that they were right. He told Milton, "All this time, I kept wondering if there was something devil-ish in me." He remembered how he had sensed a connection between his bizarre dreams and the bromide drug and had resisted taking it, only to have the doses forced down his throat. Annemarie, too, had often felt anguish over her memories of that time. "I didn't know what to do with the slurs they made against him. They accused him again and again about it. In the end, it was just too painful for me to bear, and I tried to thrust it from my mind."

That evening, Milton reported his findings to a members' meeting. Since Georg was present, Doug asked him if he could throw any light on what had happened. "I can't recall exactly what Cyril told me," Georg said. "But I knew . . ." He trailed off, unable or unwill-ing to elaborate. It soon became clear to Georg, and to everyone else, that he had still not yet fully acknowledged his share of respon-sibility for a fateful chain of events — one that deeply affected even the next generation.

Many in Woodcrest, hearing these details for the first time, were so appalled that they were ready to give Georg the boot immediately. But Heiner stood up for him. "One thing is for sure: I want to fight for Georg. I love him. I don't understand why he refuses to recognize what he did. But I am still not going to give up on him."

Though Georg again asked for the community's pardon, this time Heiner did not rush to assure him that everything was over and for-gotten. He had already reconciled with Georg more than once within the last decade — and trusted that he had come clean. And now those acts of forgiveness seemed hollow. He felt it was crucial for Georg to face the full impact of what he had done, if only for his own sake. How else could trust be restored? Georg conceded that Heiner's hesitation

312 ◆ Homage to a Broken Man

was just. Over the next several months, he courageously sought to give the community an honest and complete accounting for the past.

For Heiner, each new revelation from Georg reopened old wounds. "It is because I love Georg that it hurts so much," he told Doug. Again and again he struggled to forgive. Sometimes he paced up and down his room, struggling with anger and reminding himself of Jesus' warning: "If you do not forgive your brother, you will not be forgiven." At other times his resolve came more easily: he knew from experience that the first step to forgiving someone who has badly hurt you is to recognize your own guilt. And so he was merciless with himself, coming again and again to Doug to talk about instances where he felt he bore responsibility for what had happened.

Finally, after several months, Georg came to a breakthrough. There were no more tortured letters from him; he seemed to have found a new transparency and peace. Heiner told him, "Now the past is a closed chapter." The reconciliation was real. Heiner took Georg fully back into his trust, and from then on would not let anyone speak of Georg's mistakes without emphasizing that they had been forgiven. He impressed on his children that they should forgive Georg too.

In the years that followed, others in the community—including some of the fellow leaders Heiner counted on most—betrayed his trust and that of the communities they had been asked to care for. As with Hans and Georg, it was mostly a matter of people exercising the authority entrusted to them in a heavy-handed way, and lording it over others. Heiner never shied from challenging such abuses of power. But whenever someone turned around, he acknowledged their remorse and forgave them fully.

Trust was an article of faith for him. Newcomers and old-timers alike sometimes shook their heads at his endless insistence on forgiving. Why, after such and such a person had stabbed him in the back time after time, did he insist on trusting him yet again? It went against all common sense. But Heiner saw it differently. As he once explained to Christoph, "I would much rather trust and be betrayed a thousand times than live in mistrust for a single day."

Unlike Georg, Hans never showed a hint of remorse for his abuse of leadership, even a decade after his departure from Woodcrest. Heiner tried to visit him several times in Germany, hoping to reconcile, or at very least, to talk. But Hans would have none of it, and refused to so much as meet him. Consumed by bitterness, he spent his days working on a manuscript on the history of the Bruderhof from his perspective, with financial support from well-heeled friends. In one back-and-forth during 1972, Heiner wrote to Hans asking for a chance to talk heart to heart. Hans rebuffed him with a mocking reply that began, "You're a poor swine, Heiner . . . ." It would be their last exchange.

That summer, Hans-Hermann phoned Heiner from his home in Connecticut and, weeping, told him he had been diagnosed with advanced lung cancer. Heiner immediately invited Hans-Hermann to spend his last weeks in Woodcrest.

The news of his younger brother's illness shook Heiner. Fifty-six and a father of nine, Hans Hermann had left the community after the turmoil of 1961 – a dark, confusing time for him – and had spent most of the previous decade living on his own. He had only recently begun to come out from under the long shadow of the past.

Like Heiner, Fritz, Hardy, and others, Hans-Hermann had been severely punished by Hans and his followers whenever he went against them. But perhaps because he was the youngest of the three Arnold brothers (he was only nineteen when his father died), his spirit had been crushed in a way that Heiner's and Hardy's had not, and he battled self-doubt and self-accusations continually. He had gradually grown mistrustful of others, even his brothers, much as he loved them. And now, though Heiner could hardly believe it, he was dying. Heiner said over and over to his children: "He's my younger brother. We slept in the same room and were scared of the same things; went to school together and played together in the same stream and woods. And now he's going before me."

Days after Hans-Hermann's diagnosis, he moved with his wife Gertrud and their family to Woodcrest, where they lived next door to Heiner and Annemarie. Heiner visited his brother at least two or three times a day. Hans-Hermann lay on his hospital bed, skeletal and short of breath. He was losing strength rapidly. But whenever Heiner came in, he tried to raise himself from the bed, beaming and reenergized, and stretching out his arms toward him. Past misunderstandings and mistrust melted away as if they had never been. All that was left was love. The two talked about everything, and laughed and cried. And again and again, the conversation returned to their childhood. It was as if they were two boys in Sannerz once more.

Hardy, who was also at Woodcrest, joined them daily – it was the first time in decades that all three brothers had lived at the same place for any length of time. Occasionally the conversation turned more serious as they relived hard times in Primavera. At one point Hans-Hermann and Hardy told Heiner, "We never really understood you. Sometimes we even worked against you. Now we see everything with new eyes. Please forgive us for wherever we hurt you."

Emmy, now eighty-seven, was often present too, though she talked little. Mostly she just sat in an armchair at Hans-Hermann's side. Even Monika, the youngest sibling, visited now and then (she had left the community in 1960, but lived nearby). It was the closest they had come to being a family since their father's death.

Only one cloud marred their happiness: Emy-Margret. She still seemed haunted by the past. Physically, she had separated from Hans a dozen years ago, amid an outpouring of sympathy for her as the injured wife. But despite her own hurt and the stream of revelations of how Hans had mistreated others, she still defended him. In fact, she seemed so deeply bound to him emotionally that it was as if she were under a spell.

Because Emy-Margret saw herself only as a victim, she had never been able to face the possibility others saw – that she had played an important role in enabling Hans's destructive course after her father's death. Nor could she see that she was tangled in a tight web of guilt and dishonesty. Even now, as Hans-Hermann lay on his deathbed, she continued to drop malicious remarks about him and the rest of the family behind their backs, while to their faces she took pains to show her devotion and showered Hans-Hermann with tokens of affection.

He saw through her. Facing death himself, he feared for his sister's soul. He warned her that one day she too would die, and would have to give an account for how she had used her life. He asked her to stop visiting him.

Heiner understood his brother's point of view but begged Hans-Hermann to relent on his last point. "Just give her one more chance. Let her at least say goodbye."

Hans-Hermann consented. "All right, I will see her. But please tell her: *Kein Theater mehr.* No more play-acting."

When Emy-Margret came, she fell to her knees and begged him to forgive her. Hans-Hermann locked her in his gaze, and waited until she was silent. "Emy-Margret," he said finally, "I forgave you long ago. But change, repent. Stop your wicked talking. Find your childhood again."

Hans-Hermann's words pushed Emy-Margret to deeper soul-searching, and Heiner and Hardy pondered them too. They cast a revealing light on their sister's predicament. What had happened to the Emy-Margret they had known in their childhood? Then she had been innocent, candid, and full of fun, the darling of their parents and a close friend of Tata's. Now she looked desperately unhappy.

At the end of the year, Hans-Hermann's condition deteriorated. He was clearly near death; it was agonizing to watch him panting for breath. Heiner stayed at his side day and night.

Then, one morning at dawn, about a week before Christmas, Hans-Hermann suddenly pulled off his oxygen mask. He had decided it was time to go. Gertrud was with him and, sensing the end was near, she called Heiner and the family into the room. Ten minutes later Hans-Hermann took his last breath.

Years afterward, Heiner still spoke of the light in his brother's eyes, and the peace that transfigured his features as he went. Not since Tata had he seen anyone meet the last moment so consciously and joyfully, and so certain of victory. "Looking into his face, one saw something victorious. I cannot express it differently—it was the joy of accepting God's will and God's hour."

In March 1973 an unexpected phone call brought shocking news from Europe. Hans Zumpe and his current mistress had been on the way to Majorca for a holiday when their jet collided with a cargo plane high over France. Every passenger was killed, and bodies were strewn over a five-mile swath of countryside. When Heiner heard the news, he was deeply shaken. Yet his first words were of optimism: "Who knows, maybe even in his last moments he was reconciled with God."

Tragic as Hans's death was, Heiner hoped that it might help Emy-Margret forward. Until now, her husband's figure had continued to loom over her; it seemed as though she was lost in a fog and unable to find her way out, no matter how frantically she tried. Now their separation had suddenly become final. Perhaps this jolt would enable her to become free. At first, however, the impact of Hans's death seemed only to numb her. One night Emy-Margret told Heiner that she feared Hans even in death.

It was through this recognition that the peril of her situation began to dawn on her. In the months that followed, she needed hours of patient counseling. It was a long, intense battle, but she said she was determined to fight it through to the finish. Heiner supported her throughout, devoting hours of his time to her. Emy-Margret told him that ever since meeting Hans, she had adored him for his charisma, his capabilities, and his self-assurance. By the time they married, her admiration was such that it left her powerless to confront him, even when she knew he was in the wrong. Just days into their honeymoon, she had begun to see the ugliness of Hans's domineering attitude. Given her closeness to her parents and Tata, she could easily have sought their advice. But instead, she did her best to conceal her husband's faults from them, and especially from her father. Soon, her loyalty belonged solely to Hans.

After her father's death, she threw her weight behind Hans's pursuit of power, even as he grew more ruthless, and even as he persecuted her own mother and brothers whenever they dared to stand in his way. Part of what drove her was fear of how he might punish her if she opposed him. But part of it was also her own lust for influence: she relished the social prestige his role brought her.

As Emy-Margret came out with the story piece by piece, sorting and separating her conflicting loyalties and emotions, the pent-up lies and half-lies that had burdened her for decades slipped off her, and she became stronger and freer.

By the fall of 1973, she had won through to victory. It was visible to everyone. Her personality radiated the same childlike joy as it had in Sannerz, her physical features were transformed, and even her health improved. Her younger sister Monika, meeting her again for the first time since Hans-Hermann's death, exclaimed in amazement, "You are completely different, completely changed!"

Emy-Margret's transformation came at a cost. She had lost her husband without being reconciled with him. Now her attempts to make amends for where she had acted wrongly embittered old friends who sided with Hans, and even left her estranged from two of her children. But she did not doubt that it was worth it. Writing to her brother Hardy, she exulted, "Great liberation and peace has been given to me and is still being given, far beyond my hopes and prayers."

34

To the Finish

Hans-Hermann's death pushed Heiner to reckon with the likelihood that he himself did not have long to live. At sixty, he had never regained full health after the kidney infections of his twenties, nor after his emergency hospitalization in 1961. His heart condition, combined with chronic lung disease, made it a strain to walk the shortest distances. Aside from all this he had developed severe diabetes.

Annemarie, too, sometimes wondered if their time together was drawing to a close. She didn't talk about it with him — she had often found it easier to express her deepest thoughts in writing rather than in conversation — but for his sixty-first birthday she wrote, "Because I do not have anything special for your birthday, I want to write a little letter just for you. I am so thankful for the past year. It brought us so very close together, perhaps because it included some difficult times. Again and again you have let me share in what was moving you, including the hard struggles of past years. I came to understand you so well, and also what you suffered. I am pained about the many times in earlier years when I didn't understand you, and as a result acted toward you with so little love — especially during the 1940s in Primavera. But throughout this year I have felt with all my heart that we are completely one. Your love to Jesus is always an incentive to me.

"Whatever the future holds, I am absolutely confident that our bond is firm and unbreakable into all eternity. It has always been that way, but now it has become deeper, closer, and more inseparable. Completely yours, Annemarie."

Heiner found her letter on his pillow that evening. He wrote back the next morning: "My only Annemarie! Your letter yesterday was a special joy to me. I feel quite ashamed of your love and trust. It is a fact that we have experienced special grace this year. I have felt your longing for inner community very strongly, and thank you for it. There were times in the past when you seemed so self-sufficient. This past year has shown me that actually you have always longed to share, and I ask you for forgiveness.

"What happened in my own heart, especially in the years since Emmy Maria's death, is something I cannot explain. It was a mistake that I closed my heart to you and did not share its struggles. I cannot describe how terrible they were—it was not something I had any control over. A decision of the will did not help; every attempt failed.

"What held me fast was that, buried deeply under all these terrible things, still I knew I had experienced Jesus, and that experience lived on deeply beneath everything dark. Even in hours when I doubted, Jesus held me fast. In deep love, your Heiner."

Just one week after this birthday, Heiner's strength was tested as it had not been in years. Dwight Blough, a longtime friend and one of his closest confidants, was killed when a small plane in which he was flying crashed into a mountainside. Dwight had come to Woodcrest with his wife, Norann, in 1956, and before long, he had gained Heiner's notice by risking his life.

A fire had started in the building that housed Heiner's second-floor study, and as it spread out of control, Dwight rushed upstairs to help. In the end he was too late—flames were already shooting from many windows. Heiner ordered him down, but never forgot how Dwight's first impulse had been to retrieve what he could, heedless of any danger to himself.

Later, after the collapse of Primavera, Dwight had accompanied Heiner on his 1964 trip to Europe to reach out to people who had left the community or been sent away. Dwight did not speak German, and he had never been to Primavera, let alone hurt any of its ex-members. But he knew how taxing such a journey would be for Heiner, and had wanted to support him however he could. Together they had visited old comrades such as Dorli Bolli, Heiner's old Silum house parents Hannes and Else Boller, and his childhood friend Sophie with her husband Christian. The last visit was unexpectedly tragic – Sophie's sixteen-year-old son Johann Gregor, who suffered from a congenital illness, had unexpectedly died. Dwight and Heiner had stood by her side as they buried the young man at the Sparhof, a few feet from Tata and his father.

In 1968, Dwight had moved to Pennsylvania to oversee a branch of the Bruderhof there. Still, he had kept in daily touch with Heiner and others at Woodcrest. He had seen how divisiveness and competitiveness had almost destroyed the movement in the 1950s, and he was determined to help cement its unity now. This was why he had spearheaded the purchase of a small plane to facilitate transport and communication among the communities, and why he was out flying the day of his fatal accident.

Dwight's death left Norann and her twelve children (the youngest was only six weeks old) without a husband and father – and it left the large community where he had lived without a head. It also left a hole in Heiner's heart.

The day after Dwight's death, Dick Mommsen enlarged a photograph of Dwight and brought it to Heiner. Heiner could not even look at it. He was too cut by the loss of his friend.

Despite his grief, Heiner kept up a grueling work regimen. Nicky Maas, his secretary, remarked, "I don't know anyone else who uses each minute of the day as fully as Heiner does." As elder for four communities with a combined population of more than a thousand, he had no free time. Inevitably, those responsible for the movement's finances, businesses, and schools turned to him for advice with their problems and plans. But that was only one facet of his work. He continued to visit other communities and to nurture contacts throughout America and Europe, disregarding doctors' warnings that the constant trips put his life at risk. During a trip to England, he collapsed and had to be rushed to the hospital in critical condition with severe chest pain. Even that did not quell his urge to travel. What if someone was hurting unnoticed? What if there was someone who needed an ear?

To Heiner, the care of souls was not a matter of dispensing advice or passing on wisdom. It was simply the obvious response to the biblical command, "Love one another." Having gone through one hard time after another in his own life, he identified with anyone who was lonely or discouraged, and he knew what had helped him through: a personal relationship with Jesus. That was always the heart of his counsel, whether he pointed to it by means of a loving arm around the shoulder, a frank admonition, or—when the occasion called for it—a public confrontation.

As the 1970s began, the unreconciled relationships with those who had left the community a decade before still gave Heiner no peace, and he suggested founding a new community in England, Darvell, to make it easier for those in Europe to stay in touch. He and Annemarie continued to visit those they could, including Cyril Davies and his wife Margot, who received them warmly but made it clear they would not return. Will Marchant and his wife Kathleen felt similarly; all the same, Will sent Heiner a message through his son Jerry that the two years they had spent in Woodcrest at its founding were the best in his life.

To Johnny Robinson, who was still reeling from Primavera's collapse, Heiner apologized for not intervening when Johnny was sent away, despite having had serious misgivings. Yet he also reminded Johnny that the collapse did not come from nowhere—its cause was the fact that "the beloved community of Primavera had come close to inner bankruptcy," a bankruptcy for which they both shared responsibility. Heiner's point was not lost on Johnny, and eventually he did return, though by that time Heiner was no longer alive to welcome him home.

To Maureen Burn, another former member, Heiner wrote: "I know that 1960 and 1961 was a very, very hard experience. It would be a mistake to think it was only heartbreaking for those who left or had to leave. . . . But Maureen, my words of 1961 still stand, which I said to you when you left: 'You should return to us when you think that we have made an honest new beginning.'" Maureen took Heiner up on his offer, reconciled with the community, and came back.

Such correspondence with people both inside and outside the community often demanded the aid of several typists. Often Heiner received more than a hundred letters in a week asking for advice on everything from child-rearing and college plans to bereavement and sexuality. He dictated thousands of letters in reply. Children wrote, too, and got as much attention as longtime colleagues. (Some still have a shoebox full of the replies they got from him.)

Heiner's insights were treasured not only by those he addressed them to. After his death, selections from his letters and other writings reached a large audience in the form of a book, *Discipleship*. Henri Nouwen, the popular spiritual author, received the manuscript before it was published. He was so struck by its contents that he reneged on a vow to write no more forewords—and turned out one for *Discipleship* in a matter of days. In it he explained, "This is a tough book. As I began reading it, Arnold's words touched me as a double-edged sword, calling me to choose between truth and lies, salvation and sin, selflessness and selfishness, light and darkness, God and demon.

"At first I wasn't sure if I wanted to be confronted in such a direct way, and I discovered some resistance in myself. I want the Good News to be gentle, consoling, comforting, and to offer inner peace and harmony. But Arnold reminds me that the peace of the gospel is not the same as the peace of the world. . . . It asks for a choice, a radical choice, a choice that is not always praised, supported, and celebrated.

"Still, Arnold's writing is not harsh, unbending, fanatical, or self-righteous. To the contrary, it is full of love. Tough love, but real love. It is the love that flows from the broken heart of Jesus.

"Arnold does not speak in his own name. He speaks in the name of Jesus. He has heard clearly the words of Paul to Timothy: 'Before God, and before Christ Jesus, who is to be the judge of the living and the dead, I charge you: proclaim the message and, welcome or unwelcome, insist on it.'

"It is Arnold's deep rootedness in Jesus Christ that makes him a very wise, safe, and challenging guide in our spiritual journey. But there is more: every word he speaks comes from his experience in community. . . . I am very grateful for this book. It is a prophetic one."

Busy or no, Heiner made time for anyone looking for guidance. As ever, it was his way of listening that drew people. Ellen had known Heiner for twenty years, though now she lived in a different state. After she lost two young children in one year, her anguish was so immense that she sometimes felt it would drive her over the edge. One day she impulsively dialed Heiner's number, though she had no idea what to tell him. He picked up the phone. Ellen could not even introduce herself; she only sobbed into the phone. Heiner listened, not saying a word, as the minutes passed – how many, Ellen could not remember afterward. When he finally spoke, he said only, "I understand." That was all. But the way he said it, Ellen knew that he did understand. It gave her a sense of comfort, even of hope, that she had despaired of ever feeling again.

Heiner sometimes stayed in Woodcrest for months at a time, but his mind constantly ranged far beyond. "The older I get, the less important the Bruderhof is to me," he told community members one evening. He urged them: "It is not enough to live together in community, to love one another and make each other happy; to cook dinner for your neighbor, who then cooks dinner for her neighbor. More is demanded of us." He was constantly looking outward, pondering and probing. "What is our responsibility? How can we respond to the happenings of the day?" – the Vietnam War, Three Mile Island, the conflict in Israel, and the Iran hostage crisis.

Visitors to Heiner's study included hippies from New York City and from rural communes, long-haired Jesus People who talked about "getting high on God," and journalists and academics who wanted to interview him. When Southeast Asia's "boat people" made headlines in the late 1970s, Heiner saw to it that the community took in several families until they were able to find steady work and decent housing. He also befriended Vietnam veterans like Terry Fritz, a local homeless man with a history of substance abuse. When Terry committed suicide in 1977, Heiner wept as if he had lost his own son.

One day Giovanna, a young woman who had been a member of Sun Myung Moon's Unification Church, came to him for help. Giovanna had come to see the cult (in particular its belief in Moon's divinity) as idolatry and longed to return to the faith of her childhood, which she had rejected in her college years. But inwardly she had not been able to free herself from the group and still felt the weight of her past involvement in it. As she came into Heiner's study, she fidgeted nervously, feeling challenged to her core. Heiner's first words to her were, "Giovanna, here at this community we do not worship people." He was warm, but he made no bones about what he thought. "You are endangering not only your emotional health, but also your soul."

For Giovanna, that conversation proved to be a crucial step forward. Years later, she recalled: "What struck me most in that first meeting was his integrity. There was no compromise. I had never met him before, but I knew, 'Here is a man of God. He will understand.' And he did. He represented Jesus' words without conceding an inch. Because of that you could trust him totally."

Heiner sharply rejected any attempt to cast him as a guru – and there were plenty of people who tried to do so. But still he felt it was his job to be available to anyone who came to him in good faith. When Sibyl's daughter Xaverie was in high school, she waited for weeks before asking for a talk with him. Part of her was shy; part of her respected Heiner so deeply that she was certain an appointment with him would be decisive for her life. Finally she plucked up her courage and asked to see him.

When she came into Heiner's study, he was finishing a bowl of ice cream. She began to pour out everything she had planned to say, not forgetting any details: her search, the mistakes she had made, her doubts, her insecurities. It took a while, and Heiner kept right on eating his ice cream as he listened. When she finished, she looked up at Heiner expectantly. Now at last, she thought, the moment had come. He would open her eyes with a life-changing insight.

There was a pause. Then he said, "Xaverie, would you be so kind? Please take this bowl to the kitchen for me." And with that he ended the interview.

When someone was in distress, however, Heiner would stop at nothing. Barry was sixteen. Puberty had left him confused, especially because he felt a strong tug of sexual attraction not only to girls (he knew that was normal) but even, to his horror, to women who were married. Embarrassed and afraid of telling anyone about his feelings, Barry turned in on himself. Finally, thinking that he would go crazy unless he got help, he visited Heiner's study one afternoon and asked to talk. When they were alone, Barry poured out everything that troubled him.

Heiner thanked Barry for his openness, and then told him how crucial it is for a young man to choose what attitude he takes to his drives. He also told him something his own father had told him at Barry's age: "If you approach the sexual sphere with the utmost honesty and respect now, it will make self-discipline easier in later life. Listen to what your conscience tells you is right." And then he added, "I will think of you."

But that wasn't the end of the story. When Barry came home that evening, he found that Heiner had been there before him and dropped off a letter on his bed. "Dear Barry," it began, "I am sorry I wasn't more helpful to you this afternoon, when you opened your heart to me about the temptations that torment you. This is something where no man can help another find the way out, at least not alone. Jesus must enter into the picture. Jesus says, 'If you want to follow me, deny yourself and take your cross upon yourself.' If we are willing to do this, Jesus can come as a power to us and free us, which no other man can do. Your friend, Heiner."

◆ ◆ ◆

From the mid-1960s on, Christoph was Heiner's right-hand assistant, helping him in his counseling work. In 1974, the community formally asked him to support his father in his tasks as senior pastor. He and Verena were busy with their own growing family by now, but Heiner still relied on him heavily, and Christoph regarded supporting him as his first priority. When his father would call, he would appear within minutes—to give pastoral support in the event of a sudden medical emergency, to assist in a difficult counseling case, to drive him somewhere, or to bring food to the house for an unexpected party of visitors.

Often, especially when Heiner's asthma was bad, he looked so exhausted that Christoph would urge him to skip the day's communal events and rest at home. Sometimes he complied, but sometimes he would not, especially in the case of an evening gathering for prayer and singing. Then he would insist on going, no matter how labored his breathing or high his fever. "I have to see the brothers and sisters. My strength comes from the brotherhood."

On such occasions Christoph would pass the word around beforehand, "My father is weak tonight, please be considerate of him." But the moment Heiner was in the meeting, his weakness vanished.

Transformed by the presence of people he loved, the exhausted man of a few minutes before became vibrant—and his energy would last the rest of the evening. Back at home afterward, he would sit in his large armchair, with Annemarie, the children and their spouses, chatting, joking, expounding on topics he'd been mulling over, or asking their input on an issue of current concern to him. Emmy or Hardy would drop in, or Georg would come for a glass of wine, and they would sit together and reminisce. Sometimes he grew so animated that afterward he could not get to sleep.

Heiner spoke often of his relationship to his father, and sensing that he might not have long to live, he felt an obligation to pass on the torch he had received from him. Eberhard had been far more than a parent to him: ever since he had learned of Heiner's encounter with Jesus as an eleven-year-old, a deep spiritual bond had held them together as well. Now the same relationship bound Heiner and Christoph.

One night Heiner worked almost till dawn writing a letter to his son and his wife, then sealed it and put it in a safe with instructions that it should be opened only after his death. It was addressed to Christoph and Verena and began, "You, dear Christoph, have carried so very much with me in recent years, and so I have some thoughts to share with you for the time when I am no longer among you. What remains as a basic direction for the future is your grandfather's last letter from Darmstadt. Let yourselves be guided by this always. . . . Never give way in questions of inner freedom and genuineness. Never deny God's greatness and God's kingdom on this earth. In all things hold fast to faith in God."

The letter then went on to review the community's history so that Christoph might be reminded of it in the future. "In the early life in community the little circle was deeply gripped by the love of Jesus, overflowing with love for one another. The burdens that this little group was able to bear were amazing. Even the children, because they too were filled with the love of Jesus, helped bear the burdens without realizing it and took it on to help beggars and other needy people in some way.

"Then, especially in Primavera, the true Jesus . . . was increasingly rejected. And so it came about that the Bruderhof life gradually turned into the opposite of what it had been to begin with. I know I am expressing this very crassly.

"I ask myself constantly: How was it possible for this community, founded in Christ, as represented by Opa, Oma, and Tata, to develop that way and to be so thoroughly twisted into the opposite? How was it possible, after the beginning had been so clearly founded on Christ, that it was twisted so completely into the opposite later on?

"The contrast with the spirit of the beginning was so crass and obvious that I am wondering now why I did not recognize it in all its horror. At this point I don't want to go into the historical details or the guilt, which we Arnolds certainly also shared. . . .

"In the end we are all poor people, really very poor. Without the crucified Christ not one of us can find the way to God. But that is our joy, our faith, our proclamation. . . .

"Jesus Christ must remain the center at all times. The community needs constant renewal from within. By that I mean an ever new encounter with God."

Then, remembering what his own father's blessing had meant – and still meant – to him, he closed the letter on a personal note: "For you and Verena and your beloved children I wish God's blessing on your future. . . ."

Heiner made other preparations with an eye to the future. Whenever he had a few spare minutes, he dictated his thoughts on pastoral care to Nicky or Hela, his secretaries. Christoph, who had worked in publishing, helped collect these thoughts into two volumes. *In the Image of God* addresses marriage and sexuality, while *Freedom from Sinful Thoughts* focuses on a little-mentioned but widespread source of misery—and draws heavily on Meister Eckhart, the young Heiner's favorite author.

At first Heiner gave out only a few dozen copies, mostly to those who came to him for counseling. But the books circulated, and soon letters began to come from grateful readers. The community decided to have the manuscripts published, and the response increased. Complete strangers wrote, telling Heiner, for instance, that reading *Freedom from Sinful Thoughts* had been a turning point in their lives. (A handful even claimed that reading it had saved them from committing suicide.) Both books sold without fanfare, but steadily, year after year.

Seeing his own name on the spine of a book greatly amused Heiner, and he teased his old teacher Trudi, who now lived at Woodcrest, about it mercilessly. "You always said I was so hopeless as a pupil," he would remind her.

"*Ja*, Heiner. You were just too much for me! I tried to teach you English, but you refused to learn it."

"And then it was time to start me on French. I still remember: you told Papa in front of me, 'There is no hope for Heiner,' and he decided that I shouldn't go to the university. And today, Trudi, I am an *author*." They burst out laughing.

Now it was Heiner and Annemarie's grandchildren who were in school. When they visited, Heiner always greeted them warmly, using the special nicknames or terms of endearment he had picked for each one. Christoph's son Heinrich felt a special connection because he shared his grandfather's name. He visited his Opa daily on the way to school, and was usually sent on his way with a hug and a kiss.

As Heiner's grandsons grew up, he tried to pass on his ideas about what it means to be a man. "When Hardy and I were teenagers," he told them, "Hardy was dashing and brilliant. A university student. I was going to agricultural school with peasants' sons. But when Hardy and I wrestled, I could take him to the ground, even with one arm behind my back."

He still loved to ride. He had Heinrich and Nathan (Maria's eldest son) saddle up the horse and lead it outside his study. Because of his weakness, he needed help to mount. But once in the saddle, he rode easily, holding the reins in one hand as he cantered through the fields and woods behind his house.

The younger grandchildren were treated to stories about Sannerz and Berlin: "We were riding on a train with Tata," he said, his eyes bright as he acted out a favorite. "An elderly lady, very dignified in a black dress, is sitting in our compartment. Suddenly Hardy gasps and points at her face. 'Look Tata! Look at her nose. She has a wart.' Tata tries to shush him, and says it's nothing. 'No,' Hardy keeps saying, 'There *is* a wart. Don't you see it?' Finally the lady gets up and flounces angrily out of the carriage."

Heiner had a heart for children and often defended them against adults. Few things made him more furious than when adults labeled children based on their academic performance and pushed them. One afternoon, Christoph and Verena's thirteen-year-old Emmy Maria walked in on a discussion about problems at Woodcrest's school. "The stupid arrogance of teachers," he was saying, "who were good in college and think of themselves and those of their choosing as academics—as if they were better than other people!" His eyes flashed. Suddenly he noticed Emmy Maria in the room. He wagged his finger at her. "Don't you ever tell your teachers what you just heard me saying."

Still, Emmy Maria knew that if she ever disobeyed one of those teachers, she would have to reckon with her grandfather. The ultimate discipline for any of Heiner's grandchildren was to be told, "Go and tell Opa what you did." Not that Heiner scolded or punished them. But having to face him and tell him about your misdeed—lying or being disrespectful—that was worse than any punishment. Of course, he wouldn't let a child go without assuring him or her that he knew things would change. "I know that tomorrow will be different, yes? Now, give me a hug."

From the early 1970s on, Heiner's diabetes required him to receive regular insulin injections. These caused him to gain weight steadily, and he became a heavy man for the first time in his life. Soon other complications developed, and his doctors forbade him to smoke or eat salt. Heiner had no patience for these prohibitions. In the evenings, when his family was busy with other things, he would steal upstairs in his slippers to visit his old friend Rudi Hildel—they had grown up together at the Sparhof—pad right across the living room, and reach into Rudi's shirt pocket, where he knew there would be a pack of Pall Malls. After sharing a cigarette or two with him, he would cheerfully return downstairs.

Every couple of months, Ben, a son of Hans and Emy-Margret and an amateur winemaker, appeared from Connecticut with a gallon of his latest batch, and Heiner and he would set about their ritual of sampling the delivery. "You know, Ben," Heiner once told him, "The first miracle Jesus performed was to turn water into wine. There are many Christians who wish it had been the other way around. *Aber das ist einfach nicht das Evangelium!*—But that is simply not the gospel!" Sitting at the dinner table, covering his food with a heavy sprinkling of forbidden salt, he would pull out a similar argument: "Jesus tells us to be the salt of the earth. And then the doctors tell me, No salt!"—with which he would then shake on even more, to drive home his point.

Though only in his sixties, he looked like an old man. Annemarie, on the other hand, was full of energy and activity. They were still a single unit, kidding each other constantly, arguing over some practical question with obvious mutual affection. Before leaving the house, she would bustle around him, combing his hair, scrubbing a stain out of his jacket, or spritzing him with cologne while he sat and smiled. "*Ach*, Annemarie, is it really necessary?" he would say in a half-hearted show of resistance.

It was impossible for anyone to think of him without her, least of all Heiner. In fact, he was so certain that she would outlive him that one day he talked with Christoph about how best to support her after his death. Maybe, Heiner suggested, Christoph could persuade her to write a history of the community from Sannerz on. She would do it better than anyone, he felt. You could see from the countless letters she wrote that she had a gift for storytelling and description.

But one afternoon in September 1979, everything changed: Annemarie was diagnosed with cancer of the lymph nodes. It was not a complete surprise – she had suffered from weakness and chest pain for weeks, and Monika, now a doctor, had arranged for testing. Yet until now, such an outcome had seemed inconceivable. Both Annemarie and Heiner wept when Christoph and Monika broke the news to them. But then Annemarie pulled herself together, and looked Heiner in the eye: "Now every day, every moment, counts. We must not miss any chance to show love to our brothers and sisters, to the children, and to our guests."

The cancer advanced rapidly, and by January she who had spent her life serving others was an invalid who needed to be cared for – something she found hard to accept.

As if that wasn't enough, Heiner's mother came down with pneumonia just that winter. For the last few years, Emmy had lived in an apartment upstairs, where Verena, Emy-Margret, and others took care of her. At ninety-five, Emmy was more contemplative now, and sometimes a little confused. But her fire remained. "In times of struggle I am strong," she would say, unfazed by bad news or problems that disconcerted others. She talked daily of "passing into eternity" – and like a little girl looking forward to Christmas, she eagerly awaited that moment. "Tata always told me, 'When you die, you'll just go to sleep like a child.'" She also spoke daily of "meeting my Eberhard," and of the forty-five long years she had survived him. Sometimes in her love for Heiner she mistook him for her husband, looking at him with her radiant blue eyes, and saying, "My Eberhard. My Eberhard." No one corrected her.

One evening three weeks after Christmas, Emmy's ninety-fifth birthday, Verena called Christoph and Heiner to Emmy's room: "She won't be with us much longer." Minutes later, she slipped away, just as Tata had told her she would—with the peace of a child. For years, Heiner had told his children, "Something significant will happen in heaven when Mama passes away." Now that moment had come. It was a deep loss for the family, but not an unbearable one. They had only to think of her joy at being reunited with her husband after so many years of loneliness and heartache.

It hurt Annemarie that she was not well enough to prepare her mother-in-law's body for burial or to set up the room in which she was laid. She had always felt it a privilege to do this "last service of love," as she called it, for members of the community.

But there would be more losses to come. Only a few days after Emmy's death, Dora, a woman Annemarie had known for almost fifty years, passed away too. Annemarie was too weak by now to attend a funeral, but she still got out of bed, dressed herself in black, and stood, feverish and trembling, as Dora's burial procession passed the front door of her house.

Seven days later Ruth, an old classmate of Heiner's, died. For her funeral, though even more sickly than the previous week, Annemarie dressed in black again. It was clearly more than she had strength for, but she insisted on doing it out of respect for Ruth.

All three women had been close to Annemarie for many years, and their deaths cut her deeply. With each one, she went noticeably downhill. Heiner recognized that she was dying before the doctors did. They assured him that Annemarie's cancer had a low mortality rate, that the test predictions were good. But one day he told Milton, "Just by looking at her I can see she is getting weaker. Every day you tell me about the next test you're going to do, that her potassium is up, that her heart condition is improving. But you never tell me that she is dying, that I'm going to lose her."

Milton was taken aback. He was hearing what he himself didn't want to admit, even to himself. But now he realized, "Heiner's right. She's near the end."

In the last weeks of her life, Heiner poured every ounce of his strength into supporting her. He hardly left her side except to spend time with the grandchildren. She was in agony – that was hard enough – but worst of all, she lost the ability to speak for long periods. One night it returned, and she surprised everyone in the room by calling for Emmy Maria. She was agitated, and to calm her, Roswith brought in her own baby daughter, who was named after the child her mother had lost four decades before. As Annemarie held the baby, she grew peaceful again.

On March 15, at seven in the evening, Milton called Heiner and the children to her bedside. Her pulse was irregular. Outside the window by her bed, the community was singing. Annemarie seemed to be trying to speak, but could not. She turned her eyes to Heiner. For several minutes she looked into his eyes – a conscious farewell. Minutes later, Heiner, in tears, came into the living room to tell the grandchildren that she was gone.

After Annemarie's death, Heiner spoke of her constantly and read and re-read her letters and diaries. Though no longer beside him physically, she was still present to him in other ways, and he was not willing to let go of her yet. One day not long after the funeral, he was sitting together with his daughters, having coffee. They were talking about their families, and having a good time. Heiner didn't join in. In fact, he soon let them know that he was hurt by their levity. How, he wanted to know, could they let life return to normal so quickly? Couldn't they see that he was still grieving for Mama? And why weren't they taking her death just as seriously?

Some time later he had each of the children write down their memories of their mother for him, and he asked for these to be read aloud to him – more than once. "I want to know how much I have lost," he explained, tears streaming down his face. "Now I see the beauty of her soul."

The first Christmas after her death, he called his grandson, Nathan, to his room and gave him an old guitar. "This was your Oma's," he told the fourteen-year-old. "I bought it for her in Asunción. We used to play together . . ." He burst into tears. Nathan sat by him on the bed, wanting to comfort him but feeling helpless to do so.

The next two years were bitter and lonely. Till now, Heiner used to turn to Christoph. But after Annemarie's death, even this source of strength was undermined: his daughters, envious of the special bond between father and son, vied for their father's attention and pushed their brother aside. Meanwhile, they tried to draw Heiner onto their side in conflicts with each other and in the community at large. These painful divisions within his own family weighed on Heiner and depleted his strength until he was no longer able to guide the community.

What gave him the most comfort was children. During the last weeks of Annemarie's sickness, many of her grandchildren and their peers had started meeting on their own to pray for her. They had often appeared outside her window to sing to her, to her joy, and several times she had even rallied physically for hours or days after they came. After her death, the little movement intensified. More and more children attended their meetings. They sang around campfires, went on hikes, and put on plays that they had written. Seeing them reminded Heiner of his childhood and the Sun Troop, and he asked Christoph to keep in touch with them and shield them from well-meaning interfering adults.

Sometimes they came directly to him, telling him about their activities and asking him for advice. Usually he answered with a story: about his father and mother, about Sannerz, about the dogs he had had as a boy. He also told them Bible stories, and stories about Saint Francis and the lepers. About Rachoff. Heliopher. Sadhu Sundar Singh . . .

For months it had been clear he was dying. But for family members it was still a blow when in the spring of 1982 his body gradually began to shut down. Through June and July he never left his house, though he still invited his grandchildren and their friends to come in and see him. He also asked to see people close to his heart.

Over the past two years, he had become more and more concerned about mission—not in the sense of converting people or recruiting them as members, but simply in the sense of the Gospel passage where Jesus says, "I was hungry, and you gave me meat; thirsty, and you gave me drink; a stranger, and you took me in; naked, and you clothed me; sick, and you visited me; in prison, and you came to me."

In response to these words—words that had burned in him all his life—Heiner urged the community to free members from their workplaces and send them out two by two to visit nursing homes, prisons, slums, and other places of despair. "I long that we can become more active," he said. "The time is urgent; so many people live in anguish. There is lots of room to do outreach. May it be given that a light is kindled, and that the message of love, the new way of love, is proclaimed throughout the world."

The breadth of this vision did not exclude those right around him—people like Giovanna, who was still seeking his help. When she came to see him for the last time, she was startled at how frail he had become. "Come sit down," he said, "I've been wondering how you were getting on."

"He is so near his own end," she said to herself, overwhelmed, "and yet he has been thinking of me!" Years later she recalled, "I spilled out things which I had never planned to tell him and which I could not even verbalize to myself. It was as if something had been released in me. He listened with such compassion—no hint of condemnation— that I felt free to express myself. I think it was because I could feel his reverence. He saw every person as a fellow child of God.

"When it was time to go, he said to me, 'Please come see me again, whenever you need to talk. Do not wait. You can come any time.' As I left his room, I felt that I had begun to be healed."

Heiner himself often wondered if he had failed. He had never wandered from village to village as he had imagined he would as a boy. He worried that he had not answered the call of his childhood. He had spent his life on the knife's edge, and seldom known security and peace. Ever since the day of his conversion, he had moved in the midst of a battle, receiving wounds with every step. He approached death as a broken man.

But to me, the grandson who barely knew him, that brokenness was his greatest gift. To me, Opa was broken like Sundar Singh, who was driven from his home and died a beggar. Broken like Heliopher, who tore out his heart for his people. Broken like Rachoff, who died in a prison but shouted at the top of his voice, "Brother Jesus, I am coming, I am coming!" and ran with his arms outstretched toward the rising sun.

Epilogue

Woodcrest, July 24, 1982

Anne Schwerner didn't want to stare at the body. It rested on the bed where he had died yesterday, looking natural; and yet no sleeping man's head ever lay so neatly at the very center of the pillow. He held nine roses, one for each of his children, including Emmy Maria and Marianne. Christoph had closed his eyes for the last time and, with Milton's help, washed and dressed him. Anne could see that the mortician had not been allowed to interfere. The twenty-four hours since his death had gently relaxed his face. He looked confident, like a child.

Rather than stare, Anne let her eyes travel around the room. Her husband Nat sat solemn and silent, as did ten or twelve other people—faces she didn't know. The yellow walls of the bedroom displayed dozens of photographs. She recognized Annemarie in many of them, looking into the camera with the happy impatience of someone made to stop and pose in the middle of an urgent errand. All those snapshots of beaming children arrayed in circular brass frames must be his grandchildren. Mounted on the wall near his head hung a small homemade cross, just two strips of wood glued together and painted black.

The two air conditioners were set on high, and running noisily. She signaled to Nat that she needed to go outside. Chairs squeaked as the other mourners shifted to let them past. They stood in the bright heat again, by a bed of roses and geraniums—one of Annemarie's gardens, Anne supposed. The world seemed to have been turned on mute. Then, as though the sound came through thick glass, she could hear someone inviting her and Nat for coffee. She said she had to go straight home.

It made no sense. What was she, an atheist, doing here? Why was it so hard to say goodbye to this man with his homemade cross?

The Life of
Heiner and Annemarie Arnold
in Pictures

Rifton, New York, 1962

Top: The Arnold family in 1915: Emmy, Emy-Margret (age four), Heiner (age one), Eberhard, Hardy (age three). **Bottom left:** Heiner with his stuffed monkey at age five, shortly before the family left Berlin for the backwater village of Sannerz (1919). **Bottom right:** Else von Hollander, holding her nephew Heiner shortly after his birth on December 23, 1913. **Opposite:** The Arnolds' townhouse in the Wilmersdorf borough of Berlin. On the lower veranda (left to right) are Heiner, Hans-Hermann, and Hardy.

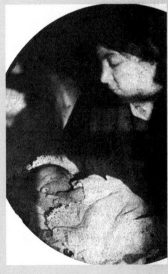

Tyrol and Berlin 1913–1920 ◆ 343

Top: Destitute but happy, the Arnold children after moving to the Sannerz settlement (ca. 1921). Left to right: Hans-Hermann, Heiner, Monika, Hardy, and Emy-Margret. **Bottom:** At this Youth Movement conference at Pentecost 1921, Heiner met his childhood friend Christel Girbinger.

Top: Members of the Sannerz community in 1924: 1. Eberhard Arnold; 2. Moni von Hollander; 3. Emmy Arnold; 4. Lotte Henze; 5. Karl Keiderling; 6. Else von Hollander; 7. Hans-Hermann Arnold; 8. Emy-Margret Arnold; 9. Trudi Dalgas; 10. Hardy Arnold; 11. Sophie Schwing (holding child); 12. Heiner Arnold; 13. Monika Arnold.
Bottom left: Eberhard and Emmy in Youth Movement dress, 1921. **Bottom right:** Karl Keiderling, a young anarchist, arrived in Sannerz in 1922 and became Heiner's mentor and friend.

Sannerz, Germany 1920–1928 ◆ 345

Top left: Sadhu Sundar Singh, whose story inspired Heiner to want to become an itinerant evangelist. **Top right:** Else von Hollander, or "Tata," was the adult who was closest to Heiner after his parents. **Bottom:** The Sun Troop's founding members (1928): Luise Kolb, Heiner Arnold, and Sophie Schwing.

Top left: Pupils from the Sannerz community school with their teachers on a field trip: 1. Sophie Schwing; 2. Heiner Arnold (carrying the Sun Troop flag); 3. Trudi Dalgas; 4. Georg Barth. **Top right:** The Sannerz villa. In summer, communal meals were eaten on the front porch. **Bottom:** Heiner and his schoolmate Hans Grimm chopping firewood for the kitchen (1922).

Top left: Emy-Margret with her fiancé Hans Zumpe (1929). *Top right:* Friedel Sondheimer, a Sparhof member, came from a prominent local Jewish family and was in special danger after Hitler seized power in 1933. *Bottom:* Trudi, the Sparhof's schoolteacher, on her wedding day with husband Walter Hüssy (1931). Her pupils wave them off from the steps of the Sparhof's school building.

Top: Annemarie Wächter, Heiner's future wife, was enthusiastic for the Youth Movement's revival of folk music. **Bottom:** The two sisters Emmy and Else with a group of children at the Sparhof (1930).

Top left: Annemarie, who had been Emy-Margret's classmate in college, arrived at the Sparhof on the day of Else von Hollander's death in January 1932. **Top right:** Else loved the legacy of Saint Francis and Saint Clare of Assisi; for this photograph, taken in her last months, she wore a monastic habit. **Bottom left:** The hut at the Sparhof where Else was nursed during her last battle with tuberculosis; she lived separately for fear of contagion. **Bottom right:** Eberhard Arnold walking with a leg cast in 1935; despite an unhealed fracture from two years earlier, he was tireless in working to protect the community from Nazi threats.

Top: The entrance to the Sparhof's burial ground, where Eberhard Arnold was was buried in November 1935 (photograph ca. 1938). None of his sons could attend the funeral: as conscientious objectors, they could not safely return to Germany. ***Bottom:*** Nazi supporters marching through Fulda in March 1933. Two months earlier, on the day Hitler came to power, Heiner had found himself a horrified onlooker of such a march; his agricultural school was located behind the building in the background.

Top: View of Silum from above, looking down into the Rhine valley between Liechtenstein and Switzerland. **Bottom:** Heiner at work in Silum (1934).

Top: Silum hikers on an Alpine peak, with Heiner (seated with violin) and Fritz Kleiner (standing). **Bottom:** Heiner's class at the Strickhof Agricultural School (1934); he is in the back row, center.

Silum, Liechtenstein 1934–1936 ◆ 353

Opposite: Heiner and Annemarie on the day of their wedding in Silum, March 24, 1936. *Top:* The newlyweds on the Channel ferry to England, thrilled to have made it off the Continent. *Bottom:* Hardy and his wife Edith née Boecker; they met as students at Tübingen University.

Top: The Birmingham Salvation Army's band plays for the Ashton Fields community; Heiner, who had invited them, helps lead the way. **Bottom left:** Hans-Hermann Arnold, Heiner's younger brother. **Bottom right:** Emmy Arnold, now a widow, in Ashton Fields in 1936.

Top left: Heiner with two coworkers – Stanley Fletcher and Arnold Mason – in the Ashton Fields courtyard. **Top right:** Johnny Robinson, an agnostic and socialist, with his soon-to-be-sold motorcycle. **Bottom:** The first group of emigrants departs Ashton Fields for Paraguay in November 1940. For fear of the ship being attacked by German U-boats, they kept the departure date secret even from their close families.

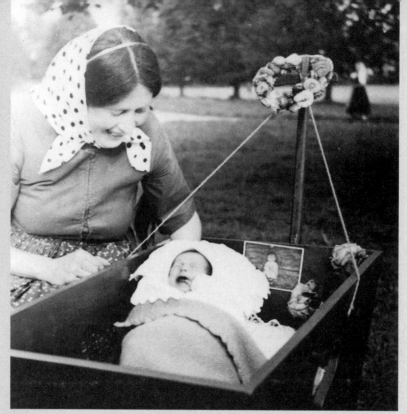

Top: Emmy Maria with her mother Annemarie (1938). Heiner crafted the wooden wagon for his firstborn daughter. **Bottom:** Proud father with his second child, Roswith (1939).

Left: Fritz Kleiner kept up a ferocious work ethic during the day, but after quitting time became a good comrade (1937).

Top left: The SS *Avila Star,* on which the Arnolds traveled, would be sunk by a German submarine one year later. **Top right:** On the ship en route to South America: Roswith and her baby brother Johann Christoph (1941). **Bottom:** Arrival at a new home in Paraguay: the last group of pioneers are welcomed to the Primavera settlement. On the left, a hastily built dormitory shed; center left and standing, Alfred Gneiting and Fritz Kleiner.

Top: The hut (left) where Heiner lay during his near-fatal sickness in September–December 1941. Bottom left: Heiner and Annemarie's family reunited in 1942 after his long illness. Below right: Christine Kleiner, daughter of Fritz, was the third baby to die in Paraguay. Bottom right: Cyril Davies, the doctor.

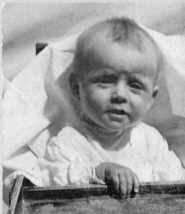

Top: In this family portrait from 1945, Heiner is conspicuously absent. At the time the picture was taken, he was working at the Santa Isabel leper colony, having been separated from his family the previous year. **Bottom left:** Patients line up for treatment in the courtyard of the Primavera hospital, which treated thousands in this impoverished region of Paraguay. **Bottom right:** Two Primavera men saw boards in a pit. Adults in the community worked heroically to provide a home for the children and infirm.

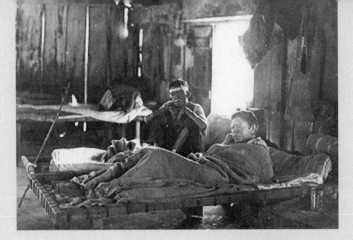

Top: Patients in the hospital ward of the Santa Isabel leper colony in Sapucai, Paraguay (1940s). *Middle:* Santa Isabel residents outside one of the homesteads where healthier lepers lived. *Bottom:* Heiner's house in the leper colony (center right). As director of agriculture, he lived outside the area reserved for the lepers.

Santa Isabel, Paraguay 1944–1946 ◆ 363

Right: Marianne Arnold, July 24–25, 1947 (sketch by Stanley Fletcher).
Bottom: Heiner at Marianne's graveside (1961).

Top: Between trips to North America: Heiner with his brother Hardy in Paraguay (1953). ***Bottom left:*** Johann Christoph with his pet. ***Bottom right:*** Heiner and Annemarie boating on the Tapiracuái River, Paraguay (1953).

Top right: Fundraising team: Will Marchant and Heiner in Pendle Hill near Philadelphia (1951). **Middle left:** Grace Rhoads. **Middle right:** Tom and Florrie Potts. **Bottom:** Heiner and Will visiting Koinonia Farm, an integrated cooperative in Georgia founded by Clarence Jordan.

Top: A new family arrives in Woodcrest (ca. 1956). The community struggled to provide housing for all the new North American members. **Bottom:** A summer celebration at Woodcrest in 1956. Heiner and Annemarie grew to love the new community's informal tone. In photograph: 1. Annemarie; 2. Jörg Barth, Georg and Moni's son; 3. Heiner; 4. Arnold Mason; 5. Roswith; 6. Duffy Black.

Top left: The men do the washing up after lunch on the porch of Woodcrest's main house. **Top right:** Annemarie and Harriet Alexander, her coworker, discuss the community's daily practical arrangements. **Bottom:** Sibyl Sender, with Annemarie's enthusiastic participation, leads a group of Woodcrest women in a protest rally against beards (ca. 1962).

Left: Camping trip: Heiner with daughters Maria, Monika, and Else (1959). **Bottom:** At the Arnolds' house, Sunday afternoons were dedicated to spending time together as a family, including with Emmy Arnold (1960).

Right: En route to Primavera: Heiner and Doug Moody in Asunción, Paraguay (1961). *Below:* Reunion: Heiner and Georg Barth in front of the Sannerz villa (1961). *Bottom:* Emmy Arnold and Dwight Blough (1973).

Left: At the SCLC offices in Selma, Alabama in March 1965; Heiner came to respond to Martin Luther King Jr.'s call for American clergy to march in Selma after Jimmie Lee Jackson's murder. **Below:** Heiner resting during the Selma march. **Bottom:** Nat and Anne Schwerner (on left and right), parents of the murdered civil-rights activist Michael Schwerner, at the wedding of Heiner's son Johann Christoph to Verena Meier (May 1966).

Top: Joking with grandson Nathan Maendel (1968). **Bottom:** The Arnold family in 1965: standing, Heiner, Annemarie, Roswith, Johann Christoph, Edith, Lisa, Maria, and her fiancé David Maendel; sitting, Else, Emmy, and Monika.

Left: Johann Christoph escorts his father shortly after receiving news of Hans Zumpe's death in a plane crash (March 1973).
Below: Annemarie with her granddaughter Margrit.
Bottom: Heiner in his study, drawing a happy face for the author as a two-year-old (1978).

• • •

Acknowledgments

I would never have been able to complete this project without the encouragement and help of Christoph and Verena Arnold; this book is dedicated to them in gratitude. In the same way, I thank my parents and David and Roswith Mason for their constant support during the long process of researching and writing.

It would be difficult to overstate the contribution of Carolyn Weeks, who helped organize my grandparents' papers and prepared a detailed chronology of their lives. I thank my editor Chris Zimmerman for his coaching and his attention to the prose.

Among those who actively contributed to this book by giving interviews, supplying documents, and commenting on drafts, I thank especially Reuben and Margrit Zimmerman, Peter and Lisa Maas, David and Maria Maendel, David and Edith Moody, Doug and Ruby Moody, Sibyl Sender, Sophie Löber, Peter and Kate Cavanna, Ruth Land, Jennie Harries, Stan and Hela Ehrlich, Art and Mary Wiser, Dick and Lois Ann Domer, Alan and Nellie Stevenson, Derek and Madge Wardle, Klaus and Heidi Barth, Rudi Hildel, Jörg and Renate Barth, John and Nancy Winter, Milton and Sandy Zimmerman, and my grandparents Arnold and Dorothy Mommsen.

Many others who knew my grandparents contributed to this book either directly or (in the case of those no longer living) through their written recollections: Don and Eve Alexander, James and Harriet Alexander, Hermann Arnold (Heiner's cousin), Stefan and Gill Barth, Josef and Ruth Ben-Eliezer, Francis and Sylvia Beels, Duffy and Susie Black, Christoph and Maidi Boller, Hugo and Margery Brinkmann, Norann Blough, Maureen Burn, Mary Cawsey, Freda Dyroff, Seppel and Christine Fischli, Stanley Fletcher, Donna Ford, Gary and Susan Frase, Alfred and Gretel Gneiting, Jakob and Juliana Gneiting, Dorie Greaves, Kathleen Hasenberg, John and Gwen Hinde, Pep Hinkey, Franz Hüssy, Walter and Trudi Hüssy, Karl and Irmgard Keiderling, Roland and Lotte Keiderling, Carroll and Doris King, Ilse von Köller, Howard and Marion Johnson, Martin and Burgel Johnson, Edna Jory, Christel Klüver, Julie Lien, Rahel Löber, Nicky Maas, Harry and Lotti Magee, Allister and Judy Marchant, Will and Kathleen Marchant, Olgi Martin, Arnold and Gladys Mason, Johnny and Biene Mason, Miriam

Potts Mathis, Andreas and Fida Meier, Susi Fros Meier, Sharon Melancon, Toby and Johanna Mommsen, Dorie Kaiser Moody, Don and Marilyn Noble, Paul and Mary Pappas, Tom and Florrie Potts, Martin and Susanna Rimes, Robert and Olwen Rimes, Eileen Robertshaw, Johnny and Betty Robinson, Yvonne Sanderson, Mary Ann Sayvetz, Geoff and Molly Thorn, Nancy Trapnell, Jerry and Nancy Voll, Nathan and Lucy Warren, Gerd and Gertrud Wegner, Anne Wiehler, Emmy Wilson, Giovanna Wood, Arthur and Phyllis Woolston, Rosemarie Kaiser Woolston, Wilfred and Nina Wright, Jonathan and Joyanna Zimmerman, Marianne Zimmermann, and Ben and Marianne Zumpe.

Many of those named above helped in fact-checking my drafts. After writing the first version of each chapter, I sent it to a list of around twenty people who had knowledge of the time period covered to request their review. I benefited immensely from their enthusiastic participation. They not only pointed out mistakes and discrepancies, but also challenged simplistic interpretations, filled in missing background, and enriched the story with new details. Any remaining errors are of course my own.

Finally, I thank my most critical reader, my wife Wilma, for her unfailing patience and encouragement.

Sources

In writing this book, I was fortunate in having access to a wealth of primary documents. These unpublished sources, which I have on file, were obtained from various collections of family and personal papers and from Bruderhof historical documents.

For starters, there were my grandparents' papers collected by family members: certificates and medical records, photographs, speaking notes, autobiographical writings, poems, journals, and – last but not least – letters. Thousands of letters from and to them survive (not least regular detailed reports from my grandmother Annemarie to her relatives in Germany). Their correspondence from 1951 alone, for instance, fills a two-hundred-page binder, and their correspondence from other years tops even that. The rest of my grandfather's family – including his aunt Moni Barth; his sisters Emy-Margret and Monika; his brothers Hans-Hermann and Hardy; and Hardy's wife Edith – were all prolific letter writers on a similar scale. Supplementing these were the voluminous publications, notes, and correspondence of Eberhard and Emmy Arnold.

More than a dozen veteran Bruderhof members (or their families) made their diaries and letters available too, so that for each year of my grandfather's adult life I could turn to multiple sources, often with differing points of view, to corroborate important events and dates. Hans Zumpe's daughter Heidi Barth allowed me to read her father's diary from the 1940s, as well as other family papers. Anecdotes, details, and color were provided by interviews with more than sixty people involved in my grandfather's life in various roles, as siblings, longtime friends, fellow community members, pupils, or coworkers. Their names appear in the acknowledgments.

◆ ◆ ◆

Turning to the published sources, I invite the interested reader to read my grandfather's own books. *Discipleship: Living for Christ in the Daily Grind* (Plough, 1994, 2011), with a foreword by Catholic writer Henri Nouwen, is a devotional collected from his letters and pastoral writings. *Freedom from Sinful Thoughts* (Plough, 1973, 1997) yields rich insights into his pastoral practice. *In the Image of God* (Plough, 1979) addresses the topics of relationships, sexuality, and marriage.

Another essential starting point was the literature by my grandfather's parents. Emmy Arnold's memoir, *Joyful Pilgrimage: My Life in Community* (Plough, 1999), gives my grandfather's family background and covers the first twenty-two years of his life. Eberhard Arnold's published works include *God's Revolution: The Witness of Eberhard Arnold*, ed. John Howard Yoder (Mahwah, NJ: Paulist Press, 1984; Plough, 1997); with Thomas Merton, *Why We Live in Community* (Plough, 1995); *Salt and Light: Living the Sermon on the Mount* (Farmington, PA: Plough, 1998); *Innerland: A Guide Into the Heart of the Gospel* (Farmington, PA: Plough, 1999); *Eberhard Arnold: Modern Spiritual Masters* (Maryknoll, NY: Orbis Books, 2000).

Of the secondary literature on the Bruderhof, an excellent introduction is Markus Baum's *Against the Wind: Eberhard Arnold and the Bruderhof* (Plough, 1998). Other carefully researched sources include Antje Vollmer, *Die Neuwerkbewegung 1919–1935: Ein Beitrag zur Geschichte der Jugendbewegung, des Religiösen Sozialismus und der Arbeiterbildung* (doctoral dissertation, University of Augsburg, 1973); Helmut Gollwitzer, "Einiges zu Eberhard Arnold und den Bruderhöfen," in *Neue Wege* (1988) 232–237; Thomas von Stieglitz, *Kirche als Bruderschaft: Das hutterische Kirchenbild bei Eberhard Arnold aus heutiger katholischer Sicht* (doctoral dissertation, University of Paderborn, 1991); and Michael Cole Barnett, *The Bruderhof (Society of Brothers) and the Hutterites in Historical Context* (doctoral dissertation, Southwestern Baptist Theological Seminary, 1995). Yaacov Oved's *The Witness of the Brothers: A History of the Bruderhof* (New Brunswick, NJ: Transaction, 1996) is a wide-ranging survey by a sociologist, marred at times by inadequate grounding in the archival sources. Another, shorter sociological work is Michael Tyldesley's *No Heavenly Delusion?: A Comparative Study of Three Communal Movement* (Liverpool: Liverpool University Press, 2003). More recently, Ian Randall's concise study *"Church Community Is a Gift of the Holy Spirit": The Spirituality of the Bruderhof Community* (Oxford: Regent's Park College, 2014) gives a modern evangelical view and includes an overview of the literature in English. Emmy Barth's *An Embassy Besieged: The Story of a Christian Community in Nazi Germany* (Eugene, OR: Cascade, 2010) focuses on the period 1933–1937.

Memoirs by my grandfather's coworkers include *May They All Be One: A Life of Heini Arnold* by Richard E. Domer, Winifred Hildel, and John

Hinde (Plough, 1992), which was published on the tenth anniversary of his death; and Merrill Mow's *Torches Rekindled: The Bruderhof's Struggle for Renewal* (Plough, 1991). While interesting as oral history, these books were not relied on unless corroborated by other documentation.

◆ ◆ ◆

In addition to the sources described above, I used the following sources for specific sections of the book:

For chapters 2 to 9, I turned to a variety of unpublished memoirs, including especially: Emy-Margret Arnold Zumpe, "Childhood Memories," 1980s;, Hardy Arnold, "Memories of the Beginning Time in Sannerz," 1978; Trudi Hüssy, "Children in Bruderhof Life," 1981–82; Emmy Arnold, "Community is Born," in three notebooks, 1940; and Emmy Arnold, "From Our Life" (Das geschlossene Buch), 1938–1943.

In chapter 2, for the background to street fighting in revolutionary Berlin in 1919, see Pierre Broué, *The German Revolution 1917–1923* (Leiden: Brill, 2004). For the Arnolds' background in the Christian revival movement, see Ian Randall's *Church Community;* Eberhard Arnold's work with the Furche publishing house is described in Karl Kupisch, *Studenten entdecken die Bibel: Die Geschichte der DCSV* (Hamburg: Furche Verlag, 1964). Those interested in the *Jugendbewegung* (German Youth Movement) will find a helpful overview in Walter Laqueur's *Young Germany: A History of the German Youth Movement* (New York: Basic Books, 1962). Eberhard's activity as a lecturer is described in Baum, *Against the Wind*, 47, 79–84; the quote, "We people of today need an upheaval . . ." is from Eberhard Arnold, "Jesus und der Zukunftsstaat," lecture in Hochschule für Musik, Bahnhof Zoo, Berlin, April 1919.

Chancellor Georg Michaelis's involvement with the German National People's Party is discussed in Bert Becker, "Revolution und rechte Sammlung: Die Deutschnationale Volkspartei in Pommern 1918/1919," in *Geist und Gestalt im historischen Wandel* (Münster: Waxmann, 2000), 219. The influence of Gustav Landauer, the Jewish mystic and anarchist, is explored in Michael Tyldesley, "Gustav Landauer and the Bruderhof Communities," in *Communal Societies*, Vol. 16 (Amana, IA: Communal Studies Association, 1996), 23–42. See also Landauer's classic manifesto *Aufruf zum Sozialismus* (Berlin: Verlag des Sozialistischen Bundes, 1911).

Eberhard's brush with the Kapp Putsch is discussed in Baum, *Against the Wind*, 121–122; for the context, see William Mulligan, *The Creation of the Modern German Army: General Walther Reinhardt and the Weimar Republic*, 1914–1930 (New York: Berghahn Books, 2005), 138–168. Eberhard and Emmy's shift toward a radical Christianity and their decision to start a communal settlement is documented extensively in Vollmer's *Neuwerkbewegung*. Eberhard's reference to "the dying metropolis" comes from a letter to Max Zink, June 9, 1920.

For chapter 3, I used Emmy Arnold's *Joyful Pilgrimage* extensively as well as Vollmer and Baum. The Eberhard Arnold statement, "We want to be part of the stream of the Spirit that began at Pentecost . . ." is a composite quote taken from his letters to Johannes Schneider on June 30, 1920 and to Josef Berdolt on June 19, 1920. For the relationship to his cousin Rudolf Bultmann, my source is Eberhard's correspondence from the 1920s, e.g. a July 17, 1925 letter to August Dell reporting on a visit to Bultmann.

"I declare war on the existing church systems . . ." (also chapter 3) is quoted from Eberhard Arnold's letter to Emmy von Hollander on September 4, 1907. Eberhard Arnold's reference to a "communism of love" comes from his essay "Familienverband und Siedlungsleben: Wege zur Hingabe an die Gemeinschaft," in *Das neue Werk*, no. 3, May 1920 (Sannerz: Neuwerk-Verlag). For Christian "Christel" Girbinger, the revolutionary Bavarian carpenter, see Vollmer, *Neuwerkbewegung*, chapter 3, as well as Girbinger's article for Sannerz's magazine: "Entscheidung," *Das neue Werk*, no. 10, November 1921.

In chapter 4, for background on Dutch reform educator and pacifist Kees Boeke and the Bilthoven school, see H.W. von der Dunk, "Boeke, Cornelis (1884–1966)," in *Biografisch Woordenboek van Nederland* (accessed online November 2013). The near-breakup of the Sannerz community in 1922 is described in Vollmer's dissertation (chapter 3) and in Emmy Arnold's various memoirs, as well as an unpublished memoir by Trudi Hüssy, "The 'Neuwerk Crisis' 1922," 1973.

For chapter 5, Eberhard Arnold's authority as a spiritual leader is vividly evoked by Hans-Joachim Schoeps in his autobiography *Die letzten dreißig Jahre – Rückblicke* (Stuttgart: E. Klett, 1956), 43–48. For Sadhu Sundar Singh, see A. J. Appasamy, *Sundar Singh* (Cambridge, England: Lutterworth, 1958, 2002). The story Heiner heard read aloud about Rachoff, the wandering Russian evangelist, was Karl Josef Friedrich's novella "Der Fall Rachoff," in *Die arme Schwester der Kaiserin und andere Gottesfreundgeschichten* (Berlin: Furche Verlag, 1919); Friedrich's story is based on published reports of the life of Vasily Osipovich Rakhov, born ca. 1861. Accounts of the death of the historical Rachoff/Rakhov vary.

In chapter 8, the relationship to the Prince of Schönburg-Waldenburg, a family friend, is described in Emmy Arnold, *Joyful Pilgrimage*, 84–85. For a biography of Schönburg-Waldenburg, who was a generous patron of cultural and church causes, see Robby Joachim Götze, *Günther Fürst von Schönburg-Waldenburg (1887–1960)* (Glauchau, 1997). The episode in which local Nazis would later approach the prince is recounted in Trudi Hüssy, "Begegnungen, Erleben, und Gestalten," memoirs for Emmy Arnold, December 25, 1954; Hans Zumpe, "Unsere Auseinandersetzungen mit dem nationalsozialistischen Staat: Bericht über die Jahre 1933–1937 in der Geschichte unserer Bruderhöfe," unpublished manuscript, 1945.

In chapter 9, Sannerz's connection to Karl Barth is discussed in Baum, *Against the Wind*, 84–87, including the fact that Eberhard was the respondent to Barth's pivotal lecture at Tambach in 1919, a turning point for twentieth-century theology (Baum, *Against the Wind*, 84–87). For relationships with Tillich, Buber, Ragaz, and Siegmund-Schultze, see Baum generally as well as: Michael Tyldesley, "Martin Buber and the Bruderhof Communities," *Journal of Jewish Studies* 45 (1994/2) 258–272; Vollmer, *Neuwerkbewegung;* Helmut Gollwitzer, "Einiges zu Eberhard Arnold und den Bruderhöfen," in *Christ und Sozialist* no. 1, 1988.

Eberhard's visit to the North American Hutterites in 1930–1931 is documented in Eberhard Arnold et al., *Brothers Unite: An Account of the Uniting of Eberhard Arnold and the Rhön Bruderhof With the Hutterian Church* (Plough, 1988), which includes correspondence between Heiner and his father. For the Hutterites generally, see John A. Hostetler, *Hutterite Society* (Baltimore: John Hopkins University Press, 1974, 1997).

On Else von Hollander's worsening health and activities in this period, see Eberhard Arnold et al., *Else von Hollander, January 1932* (Plough, 1972), a collection of memories made after Else's death in 1932. This book, supplemented by unpublished sources, forms the basis for the account in chapter 10. For Annemarie's family background and her arrival at the Sparhof, see Annemarie Wächter, *Anni: Writings and Letters of Annemarie Wächter*, ed. Marianne Wright and Erna Albertz (Rifton, NY: Plough, 2010).

Chapters 11 and 12, in their descriptions of Hitler's rise to power and the Bruderhof's experiences under the Nazi regime, rely heavily on Emmy Arnold, *Joyful Pilgrimage;* Hans Zumpe, "Auseinandersetzungen"; Hans Meier, *Solange das Licht brennt: Lebensbericht eines Mitgliedes der neuhutterischen Bruderhof-Gemeinschaft* (Klosters, Germany: Pflug-Verlag, 1990); Marjorie Hindley, "'Unerwünscht': One of the Lesser Known Confrontations with the National Socialist State, 1933–1937," in *German History* vol. 11 no. 2 (1993), 207–219; Emmy Barth, *An Embassy Besieged;* Achim Buckenmaier, review of Embassy Besieged, in *Theologische Revue* 2011, 479–480; and "Der Bruderhof," in *Evangelischer Widerstand,* online exhibit (Munich: Forschungsstelle für Kirchliche Zeitgeschichte, 2015), at *de.evangelischerwiderstand.de.* I also benefited from conversations with Professor Thomas Nauerth at the University of Osnabrück, who is preparing a richly documented book-length study of the Bruderhof under National Socialism (1933–1937).

The interaction with the Zionist training farm at the Gehringhof (chapter 12) is described in Oved, *Witness of the Brothers,* 70–71. Of the "volley of letters" that Eberhard wrote to Nazi officials on the community's behalf, one was an open letter to Reich Bishop Ludwig Müller, "An den Reichsbischof der evangelischen Kirche Deutschlands, Berlin," *Mennonitische Blätter* no. 80 (12/1933), 117–119; this was the last writing Eberhard managed to have published under the regime. The local Nazi epithet for Bruderhof members—*Edelkommunisten* ("idealistic communists")—is attested in a June 1934 report to Gestapo central headquarters in Berlin (Staatsarchiv Marburg, Bestand 165, Nr. 3949 fol. 31; I am grateful to Professor Nauerth for the reference). The description of Eberhard's fractured leg is based on an author interview with Dr. Jonathan Zimmerman, who investigated the episode and its aftermath (September 18, 2003). Eberhard's quoted words to the community—"It is something great when people are found worthy to be cast into prison or killed for the sake of the gospel . . . "—are from November 12, 1933 and appear in Barth, *Embassy Besieged,* 96–97.

In chapter 13, the settlement at Silum is described in Barth, *Embassy Besieged,* 157–165; for a history, see Herbert Hilbe, "Almbruderhof," in *Historisches Lexikon des Fürstentums Liechtenstein,* vol. 1 (Zurich: Chronos, 2013). Eberhard's declining health on account of the unhealed leg fracture is documented by Baum, *Against the Wind,* 184, 189, 198. The Strickhof, described in chapter 14, is the Kantonale Landwirtschaftliche Schule Strick-hof-Zürich, an institution that still exists.

In chapter 15, Martin Niemöller's statement, "If Hitler calls me back to my post, I will go . . ." is reported in Barth, *Embassy Besieged*, 124. For Niemöller's later views, see also Matthew D. Hockenos, "Martin Niemöller, the Cold War, and His Embrace of Pacifism 1945–1955," *Kirchliche Zeitgeschichte* (KZG/CCH) 27 (2/2014), 87–101. For Heiner's brother Hardy's dialogue with Dietrich Bonhoeffer, see E.C.H. Arnold (Hardy), "Bruder-hof-Korrespondenz 1934," *Dietrich-Bonhoeffer-Jahrbuch* 2 (2005/2006) 75–87; see also Charles Marsh, *Strange Glory: A Life of Dietrich Bonhoeffer* (New York: Alfred A. Knopf, 2014), 217. Documents relating to Eber-hard's confrontation with Leonhard Ragaz are discussed in Barth, *Embassy Besieged*, 217–220; for a biography of Ragaz, see Markus Mattmüller, *Leonhard Ragaz und der religiöse Sozialismus: Eine Biographie*, 2 vols. (Zollikon/Zurich: EVZ, 1957, 1968).

Rumors of lynchings of Jewish refugees in Liechtenstein (chapter 15) were unfortunately not unfounded. Fritz and Alfred Schaie (artist name: Rotter) were Jewish theater directors from Berlin who, after fleeing to Liechtenstein in January 1933, were ambushed by Nazis in Gaflei. Fritz and his wife Gertrud fell to their deaths; Alfred and a second woman escaped with injuries. The perpetrators were given a one-year prison sentence. See "Nationalsozialistische Umtriebe von Liechtensteinern" in Liechtenstein-isches Landesarchiv, RF 198 463. The petition drive to expel the Bruderhof from Liechtenstein is described by Hans Zumpe, "Auseinandersetzungen"; see also local newspaper articles cited by Thomas Nauerth in his forth-coming book on the Bruderhof 1933–1937: *Liechtensteiner Heimatdienst*, September 21, 1935 and October 5, 1935; *Liechtensteiner Volksblatt*, September 21, 1935. Eberhard's speech to the citizens of Triesenberg took place on September 30, 1935; his notes survive. Eberhard's sermon on the Book of Revelation was made on October 4, 1935, partially quoted in Barth, *Embassy Besieged*, 236–240.

In chapters 16 and 17, several sources describing Eberhard's last days are cited in Barth, *Embassy Besieged*, 241–244; see also Baum, *Against the Wind*, 243–255. For Annemarie's mother Hedwig Wächter and the family's connection to Friedrich Fröbel's Keilhau school, see Annemarie Wächter, *Anni*, 2.

For chapter 18, a description of the community at Ashton Fields Farm by Hardy Arnold appears in E. C. H. Arnold, "Cotswold Bruderhof (Ashton Keynes, Wiltshire, England)," 1953, *Global Anabaptist Mennonite Encyclopedia Online*, at *www.gameo.org*. The 1937 Gestapo raid and forcible dissolution of the Bruderhof in Germany are recounted by Barth, *Embassy Besieged*, 269–277, and E.C.H. Arnold, "The Fate of a Christian Experiment," *The Spectator*, June 11, 1937. The crucial role played by two Hutterite ministers is explored in Thomas Nauerth, "Kirchenkampf unter internationaler Beobachtung," *Kirchliche Zeitgeschichte* (KZG / CCH) 27, 181–195. On new cooperatives and communes that were springing up all over England, see issues of the community's periodical *The Plough*, whose first issue appeared in spring 1938 (Ashton Keynes, England).

For chapter 20, the Blumhardt book that deeply affected Heiner is published in English as Friedrich Zündel, *Pastor Johann Christoph Blumhardt: An Account of His Life* (Eugene, OR: Cascade, 2010). The Maxim Gorky novella on which the "Heliopher" story is based is *Heartache and The Old Woman Izergil* (London: Maclaren and Company, 1905); for the version recounted here – an anonymous telling that may well be by Heiner himself – see "The Legend of Heliopher," *The Plough*, December 1938, 109.

◆ ◆ ◆

For chapter 21, the Nazi plans for occupying Britain are documented in General Walter Schellenberg, "The Gestapo Handbook for the Invasion of Britain," 1940, published as *Invasion 1940,* ed. John Erickson (London: St Ermin's Press, 2000). See also Peter Haining, *Where the Eagle Landed: The Mystery of Hitler's Invasion of Britain, 1940* (London: Robson Books, 2004). The arrival of twenty Jewish refugees in the community is reported in *The Plough*, September 1938, 104 and December 1938, 134. Yaacov Oved describes the visit of thirty members of *Hashomer Hatsa'ir*, a Zionist youth group, in *The Witness of the Brothers: A History of the Bruderhof* (New Brunswick, NJ: Transactions, 1996), 101–104. The internment of Freda Bridgwater was reported in *The Plough*, Summer 1940, 55–56. The local newspapers that printed letters attacking "the German Peace Community" included *The Evening Advertiser* (April 22, May 3, 14, 17, 1940, letters to the editor) and *Daily Mirror* (April 23, 1940, letters to the editor).

Lady Astor's defense of the Bruderhof in the House of Commons is minuted in *Hansard Parliamentary Debates,* "German Peace Bruderhof," June 26, 1940, vol. 362, cc443–4. (Responding to Captain Graham's questions, Osbert Peak, the under-secretary of state for the Home Department, remarked wittily if inaccurately: "As the Noble Lady [Lady Astor] said, this is a pacifist community which was driven out of Germany in 1934. Its members all wear brown dressing-gowns and beards and are for that reason unlikely to be employed by the enemy.") Eleanor Roosevelt wrote about her meetings with Bruderhof representatives in her syndicated column "My Day" (see *Washington Post,* September 24, 1940). For the story of the Bruderhof's emigration to Paraguay generally, see Donald F. Durnbaugh, "Relocation of the German Bruderhof to England, South America, and North America," in *Communal Societies* 11 (1991) 66–77.

The role of the *Avila Star* and other Blue Star vessels, and their eventual sinking by German submarines, is described in David Edgerton, *Britain's War Machine: Weapons, Resources, and Experts in the Second World War* (Oxford: Oxford University Press, 2011), 163–164. For the Bruderhof's first year in Paraguay, see Emmy Barth, *No Lasting Home: A Year in the Paraguayan Wilderness* (Plough, 2009). For Primavera in the 1950s, see Bob and Shirley Wagoner, *Community in Paraguay: A Visit to the Bruderhof* (Plough, 1991).

For chapters 22 and 23, living conditions in Primavera – including the sparse diet – are described in a pamphlet published for the benefit of family and friends in England: Sidney and Marjorie Hindley, "Work and Life of the Bruderhöfe in Paraguay," (Plough, 1943). On Heiner's sickness and exposure to excessive bromide doses in 1941, my description is indebted to conversations with Dr. Milton Zimmerman, his physician from the 1950s to 1982. For an older medical reference on bromism in general, see e.g. *The Pharmacalogical Basis of Therapeutics,* 3rd ed., 1965, 129–130. The danger of using bromides for long periods seems to have been widely known already in the first decade of the 1900s: see Simon D. Schorvon, "Drug Treatment of Epilepsy in the Century of the ILAE: The First 50 Years, 1909–1958," in *Epilepsia,* 50 (Suppl. 3):69–92, 2009, pp. 72–74.

Church discipline as practiced in the Primavera community in the 1940s was ostensibly based on sixteenth-century Anabaptist church orders, particularly "Concerning Exclusion" in Peter Riedemann's *Rechenschaft,* the classic Hutterite confession of faith from ca. 1542 (published in English as

Account of Our Religion, Doctrine, and Faith, trans. Kathleen Hasenberg [London: Hodder and Stoughton, 1950]). Primavera's harsh approach to church discipline contrasted starkly with the view advanced by Bruderhof founder Eberhard Arnold, who had emphasized that discipline in a church community was intended to be only restorative, not punitive, and was to be practiced in a spirit of fraternal love; see Eberhard Arnold, "Church Discipline among the Hutterian Brothers," remarks in a community meeting, May 1931.

Chapter 26 describes Heiner's work with STICA (*Servicio Técnico Interamericano de Cooperación Agrícola*), a US agricultural aid program established in Paraguay by a 1942 treaty; for background, see STICA, *Agricultural Progress in Paraguay* (Washington, DC: Food Supply Division, Institute of Inter-American Affairs, 1949).

Also described in chapter 26 is Colonia Santa Isabel, the leper colony near Sapucai, Paraguay, which was founded in 1934 by two missionaries: Malcolm Norment, an American sent by the Disciples of Christ denomination, and Dr. John Nairn Hay, an Englishman who later worked with the British Medical Service. Norment's reports on the colony were published in *World Call,* (October 1934, September 1946, September 1951, and January 1952). In 1951, the colony was taken over by the *Asociación Santa Isabel* under Franciscan leadership, and nuns from Little Sisters of Saint Vincent de Paul arrived to serve the patients. The colony still exists today as a home for healed patients. For a history of Colonia Santa Isabel, see Gerhard Ratzlaff, *Hospital Mennonita Km 81: Liebe, die tätig wird* (Asunción, Paraguay: Gemeindekomitee Asociación Evangélica Mennonita del Paraguay, 2001), 29–44. Much of the description of the leper colony in this chapter relies on Maureen Burn and Maria Weiss, *Outcast but Not Forsaken: True Stories from a Paraguayan Leper Colony* (Plough, 1989).

In 2008, Heiner was still remembered by older residents of Colonia Santa Isabel. Tomas Castillo, who first arrived at the leper colony as a sixteen-year-old in 1943, recalled working with Heiner on the STICA cooperative farm in 1945. He said Heiner rode around on a horse supervising the work and was very punctual and careful, but also very kind and caring and often did things for them and took an interest in them, asking where they were from. His Spanish was not very good, but he liked a good joke. (Source: Tomas Castillo, interview by Mark Clement in Colonia Santa Isabel, Sapucai, February 17, 2008; on file with author.)

For chapter 27, the episode involving the pet monkey and the neighbor's tomatoes is recounted by Heiner's son Johann Christoph Arnold in *Their Name Is Today: Reclaiming Childhood in a Hostile World* (Walden, NY: Plough, 2014), 39–42. The same book recounts the author's memories of his father's parenting approach, including his friendship toward people with disabilities or idiosyncrasies (p. 92).

◆ ◆ ◆

For chapter 29, the remarkable life of Koinonia's founder, Clarence Jordan, is told by Dallas Lee, *The Cotton Patch Evidence: The Story of Clarence Jordan and the Koinonia Farm Experiment (1942–1970)* (Eugene, OR: Wipf & Stock, 2011). An introduction to Jordan's vision is Clarence Jordan, *Sermon on the Mount* (Valley Forge, PA: Judson Press, 1952). The boom in the American intentional community movement in the 1940s and 50s is described by Henrik Infield, *The American Intentional Communities: Study on the Sociology of Cooperation* (Glenn Gardner, NJ: Community Press, 1955).

Thurman Arnold (also in chapter 29) had been Assistant Attorney General under Franklin Roosevelt. A pioneer of legal realism and then a legendary trustbuster, Thurman Arnold was related to Heiner through Carl Franklin Arnold, Heiner's grandfather and Thurman's uncle. See Thurman Arnold's autobiography *Fair Fights and Foul: A Dissenting Lawyer's Life* (New York: Harcourt Brace & World, 1965); Thurman Arnold, *Voltaire and the Cowboy: Letters of Thurman Arnold*, ed. Gene M. Gressley (Boulder: Colorado Associated University Press, 1977); and Spencer Webber Waller, *Thurman Arnold: A Biography* (New York: NYU Press, 2005).

◆ ◆ ◆

In chapter 31, for a contemporary portrait of the newly founded Woodcrest community, see David Stanley Tillson, *A Pacifist Community in Peacetime: An Introductory Description of the Woodcrest Bruderhof in Rifton, NY* (doctoral thesis, Syracuse University, 1957). Dorothy Day reported on the Bruderhof in *The Catholic Worker*, December 1955, 1, 7. Eleanor Roosevelt's two nationally syndicated columns about her visit to Woodcrest appeared in "My Day," *New York Post*, November 7 and November 8, 1958. Pitirim Sorokin's description of the Bruderhof appears in his book *The Ways and Power of Love: Types, Factors, and Techniques of Moral Transformation* (Philadelphia: Templeton Foundation Press, 1954, 2002).

388 ◆ Homage to a Broken Man

For the remarkable story of the Macedonia humanist community (also chapter 31), including Heiner's important role in its history, see Trevor Wiser, *The Last Inch: A History of the Macedonia Cooperative Community* (master's thesis, California University of Pennsylvania, 2008). Works by Dietrich von Hildebrand especially valued by Heiner include *Transformation in Christ* (London: Longman, 1948); *Man and Woman: Love and the Meaning of Intimacy* (Chicago: Franciscan Herald Press, 1966); and *In Defense of Purity: An Analysis of the Catholic Ideals of Purity and Virginity* (London: Longman, 1931).

◆ ◆ ◆

For chapter 33's description of the death of Michael Schwerner and Heiner's subsequent friendship with his parents, I am indebted to Cassie Schwerner, who kindly provided help and details in telling the story of her family. For the history of the case, see Seth Cagin and Philip Dray, *We Are Not Afraid: The Story of Goodman, Schwerner, and Chaney, and the Civil Rights Campaign for Mississippi* (New York: Scribner, 1988).

For chapters 33 and 34, Heiner's insistence on forgiving—including the quote, "I would much rather trust and be betrayed a thousand times . . ."—is described by Johann Christoph Arnold in *Escape Routes: For People Who Feel Trapped in Life's Hells* (Plough, 2002), 144. Johann Christoph Arnold also recounts his mother's reaction to her cancer diagnosis in *Be Not Afraid: Overcoming the Fear of Death* (Plough, 2002), 9.

Index

Further Reading

Discipleship: Living for Christ in the Daily Grind by J. Heinrich Arnold, foreword by Henri Nouwen. Perhaps the hardest thing about following Christ is translating our good intentions into deeds. Sometimes provocative but always encouraging, Arnold guides readers toward leading Christ-like lives amid the stress of modern life. Some chapters offer advice on specific problems; others grapple with broader themes such as world suffering, salvation, and the coming of the kingdom of God.

> *"A prophetic book in a time in which few people dare to speak unpopular but truly healing words." — from Henri Nouwen's foreword*

Freedom from Sinful Thoughts by J. Heinrich Arnold, foreword by John Michael Talbot. Sensitive and compassionate, but always pragmatic, Arnold provides insights into a crucial, universal struggle. For those who waver at times between obeying the voice of conscience and giving in to their lower nature, this book offers sound advice for coming through the battle. Drawing on years of experience as a pastoral counselor, Arnold guides the reader from the throes of frustration and guilt to a life of freedom and joy.

> *"An excellent little book." — Richard Foster*

A Joyful Pilgrimage: My Life in Community by Emmy Arnold. In the tumultuous aftermath of the First World War, Emmy Arnold and her husband, the theologian Eberhard Arnold, abandoned their affluent Berlin suburb to start a new life and "venture of faith," founding what became known as the Bruderhof. After twelve years of community living they found themselves facing down the Nazis. More than just a memoir, this book is a summons to radical Christianity.

> *"Very moving. . . . Emmy Arnold's book is a simple and direct account of a Christian life stripped to the essentials." — Thomas Merton*

Anni: Letters and Writings of Annemarie Wächter, ed. Marianne Wright and Erna Albertz. A young woman coming of age in a time of cultural upheaval (1920s Germany) questions the meaning of life, faith, and friendship in this compelling true story told through her diary and letters.

"It is infinitely reassuring to know there is an absolute truth, an infinitely great love." – from the book

Salt and Light: Living the Sermon on the Mount by Eberhard Arnold, foreword by Jürgen Moltmann. A man who was ready to risk everything in his own quest to live out Jesus' self-sacrificing demands calls all of us to live for the Sermon's ultimate goal: building a just, peaceable society motivated only by love.

"Simple, luminous, direct." –Thomas Merton

Plough Publishing House
www.plough.com